Frontiers of Urban
&
Restoration Ecology

Essays in urban and restoration ecology dedicated to the memory of Dr Oliver Gilbert

I0120325

Supported and sponsored by:

Sheffield Hallam University

L Y Landscape
C Conservation
F Forum

British Ecological Society
Peatlands Research

International Urban Ecology Review 6

Edited by Ian D. Rotherham and Christine Handley

ISSN: 1367-7519

ISBN: 978-1-904098-72-0

9 781904 098720

December 2021

Published by:

Wildtrack Publishing, Venture House,

103 Arundel Street, Sheffield S1 2NT

Front cover: photograph credit Ian Rotherham

Contents

Foreword

This volume arose from a 2-day conference held in Sheffield to celebrate the life and legacy of Dr Oliver Gilbert. It was organised by South Yorkshire Biodiversity Research Group and with Sheffield Hallam University.

A tribute to Oliver Lathe Gilbert

7th September 1936 – 15th May 2005

Oliver pictured in the British Lichen Society obituary by Wiliam Purvis

Oliver Lathe Gilbert

Alan Fryday

When I first got interested in lichens in the early 1980's I was living near the north-east Yorkshire coast and, in that pre-internet age, had only books to guide me into this exciting new world. My main reference was Ursula Duncan's *"Introduction to British Lichens"* but many of my collections did not appear to be included in that work so I needed to send my collections to a British Lichen Society referee. I chose to send them to Oliver because he lived in Yorkshire, and so was probably more familiar with the species I was collecting. It was undoubtedly one of my better decisions. Not only was Oliver able to name many of my collections but, over the years, he became a colleague, a friend and, ultimately, my PhD supervisor.

Working with Oliver was never dull. My first experience of fieldwork with him was when he invited me to join him on a survey of the lichens of the Ben Nevis massif. The first day out on Aonach Beag he nearly got me killed! It was typical West Highland weather – raining, with low clouds – but, always in search of unusual or different habitats, Oliver spotted where a snow-bed had pulled away from a rock face revealing some newly-exposed rocks. Reaching them involved climbing up the steep snowbed but no problem as we could use our hammers and chisels as makeshift ice-axes. We reached the rockface; I stood up to look at it...and slipped! I slid back down the snowbed – Oliver later described me as disappearing into the mist – and continued for several metres over the rocks at the bottom. Miraculously, no bones were broken but I was badly bruised. Did Oliver suggest calling it a day? No chance. We carried on, Oliver at the top of the snowbed, continuing to look for lichens, me at the bottom, wondering what I had got myself into. We then ascended a steep, narrow gulley full of loose crumbling rocks that required all my climbing skills to navigate and reached the summit plateau from where we had a long hike back to base.

But the excitement wasn't over. During dinner in the local inn that evening Oliver got into conversation with someone who turned out to be a helicopter pilot. He was interested in what we were doing and offered to drop us off on the summit of Ben Nevis on his way back to Inverness the following day. I was relieved – there was no way I could have hiked up the mountain – and early the next morning we were deposited fresh and raring to go on the summit of Ben Nevis. A couple of hours later, the first hikers arrived and were amazed to find us already there. It had taken them almost 4 hours to climb the mountain "Oh, it didn't take us that long" replied Oliver, without any explanation!

Oliver had a 'broad-brush' approach to lichenology. He was interested in the broad sweep of a new problem and was content to leave the details to those that came after. When I started my PhD research (describing the lichens that occurred in various montane NVC communities) he suggested a quadrat size of four metres but I soon realized that to properly survey an area that size for lichens would take all day (literally!) and by the end of my field work I was working with 50-cm quadrats or smaller. He was always in a hurry. No sooner had he finished one piece of fieldwork then he was planning the next. He would spend a few days identifying his collections, write it up and submit the manuscript for publication, all within a few weeks. He was an editor's nightmare! The then editor of *The Lichenologist* told me his submitted manuscripts more resembled notes from his diary than a piece of scientific research. His broad-brush, idiosyncratic approach applied to other things. He liked to do crosswords but considered them finished when he had done 90% of them *"...there's always a few clues you're never going to get"*; and then there was his homeopathic approach to tea!

Oliver was an ecologist, interested in what lichens were growing in a particular habitat, whether it was a remote Scottish mountain or a disused WWII airfield – both were equally interesting and deserving of attention. He wasn't interested in finding new species; in fact, I suspect he disliked them because they were too much work and distracted from his objective of describing the species that occurred in a habitat. He once told me *"If I can't ID it in 30 mins, it goes in the bin!"* and when I proudly showed him a new species I had discovered he replied, somewhat dismissively, "Well, if you're going to collect things like that, you deserve to find new species." I'm not sure it was a compliment!

Oliver has left behind a prodigious amount of work on the lichen ecology of a wide variety of habitats in the British Isles, but his major achievement was the rediscovery of the rich lichen biota of the Scottish Highlands. Because of his pioneering work, we now know that the lichen biota of the mountains of the Western Highlands is of international importance, being unique in Europe and probably the world. However, perhaps his most important legacy will be his endless energy and enthusiasm and his unique ability to recognize an ecological niche that everyone else had missed or ignored. Now, 20 or so years after his death, he is an inspiration to another generation of lichenologist. Mention his name, and someone will say how important one of his papers was in preparing for their own research, or they will quote a passage from his book '*The Lichen Hunters*' that has inspired them.

Oliver once remarked to me that he had written numerous papers and articles and given countless presentations and lectures but now he had been asked to give the eulogy at the funeral of a good friend he was nervous and didn't know what to say. At the time I didn't think much of it but now, when I find myself in a similar position with respect to Oliver, I understand completely! Delivering facts is easy, whereas summarising, in a few paragraphs, the contributions of a departed friend is something entirely different. He never told me what he said for his friend's eulogy or if it was well received, but I hope he would have liked this short reminiscence.

Oliver Gilbert – a personal reminisce

Brian Coppins

I may have first met Oliver at one of the BLS AGMs in the late 1960s, but I first really got to know him during the Northumberland leg of the 'pioneering' excursion through the North of England with Francis Rose and David Hawksworth in May–June 1969 (Rose *et al.*, 1970). In those days, the general impression amongst lichenologists down South was that there were no notable corticolous lichens in the 'North' – all having been wiped out by SO_2 air pollution. Francis was of the opinion "this can't be so" and, with Turner & Dillwyn's '*Botanist's Guide through England and Wales*' (1805) in hand, led the excursion to dispel the doubters – which he did. Oliver and Margaret Johnson (Ford Castle Field Centre) were our enthusiastic field companions and contemporary local guides. Thereafter began 35 years of close friendship and collaboration.

Oliver began collecting records for his 'Lichen Flora of Northumberland' (Gilbert, 1980) in 1965, and I joined him many times for field trips in the county, first while I was an undergraduate at Hull University, and later once I was ensconced at RBG Edinburgh (and Oliver had moved to Sheffield). These were wonderful days out, often ending with some fine dining in a country pub, or going back to his parental home in Corbridge, via the local pub, with a large jug of ale to aid the identification of the day's haul. One of my greatest achievements concerning Oliver was to improve his microscope techniques. When we had our first microscope session together, I was horrified, or rather amused, when Oliver cut too thick a section of an apothecium, mounted it in too much water, and after tapping out the preparation, wondered why he couldn't find any spores. Of course, the spores had dispersed to the four corners of the cover-slip! His technique improved after a little tuition and spores were revealed.

There are lots of stories to be told from our early exploits together, but one comes to mind during a visit to Hound Dean, Warkworth, in 1969, along with William Purvis (then an undergraduate at Sheffield). On a wooded slope, we spotted a dirty white fluffy bundle, and on getting closer realised it was a ewe that had got her fleece entangled in the barbed wire of a dilapidated fence. She was very distressed and had been there for perhaps some days as she had de-barked the hazel stems close by. Oliver stood astride the unfortunate animal, holding her head, while William and I cut away her fleece from the wire – a job which would have been very difficult had our knife blades been less than 3 inches long! The ewe didn't thank us for her freedom, but we were soon after rewarded by the discovery of *Ramonia chrysophaea* for the first time in Northumberland.

Oliver would never have described himself as a taxonomist, despite his improved technique with the microscope. However, he kept taxonomists such as Peter James, myself, and Alan Fryday well supplied with tricky specimens from his varied exploits from the highest mountains to the coastal salt marshes. Although he never actually collected it himself, in 1996 Alan and I described in his honour *Catillaria gilbertii*, a denizen of one of Oliver's favourite hunting grounds, Ben Lawers, and a few other sites in the Grampians. It remains to be discovered outside of Scotland. This species is unusual in having double the number of spores per ascus, and the specific epithet is even more appropriate as Oliver was a twin. From his studies of the Magnesian Limestone outcrops and quarries, in 1984 he described for himself *Lecanora campestris* subsp. *dolomitica*, a taxon that still holds good today and is probably deserving of species rank. His investigations of the lichens of salt marshes – scarcely considered a lichen-rich habitat – revealed a puzzling lichen growing on the old dried stems of Shrubby sea-blite (*Suaeda vera*), subsequently described by Oliver and myself in 2001 as *Caloplaca suaedae*.

Oliver was very much an ecologist of the 'old school', relying more on good observations rather than advanced statistics and ordination to present his results. His many, often pioneering lichenological papers on a wide variety of under-worked, overlooked or seemingly unpromising habitats are a joy to read being very narrative in style. Most of these papers were submitted for publication in *The Lichenologist*. To the chagrin of the Senior Editor, Dennis Brown, they were too 'narrative' in style, often almost bereft of references and pertinent cross-referencing – and as for punctuation, or rather lack of I'll say little more! On several occasions Dennis was tempted to reject the paper outright, even though he knew that with better presentation it would be ground-breaking. This is where I as an Assistant Editor and a good friend of Oliver came in. Dennis allowed me to rescue the manuscript and knock it into shape – after negotiations with Oliver, appropriate reference citations and grid references, as well as commas, semi-colons and colons were inserted; all to Dennis's satisfaction.

These are just a few words from me about my interactions with Oliver. Although he left us in 2005 to carry on the good work under his inspiration, I still hear in my head the *"Oh! Hello Brian"* as I answered the telephone – usually the prelude to news of some good finds, or to talk over his latest venture.

A reminisce of Oliver Gilbert, some personal recollections

Sandy Coppins

It was through Brian that I met Oliver the lichenologist, but that quickly developed into Oliver as a good friend. He was a great companion to set out with for a day in the field. In the mornings he would step outside, scan the sky, back straight, hands on hips, head up, breathe deep the air, and he would reckon on the day, what it held and anticipate the excitement in store. And it wasn't always the wilds of the Cairngorms (although the uplands exerted a special pull), but he was equally intrigued to seek out undiscovered, unrecorded habitats and niches. So, he might head for a disused airfield, or be curious about the influence of metal run-off onto concrete at the feet of giant pylons. Recognition of the urban habitat and the potential niches where lichens may lurk were really an 'Oliver speciality', but something that made lichens accessible to anybody who cared to look – unpromising habitat? Not if you looked. Almost everywhere was a happy hunting ground. The chapter in the *New Naturalist Lichens* (2000) – *'Work, Wealth and Wheels'* is a classic, a delight to read.

He was of a slightly built frame, lean, energetic but not in the least frenetic, always keen to press on, but mindful of the abilities and stamina of his companions. His ready smile was open, broad and immediately put you at ease, and the slightly dishevelled look from the wild bush of grey hair like a tonsure around his tanned bald head – here was someone you warmed to; you never felt over-awed by Oliver. There is a lovely portrait photo of him used by his former student, William Purvis in the tribute to him in *The Lichenologist*. He also had a distinctive pleasant, slightly gravely voice, and a contemplative was of saying *"Yers"* when considering a matter. And he had very distinctive handwriting – it took a bit of getting used to, but was instantly recognisable as Oliver.

It is typical of Oliver that he should write '*The Lichen Hunters*' (2004). It sets out all the joy and enthusiasm he loved about going out with like-minded companions to hunt for lichens. The title says it all, looking for lichens was a hunt, a discovering, excursions made for pleasure, light-hearted yet serious recording. *The Lichen Hunters* is a good story, written like a journal, with phrases like *"This put us in high spirits"* after finding *Lecanora achariana* on boulders at a high-level Welsh lake. And habitats, sections of a site, were always "worked" – well, what else would you call happily searching nooks, crannies, niches for lichens? And yet he paced himself, never working beyond the limits of himself or his companions, knowing that a good, enjoyable day in the field was not gauged by how far you walked, or how many species you recorded, but a satisfaction of a day well spent.

And indeed, the book is a joy to read. Oliver's enthusiasm for his subject and the people – colleagues, yes, but they were also his friends, his companions, who shared with him this passion for seeking and exploring habitats for lichens. He was generous in describing these companions, giving wonderful anecdotes, allowing them to express their adventures, sharing the excitement and love of the hunt. He was easy going, always brewing up new ideas and thoughts based on his observations, but never pushy. There is a special spirit in the book, an open, honest, almost naïve enthusiasm, describing these early years discovering lichens, their ecology and communities. Those were heady years when lichenology was suddenly attracting enthusiasts prepared to devote long days not only in the field, but in the laboratory. The excitement of such expeditions are rarely experienced nowadays, with concerns about Health and Safety somewhat dulling the edge of adventure.

He was a great rock climber and mountaineer as well, and when he developed kidney problems and had to dialyze twice a week, he made supreme efforts to still build an active life in the field. He would organise his dialysis to take place in different hospitals, so he would not have so far to travel. I believe his most ambitious escapade was to climb the Old Man of Hoy in between his dialysis. Crazy man.

We have good memories of going to stay in his little remote cottage in Yorkshire, near the Ribblehead Viaduct, with our collective families of young teenage kids. Oliver took them all potholing. I 'volunteered' to stay aloft, and watched them all (including Brian) clamber up a waterfall and disappear into a black hole. Oliver had told me where he anticipated they would emerge out of a bit of limestone pavement. Just after they had gone, and I was climbing up out of the gully, I saw at the top a line of orange boiler-suit-clad persons, looking down. They had on hard hats with lamps, and all the right sort of equipment. (Oliver and all were wearing old clothes, boots, and hard hats and carried candles). The leader of the pukka pot-holers asked if a team had just submerged, and were they correctly equipped? *"Oh, yes"* I said, *"Oliver's in charge, and they're all carrying torches or candles."* Looks of disbelief...... Well, needless to say, Oliver, Brian & the kids all emerged, wet but grinning, and we trooped back for a big beef stew and dumplings, recounting adventures.

Near to the cottage there was also a notorious cliff above a pool, known as "Tim's Leap". Oliver again – the oldest – led the way by leaping off, followed by the others with great screams of fear and shock as they hit the cold water. Ah, memories, memories.

I do recall very clearly, the time when Oliver received a phone call to say a match had been found to replace one of his kidneys. He was staying with us, together with a group of other BLS members, as the AGM was held in Edinburgh that year

(2004). We'd been into the Botanic Garden most of the day, and were at home late in the evening, just opened a bottle of malt, when the phone rang. It was for Oliver. I can recall his gravelly, burring voice, as he replied, *"Yes, yes, of course"* and gave our address. Then, he put the phone down, and turned to us all and said – *"I've a chance for a kidney transplant."* (You know, recounting this now – and I don't think I've ever written this down – brings tears of emotion). Oliver had a twin brother, who also had failed kidneys; the brother had also gone for a transplant, but had died during the operation. So, you can see, sense the immense drama, the tension in that room, as we stood there, knowing that Oliver had just made the biggest decision of his life.

A Police car came to take him from East Linton to Sheffield – it was gone midnight, and it was reckoned a speeding police car could accomplish the journey precisely from door to door more quickly than arranging a helicopter. Later, Oliver said it was the most exhilarating ride of his life, zooming down the motorways, all the speed cameras flashing......

The operation was a partial success; it seemed to be going well, then his body started to reject the organ. Oliver deteriorated, was taken into a hospice and told he would need a colostomy, which together with other complications, would mean he would be virtually bedridden. He realized that this would impede his lifestyle, and put an end to his freedom. Oliver had three adult daughters, and he called them together and told them that what he wanted to do was to choose to stop dialysing, and so choose to die rather than live the rest of his life an invalid. They knew their dad. And so that is what happened. Oliver made a choice, and chose death. How strange to chose your time of dying; yet what courage. That is so typical of Oliver, courage, spirit and determination, even at the end, to make this decision.

Now, here's the strangest thing – at that time (May 2005), I was organising a thing we called the Rockers' Workshop; it was an international gathering of lichen experts to help train our lichen apprentices in saxicolous lichens. In normal circumstances, Oliver would have been one of the key tutors, but, it was not to be. Oliver died a few days before the start of the Workshop. It was held at Mar Lodge, Braemar, Aberdeenshire. The first evening, as we were all gathered for supper together, I stood, and said a few words about Oliver, and asked for a minutes silence to think about him. And – the lights flickered, and dimmed…… There was a sort of gasp in the room. The lights never flickered again for the duration of the week. I still get tears and goose-pimples when I remember this. We remember Oliver with fondness, and still keenly feel the loss of a great mate.

Oliver, at Fyfield Down NNR, Marlborough, 2003

Vince Giavarini's eulogy when Oliver was awarded the prestigious Ursula Duncan Award at the 2004 BLS AGM, January 2004:

'Unselfishly, Oliver always encouraged others to join his expeditions, the two Brian's: Foxy and Coppins, Alan Fryday, William Purvis, I (Vince), and many others, have all revelled in his companionship. His New Naturalist Book on 'Lichens' written by a master storyteller in the true New Naturalist tradition is, for a lichenologist, not only a good read by which to while away many a dark winter evening, but also an inspirational journey which it is hoped, will move and captivate many of the next generation of lichenologists.'

Chapter 1: Introduction: Sheffield's forgotten environmental hero - pioneering ecologist Dr Oliver Gilbert

Ian D. Rotherham

Figure 1. Oliver searching for lichens at Stonehenge

In 2015, Sheffield hosted a unique, 2-day event (13th & 14th November) to honour and to commemorate a remarkable global champion for local wildlife and for urban ecology. Dr Oliver Gilbert of the Sheffield University Landscape Department was a truly international figure in ecology and lichenology; and his outspoken views on the benefits of exotic, sometimes invasive, urban plant species gained him coverage on the front pages of national newspapers. He was a key 1980s actor in the establishment of the Sheffield City Wildlife Group which ultimately morphed into a hugely successful 'Sheffield Wildlife

Trust'. Sadly, in May 2005, he passed away. This was around ten years previous to the commemorative event.

So, a decade after Ollie's premature death Dr Paul Ardron and me, together with other long-term friends and associates, organised this conference with generous support from the *British Ecological Society* and help from the *British Lichen Society* too. A remarkable line-up of speakers came together encompassing Oliver's many interests and celebrating his contributions to urban ecology, lichenology, exotic plants, and urban and post-industrial landscapes. Dr Gilbert's work spanned over fifty years, and invited speakers delivered illustrated lectures on fascinating topics reflecting his many interests from 'alien' species, lichens, and urban woodlands, to post-industrial flora. Indeed, this was a stunning line-up of nationally-renowned speakers on topics around urban wildlife, post-industrial ecology and heritage, and exotic or alien species too.

Oliver was one of the first academic ecologists to study urban environments, establishing terms like *'the urban commons'*, and his book *The Ecology of Urban Habitats* is still the primary text in the field. Often controversial and outspoken, and pioneering academic interest in urban habitats and urban ecology before they became fashionable, he challenged conventional thinking on invasive aliens like sycamore and Japanese knotweed. Ollie *'discovered'* ancient wildflower meadows and heaths relict in parks and other urban open spaces, and then helped gain their recognition and conservation. He was also a leading light in establishing what became hugely successful as the Sheffield Wildlife Trust, and with Mike Wild of the then Sheffield Polytechnic, coordinated the first Inner City Habitat Survey of Sheffield.

In Sheffield for instance, Oliver was:

- The first ecological researcher to champion urban ancient woodlands – in Bowden Housteads, in Ecclesall woods, and in the Gleadless Valley

- A passionate founding member of the Friends of the Porter Valley
- One of the driving forces behind the greening of the Lower Don Valley in the 1980s and 1990s
- A founder of the Sheffield City Wildlife Group nee Sheffield & Rotherham Wildlife Trust
- The ecologist behind the greening of the River Don and the first person to understand and celebrate the famous forest of urban fig trees – the only wild exotic plant to be formally protected in Britain
- A pioneer of a new approach to the conservation of urban parks and helped to discover relict habitats in Crookes Valley and in Graves Park
- An early supporter of Heeley City Farm
- An advocate and pioneer of distinctive urban meadows and spontaneous wildflower communities in urban landscapes
- The discoverer of the remarkable phenomenon by which once polluted urban areas like Sheffield were being re-colonised by rare lichens from as far away as Snowdonia

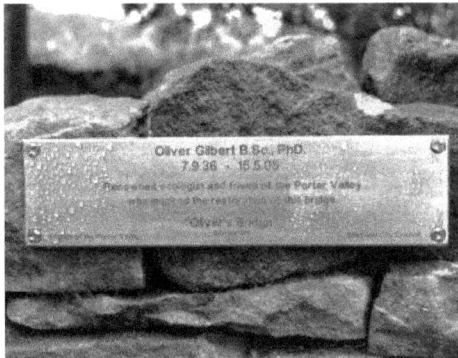

Figure 2. Commemorative plaque at 'Oliver's Bridge'

Over the two days of the event we heard speakers inform and excite amateurs and professionals alike, from students and researchers or teachers, to interested local people. The line-up included Professor Mark Seaward, Dr Penny Anderson, Professor Nigel Dunnett, Dr Jan Woudstra, Ann Le Sage, Dr Rob Francis, Dr Peter Shaw, Professor Melvyn Jones, Dr Anna Jorgensen, Penny

Anderson, Dr Peter Shepherd, Dr John Barnatt, Dr Paul Ardron and Professor Ian Rotherham. The event was joined by Oliver's family from as far away as New Zealand and Switzerland, for a very special celebration.

The follow-up book mixes those presentations and invited contributions to address and celebrate Oliver's work in pioneering urban ecology and in leading global lichenology and other fields over many decades.

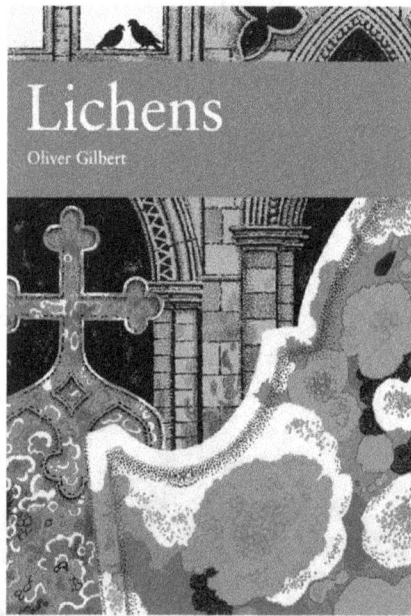

Figure 3. Oliver's definitive volume on lichens

The depth and breadth of Oliver's academic work is demonstrated by the list of publications based on the tribute in *The Lichenologist*, **37**(6), 467–475 (2005) and the publications list prepared by O. W. Purvis of the Department of Botany, The Natural History Museum, London. For anyone wanting to appreciate Oliver's published work then this is an essential read and is available on-line:
https://www.cambridge.org/core/services/aop-cambridge-core/content/view/S0024282905900042

16

I have added some missing works and made just a few corrections.

Publications (1963–2005)

Arranged under the following subject headings:

Ecology and Taxonomy of Lichens and Bryophytes
Landscape Science and Management
General Botany, Ecology, and Urban Environments

Ecology and Taxonomy of Lichens and Bryophytes

Gilbert, O.L. (1965) *Lichens as indicators of air pollution in the Tyne Valley.* In: G.T. Goodman, R.W. Edwards & J.M. Lambert (eds). *Ecology and the Industrial Society.* Blackwell Scientific Publications, Oxford, 35–47.

Gilbert, O.L. (1966) Lichen pathogens on *Lecanora conizaeoides* Nyl. ex Cromb. *Lichenologist*, **3**, 275.

Gilbert, O.L. (1968) Bryophytes as indicators of air pollution in the Tyne Valley. *New Phytologist*, **67**, 15–30.

Gilbert, O.L. (1968) *Biological estimation of air pollution.* In: Commonwealth Mycological Institute (ed.), *Plant Pathologist's Pocketbook.* Commonwealth Mycological Institute, Kew, 206–207.

Gilbert, O.L. (1969) *The effect of SO2 on lichens and bryophytes around Newcastle upon Tyne.* In: *Air Pollution.* Proceedings of the First European Congress on the Influence of Air Pollution on Plants and Animals, Wageningen 1968: Centre for Agricultural Publishing and Documentation, Wageningen, 223–235.

Gilbert, O.L. (1970) Further studies on the effect of sulphur dioxide on lichens and bryophytes. *New Phytologist*, **69**, 605–627.

Gilbert, O.L. (1970) A biological scale for the estimation of sulphur dioxide pollution. *New Phytologist*, **69**, 629–634.

Gilbert, O.L. (1970) Urban bryophyte communities in north-east England. *Transactions of the British Bryological Society*, **13**, 306–316.

Gilbert, O.L. (1970) Lichens. In: G.A.K. Harvey & J.A.G. Barnes (eds). *Natural History of the Lake District*, Warne, London, 72–75.

Gilbert, O.L. (1970) New tasks for lowly plants. *New Scientist*, **46**, 288–289.

Gilbert, O.L. (1971) Some indirect effects of air pollution on bark-living invertebrates. *Journal of Applied Ecology*, **8**, 77–84.

Gilbert, O.L. (1971) Studies along the edge of a lichen desert. *Lichenologist*, **5**, 11–17. Gilbert, O.L. (1971) The effect of airborne fluorides on lichens. *Lichenologist*, **5**, 26–32. Gilbert, O.L. (1972) Field meeting in Northumberland. *Lichenologist*, **5**, 337–341.

Gilbert, O.L. (1973) *The effect of airborne fluorides*. In: B.W. Ferry, M.S. Baddeley & D.L. Hawksworth (eds). *Air Pollution and Lichens*. Athlone Press of the University of London, London, 176–191.

Gilbert, O.L. (1974) *Lichens and air pollution*. In: V. Ahmadjian & M.E. Hale (eds). *The Lichens*. Academic Press, New York and London, 443–472.

Gilbert, O.L. (1974) An air pollution survey by school children. *Environmental Pollution*, **6**, 175–180.

Gilbert, O.L. (1974) Reindeer grazing in Britain. *Lichenologist*, **6**, 165–167.

Gilbert, O.L. (1975) *Wildlife Conservation and Lichens*. Devon Trust for Nature Conservation, Exeter.

Gilbert, O.L. (1975) Distribution maps of lichens in Britain. Map 19. *Solorina saccata* (L.) Ach. *Lichenologist*, **7**, 181–183.

Gilbert, O.L. (1975) Distribution maps of lichens in Britain. Map 20. *Solorina spongiosa* (Sm.) Anzi. *Lichenologist*, **7**, 184–185.

Gilbert, O.L. (1975) Distribution maps of lichens in Britain. Map 21. *Solorina bispora* Nyl. *Lichenologist*, **7**, 186–188.

Gilbert, O.L. (1975) Distribution maps of lichens in Britain. Map 29. *Solorina crocea* (L.) Ach. *Lichenologist*, **7**, 190–192.

Gilbert, O.L. (1975) Lichens. In: G.F. Peterken & R.C. Welch (eds). *Bedford Purlieus: its History, Ecology and Management*, (Monks Wood Symposium No. 7.) Institute of Terrestrial Ecology, Huntingdon, 125–129.

Gilbert, O.L. (1976) An alkaline dust effect on epiphytic lichens. *Lichenologist*, **8**, 173–178. Gilbert, O.L. (1976) *The construction, interpretation and use of lichen/air pollution maps.* In: L. Karenlampi (ed.). *Proceedings of the Kuopio Meeting on Plant Damages Caused by Air Pollution*, University of Kuopio, Kuopio, Finland, 83–92.

Gilbert, O.L. (1976) A lichen-arthropod community. *Lichenologist*, **8**, 96.

Gilbert, O.L. (1977) *Lichen conservation in Britain.* In: M.R.D. Seaward (ed.). *Lichen Ecology*, Academic Press, New York and London, 415–436.

Gilbert, O.L. (1977) Field meeting at Lancaster. *Lichenologist*, **9**, 83–85.

Gilbert, O.L. (1977) Phenotypic plasticity in *Cladonia pocillum. Lichenologist*, **9**, 172–173. Gilbert, O.L. (1978) *Fulgensia* in the British Isles. *Lichenologist*, **10**, 33–45.

Gilbert, O.L., Earland-Bennett, P. & Coppins, B.J. (1978) Lichens of the sugar limestone refugium in Upper Teesdale. *New Phytologist*, **80**, 403–408.

Gilbert, O.L., Watling, R. & Coppins, B.J. (1979) Lichen ecology on St. Kilda. *Lichenologist*, **11**, 191–202.

Gilbert, O.L. & Coppins, B.J. (1979) Field meeting at Melrose, Roxburghshire. *Lichenologist*, **11**, 97– 101.

Mahandru, M.M. & Gilbert, O.L. (1979) Norgangaleoidin, a dichlorodepsidone from *Lecanora chlarotera. Bryologist*, **82**, 292–295.

Mahandru, M.M. & Gilbert, O.L. (1979) Chemical studies in *Fulgensia*: structures of two new chlorodepsidones. *Bryologist*, **82**, 302–305.

Coppins, B.J. & Gilbert, O.L. (1979) George Johnston's lichen herbarium at the R.B.G., Edinburgh.. *Notes of the Royal Botanic Garden Edinburgh*, **37**, 381–385.

Gilbert, O.L. (1980) Effect of land-use on terricolous lichens. *Lichenologist*, **12**, 117–124.

Gilbert, O.L. (1980) A lichen flora of Northumberland. *Lichenologist*, **12**, 325–395.

Furness, S.B. & Gilbert, O.L. (1980) The status of *Thamnobryum angustifolium* (Holt) Crundw. *Journal of Bryology*, **11**, 139–144.

Gilbert, O.L. (1980) Lichens of the Limb Valley. *Sorby Record*, **19**, 64–67.

Coppins, B.J. & Gilbert, O.L. (1981) Field meeting near Penrith, Cumbria. *Lichenologist*, 13, 191–199.

Gilbert, O.L., Henderson, A. & James, P.W. (1981) Citrine-green taxa in the genus *Candelariella*. *Lichenologist*, **13**, 249–251.

Gilbert, O.L. & Mitchell, J. (1981) Rossdhu Park, Dunbartonshire—a major site for epiphytic lichens. *Glasgow Naturalist*, **20**, 123–132.

Gilbert, O.L. & Gibson, P.G. (1981) Lichens on farm roofs. *British Lichen Society Bulletin*, **48**, 1–3.

Gilbert, O.L., Fox, B. W. & Purvis, O.W. (1982) The lichen flora of a high-level limestone-epidiorite outcrop in the Ben Alder Range, Scotland. *Lichenologist*, **14**, 165–174.

Gilbert, O.L. (1982) Canary Islands, Tenerife: terricolous lichens of the semi-arid zone. *Lichenologist*, **14**, 90–91.

Gilbert, O.L. & Lambley, P. W. (1982) Field meeting at Ludlow, Shropshire. *Lichenologist*, 14, 185–188.

Gilbert, O.L. (1983) The lichens of Rhum. *Transactions of the Botanical Society of Edinburgh*, **44**, 141–152.

Gilbert, O.L. (1983) The lichen flora of Derbyshire. Supplement 2. *Naturalist*, **108**, 131–137. Gilbert, O.L. (1984) Lichens of the Magnesian limestone. *Lichenologist*, **16**, 31–43.

Gilbert, O.L. (1984) Some effects of disturbance on the lichen flora of oceanic hazel woodland. *Lichenologist*, **16**, 21–30.

Gilbert, O.L., Coppins, B.J. & James, P.W. (1984) Field meeting to Coll and Tiree. *Lichenologist*, **16**, 67–79.

Gilbert, O.L. & Lambley, P.W. (1984) Field meeting at Llangollen, Denbighshire. *Lichenologist*, **16**, 63–66.

Gilbert, O.L. (1984) The lichens of Choire Garbh. *New Scientist*, **101**, 42–43.

Gilbert, O.L. & Fox, B.W. (1985) Lichens of high ground in the Cairngorm Mountains of Scotland. *Lichenologist*, **17**, 51–66.

Purvis, O.W., Gilbert, O.L. & James, P.W. (1985) The influence of copper mineralization on *Acarospora smaragdula*. *Lichenologist*, **17**, 111–114.

Gilbert, O.L. (1985) *The lichen flora*. In: D. Whiteley (ed.) *The Natural History of the Sheffield Area Sheffield*. Sorby Natural History Society, Sheffield, 59–67.

Gilbert, O.L. (1985) Lichen ecology on Steep Holm. *Proceedings of the Bristol Naturalists' Society*, **44**, 27–34.

Gilbert, O.L. & Fox, B.W. (1986) A comparative account of the lichens occurring on the geologically distinctive mountains Ben Loyal, Ben Hope and Foinaven. *Lichenologist*, **18**, 79–94.

Gilbert, O.L. (1986) Field evidence for an acid rain effect on lichens. *Environmental Pollution (Series A)*, **40**, 227–231.

Coppins, B.J., Fletcher, A., Gilbert, O.L. & James, P.W. (1986) Field meeting in Sutherland. *Lichenologist*, **18**, 275–285.

Gilbert, O.L. (1986) Review of J.W. Thomson: *American Arctic Lichens. Volume 1: Macrolichens*. Columbia University Press, New York. 1984. *Lichenologist*, **18**, 100–101. Gilbert, O.L. & James, P.W. (1987) Field meeting on the Lizard Peninsula, Cornwall. *Lichenologist*, **19**, 319–334.

Gilbert, O.L., Coppins, B.J. & Fox, B.W. (1988) The lichen flora of Ben Lawers. *Lichenologist*, **20**, 201–243.

Gilbert, O.L. (1988) Studies on the destruction of *Lecanora conizaeoides* by the lichenicolous fungus *Athelia arachnoidea*. *Lichenologist*, **20**, 183–190.

Gilbert, O.L. (1988) Colonisation by *Parmelia saxatilis* transplanted onto a suburban wall during declining sulphur dioxide pollution. *Lichenologist*, **20**, 197–198.

Gilbert, O.L. (1989) Field meeting in the eastern Howgills, Cumbria. *Lichenologist*, **21**, 287–291.

Gilbert, O.L. (1989) Lichens and the greenhouse effect. *British Lichen Society Bulletin*, **65**, 1–5.

Gilbert, O.L. (1989) Review of K. Broad. *Lichens in Southern Woodlands*. Forestry Commission Handbook No. 4. Her Majesty's Stationery Office, London. 1989. *Lichenologist*, **21**, 396–397.

Gilbert, O.L. (1990) The lichen flora of urban wasteland. *Lichenologist*, **22**, 87–101.

Coppins, B.J. & Gilbert, O.L. (1990) Field meeting in Galloway. *Lichenologist*, **22**, 83–190. Gilbert, O.L. (1991) A successful transplant operation involving *Lobaria amplissima*. *Lichenologist*, **23**, 73–76.

Gilbert, O.L., Fryday, A.J., Giavarini, V.J. & Coppins, B.J. (1992) The lichen vegetation of the Ben Nevis range. *Lichenologist*, **24**, 43–56.

Gilbert, O.L. (1992) *Lichen reinvasion with declining air pollution*. In: J.W. Bates & A.M. Farmer (eds) *Bryophytes and Lichens in a Changing Environment*. Oxford University Press, Oxford, 158–179.

Gilbert, O.L. & Coppins, B.J. (1992) The lichen flora of Caenlochan, Angus. *Lichenologist*, **24**, 143–163.

Gilbert, O.L., Fryday, A.M., Giavarini, V.J. & Coppins, B.J. (1992) The lichen vegetation of high ground in the Ben Nevis range, Scotland. *Lichenologist*, **24**, 43–56.

Gilbert, O.L., Orange, A. & Fletcher, A. (1992) Field meeting in Gower, South Wales. *Lichenologist*, **24**, 299–304.

Gilbert, O.L. (1992) Accounts of the following genera (some co-authored): *Candelaria, Candelariella, Cryptolechia, Ephebe, Fulgensia, Lemopsis, Petractis, Placynthium, Poeltinula, Polychidium, Porocyphus, Psorotichia, Pyrenopsis, Solorina, Spilonema, Sporastatia, Synalissa*. In: O.W. Purvis, B.J. Coppins, D.L. Hawksworth, P.W. James & D.M. Moore (eds), *The Lichen Flora of Great Britain and Ireland*. Natural History Museum, London.

Gilbert, O.L. (1993) The lichens of chalk grassland. *Lichenologist*, **25**, 379–414.

Gilbert, O.L. (1993) The lichen flora of Derbyshire— Supplement 3. *Naturalist*, **118**, 3–8. Gilbert, O.L. & Giavarini, V.G. (1993) The lichens of high ground in the English Lake District. *Lichenologist*, **25**, 147–164.

Purvis, O.W. & Gilbert, O.L. (1994) Lichens of the Blair Atholl Limestone. *Lichenologist*, **26**, 367–382.

Gilbert, O.L. (1995) The occurrence of lichens with albino fruit bodies and their taxonomic significance. *Lichenologist*, **28**, 94–97.

Gilbert, O.L. (1995) The lichen flora of chalk and limestone streams. *Lichenologist*, **28**, 145–159.

Gilbert, O.L. (1995) The conservation of chalk grassland lichens. *Cryptogamic Botany*, **5**, 232–238.

Gilbert, O.L. & Fryday, A.M. (1995) The lichen flora of high ground in the West of Ireland. *Lichenologist*, **28**, 113–127.

Gilbert, O.L. & Ardron, P. (1995) New, rare and interesting lichens from North Derbyshire. *Sorby Record*, **30**, 48–53.

Gilbert, O.L. (1996) *Lichens*. In: T. Elkington & A. Willmot (eds*). Endangered Wildlife in Derbyshire*. The County Red Data Book.. Derbyshire Wildlife Trust, Derby, 15–26.

Gilbert, O.L. & Purvis, O.W. (1996) *Teloschistes flavicans* in Great Britain. *Lichenologist*, **28**, 493–506.

Church, J.M., Coppins, B.J., Gilbert, O.L., James, P.W. & Stewart, N.F. (1996) *Red Data Book of Britain and Ireland. Lichens. Vol. 1: Britain.* Joint Nature Conservation Committee, Peterborough.

Gilbert, O.L. (1997) *The lichens of Ecclesall Woods 1993*. In: I.D. Rotherham & M.Jones, (eds). *The Natural History of Ecclesall Woods*. Special Publication No. 1, *Peak District Journal of Natural History and Archaeology*, Wildtrack Publishing, Sheffield, 35–39.

Gilbert, O.L. (1997) Field meeting at Grange-over-Sands, Lancashire. *Lichenologist*, **29**, 483–487.

Gilbert, O.L. & Giavarini, V.J. (1997) The lichen vegetation of acid watercourses in England. *Lichenologist*, **29**, 347–367.

Gilbert, O.L. (1997) Review of N.G. Hodgetts. *The Conservation of Lower Plants in Woodland*. Joint Nature Conservancy Committee, Peterborough. *Lichenologist*, **29**, 395.

Gilbert, O.L. & McCutcheon, D.E. (1998) Lichen flora of Northumberland: Supplement 1. *Naturalist* ,**123**, 15–18.

Gilbert, O.L. & Smith, E.C. (1998) Red Data Book for Northumberland: Lichens. *Transactions of the Natural History Society of Northumbria*, **38** (2), 273–288.

Gilbert, O.L. (1999) Conserving *Calicium corynellum*. *British Lichen Society Bulletin*, **85**, 19–22.

Gilbert, O.L. (2000) A tribute to Brian William Fox. *Lichenologist*, **32**, 103–104.

Gilbert, O.L. (2000) The lichens of disused World War Two airfields. *Lichenologist*, **32**, 585–600.

Gilbert, O.L. (2000) *Lichens*. New Naturalist Series No. 8, Harper Collins, London.

Gilbert, O.L. & Giavarini, V.J. (2000) The lichen vegetation of lake margins in Britain. *Lichenologist*, **32**, 365–386.

Gilbert, O.L. (2000) *Aquatic lichens.* In: M.R.D. Seaward (ed.), *Lichen Atlas of the British Isles. Fascicle 5. Aquatic Lichens and Cladonia (Part 2).* British Lichen Society, London.

Gilbert, O.L. (2001) The lichen flora of coastal saline lagoons. *Lichenologist*, **33**, 409–417. Gilbert, O.L. (2001) *Freshwater habitats.* In: A. Fletcher, P. Wolseley & R. Woods (eds), *Lichen Habitat Management.* British Lichen Society, London.

Gilbert, O.L. (2001) *Montane habitats.* In: A. Fletcher, P. Wolseley & R. Woods (eds). *Lichen Habitat Management.* British Lichen Society, London.

Gilbert, O.L. (2001) *Species recovery programme: the Breckland rarities and* Teloschistes flavicans. In: A. Fletcher, P. Wolseley & R. Woods (eds). *Lichen Habitat Management,* British Lichen Society, London.

Gilbert, O.L. (2001) The growth and development of *Thelocarpon laureri* and *Cladonia humilis,* and observations on the recovery of *Cladonia podetia* from simulated grazing. *British Lichen Society Bulletin,* 88, 52–55.

Gilbert, O.L. (2001) Review of F. Dobson. *Lichens. An Illustrated Guide to the British and Irish Species,* 4th ed. 2000. Richmond Publishing Co., Slough. *Lichenologist*, **33**, 368–369.

Gilbert, O.L. & Henderson, A. (2001) The common names of British lichens. *British Lichen Society Bulletin*, **88**, 33–37.

Henderson, A. & Gilbert, O.L. (2001) Common names of lichens in North America. *British Lichen Society Bulletin*, **89**, 38–39.

Gilbert, O.L. (2002) A transplant operation involving *Lobaria amplissima*; the first twenty years. *Lichenologist*, **34**, 267–269.

Gilbert, O.L. (2002) Lichen flora of Devon published. *British Lichen Society Bulletin*, **90**, 62–63.

Gilbert, O.L. (2003) The lichen flora of unprotected soft sea cliffs and slopes. *Lichenologist*, **35**, 245–254.

Gilbert, O.L. (2003) Stonehenge. *British Lichen Society Bulletin*, **93**, 1–4.

Gilbert, O.L. (2003) Review of R.G. Woods & B.J. Coppins. *A Conservation Evaluation of British Lichens*. 2003. British Lichen Society, London. *Lichenologist*, **35**, 411–412.

Gilbert, O.L. (2004) The phenology of *Sarcosagium campestre* observed over three years. *Lichenologist*, **36**, 159–161.

Gilbert, O.L., Coppins, A.M. & Coppins, B.J., Giavarini, V.J. & Woods, R. (2004) What the UK BAP has done for the River Jelly Lichen. *British Wildlife*, **15**, 314–318.

Gilbert, O.L. (2004) *The Lichen Hunters*. The Book Guild, Lewes.

Landscape Science and Management

Gilbert, O.L. (1973) *Landscape*. In: *Forestry and the Countryside*. Peak District National Park Conference, Losehill Hall, Derbyshire, 12–15.

Gilbert, O.L. (1974) An ecologist's view of landscape architects. *Landscape Design*, **106**, 13. Gilbert, O.L. (1974) The place of biologists in landscape architecture. *Journal of Biological Education*, **8**, 70.

Gilbert, O.L. & Weddle, A.E. (1974) Site conservation: a new approach. *Landscape Design*, **107**, 24–27.

Gilbert, O.L. (1975) Effects of air pollution on landscape and land use around Norwegian aluminium smelters. *Environmental Pollution*, **8**, 113–121.

Gilbert, O.L. (1976) *The establishment and subsequent growth of planted trees in polluted atmospheres*. In: L. Karenlampi (ed.). *Proceedings of the Kuopio Meeting on Plant Damages Caused by Air Pollution*. University of Kuopio, Kuopio, Finland, 126–132.

Gilbert, O.L. & Wathern, P. (1976) Towards the production of extensive *Calluna* swards. *Landscape Design*, **114**, 35.

Gilbert, O.L. (1976) *Conference summing up*. Small Woods in the Landscape Conference. Peak Park Planning Board, Losehill Hall, Derbyshire.

Wathern, P. & Gilbert, O.L. (1978) Artificial diversification of grassland with native herbs. *The Journal of Environmental Management*, **6**, 29–42.

Wathern, P. & Gilbert, O.L. (1979) The production of grassland on subsoil. *The Journal of Environmental Management*, **8**, 269–275.

Gilbert, O.L. (1979) *Biological aspects (of water)*. In: A.E. Weddle (ed.). *Landscape Techniques*. Heinemann, London, 128–130.

Gilbert, O.L. & Wathern, P. (1980) The creation of flower-rich swards on mineral workings. *Reclamation Review*, **3**, 217–221.

Gilbert, O.L. (1981) Plant communities in an urban environment. *Landscape Research*, **6**, 5–7.

Gilbert, O.L. (1982) The management of urban woodland in Sheffield. *ECOS*, **3**, 31–34. Gilbert, O.L. (1982) Turf transplants increase species diversity. *Landscape Design*, **140**, 37. Gilbert, O.L. (1983) The growth of planted trees subject to fumes from brickworks. *Environmental Pollution (Series A)*, **13**, 301–310.

Gilbert, O.L. (1983) The ancient lawns at Chatsworth, Derbyshire. *Journal of the Royal Horticultural Society*, **108**, 471–474.

Gilbert, O.L. (1983) Chatsworth: the Capability Brown lawn and its management. *Landscape Design*, **146**, 8.

Gilbert, O.L. (1983) Review of: R. Bornkamm, J.A. Lee and M.R.D. Seaward (eds), *Urban Ecology: 2nd European Ecological Symposium Oxford*, 1982. Blackwell Scientific Publications, Oxford. *Lichenologist*, **15**, 103–104.

Gilbert, O.L. (1984) New directions, 7. The urban common. *Landscape Design*, *149*, 35–36. Clements, J., Bradley, C. & Gilbert, O.L. (1984) Early development of vegetation on urban demolition sites in Sheffield, England. *Urban Ecology*, **8**, 139–147.

Gilbert, O.L. (1985) A wild flower mix with a short life. *Landscape Design*, **157**, 47–49. Gilbert, O.L. (1985) Environmental effects of airborne fluorides from aluminium smelting at Invergordon, Scotland 1971–1983. *Environmental Pollution (Series A)*, **39**, 293–302.

Gilbert, O.L. & Rotherham, I.D. (1990) The ecology of urban habitats. *Applied Geography*, **10**, 239–240.

Gilbert, O.L. (1991) Diversification of an established sward using native herbs; the first nineteen years. *Landscape Design*, **200**, 15–16.

Gilbert, O.L. (1992) *The Flowering of the Cities: The Natural Flora of Urban Commons*. English Nature, Peterborough.

Gilbert, O.L. (1992) *Rooted in Stone: The Natural Flora of Urban Walls*. English Nature, Peterborough.

Gilbert, O.L. (1992) The ecology of an urban river. *British Wildlife*, **3**, 129–136.

Gilbert, O.L. (1993) Regenerating balsam poplar (*Populus candicans* Ait.) black poplar (*P. nigra* L.) at a site in Leeds. *Watsonia*, **19**, 188–191.

Gilbert, O.L. (1994) Japanese knotweed – what problem? *Urban Wildlife News*, **11**, 1–2. Gilbert, O.L. (1994) Vegetation and soils in urban areas. *Journal of the South-East of England Soils Discussion Group*, **9**, 19–27.

Gilbert, O.L. (1995) Urban commons: a colourful alternative. *Enact*, **3**, 10–11.

Gilbert, O.L. (1995) Creating wild-flower meadows: a few problems. Editorial paper. *The Journal of Practical Ecology and Conservation*, **1**, 3–6.

Gilbert, O.L. (1996) Retaining trees on construction sites. *Arboricultural Journal*, **20**, 39–45. Gilbert, O.L. & Bevan, D. (1997) The effect of urbanisation on ancient woods. *British Wildlife*, **8**, 213–218.

Gilbert, O.L. (1998) Urban ecological distinctiveness. In: M. Jones & I.D. Rotherham (eds). Landscapes—Perception, Recognition and Management: Reconciling the Impossible? *Landscape Archaeology and Ecology*, **3**, 109–110.

Gilbert, O.L. (1988) Urban scrub. *Urban Nature*, **4**, 50–51.

Gilbert, O.L. (1998) *The ancient lawns at Chatsworth*. In: *Naturschutz und Denkmalpflege*, Hochschulverlag AG an der ETH, Zurich, 217–220.

Gilbert, O.L. & Anderson, P. (1998) *Habitat Creation and Repair*. Oxford University Press, Oxford.

Ardron, P.A., Rotherham, I.D. & Gilbert, O.L. (1998) Peat-cutting and upland landscapes: case studies from the South Pennines. In: M. Jones & I.D. Rotherham (eds) Landscapes— Perception, Recognition and Management: Reconciling the Impossible? *Landscape Archaeology and Ecology*, **3**, 65–69.

Gilbert, O.L. (1998) Entries under 'Anthropocentric' and 'A.N. Other' In: P. Calow (ed.) The *Encyclopedia of Ecology and Environmental Management*. Blackwell Science, London, 47.

Gilbert, O.L. (2003) On hostile ground. *Natural History*, **112**, 72–72.

General Botany, Ecology, and Urban Environments

Raistrick, A. & Gilbert, O. L. (1963) Malham Tarn House, its building materials, their weathering and colonisation by plants. *Field Studies*, **1**, 89–115.

Gilbert, O.L. (1963) Grass diseases at Malham Tarn. *Naturalist*, **89**, 50.

Roberts, R.H. & Gilbert, O.L. (1963) The status of *Orchis latifolia* v. *eborensis* in Yorkshire. *Watsonia*, **5**, 287–293.

Gilbert, O.L. (1966) *Dryopteris villarii* in Britain. *British Fern Gazette*, **9**, 263–268.

Gilbert, O.L. (1969) Biological Flora of the British Isles: *Dryopteris villarii* (Bellardi) Woynar. *Journal of Ecology*, **58**, 301–313.

Gilbert, O.L., Jamison, D., Lister, H. & Pendlington, J. (1969) Regime of an Afghan Glacier. *Journal of Glaciology*, **8**, 51–65.

Gilbert, O.L., Holligan, P.M. & Holligan, M.S. (1973) The flora of North Rona 1972. *Transactions and Proceedings of the Botanical Society of Edinburgh*, **42**, 43–68.

Gilbert, O.L. & Wathern, P. (1976) The flora of the Flannan Isles. *Transactions and Proceedings of the Botanical Society of Edinburgh*, **42**, 487–503.

Gilbert, O.L. & Holligan, P.M. (1979) *Puccinellia capillaris, P. maritima* on North Rona, Outer Hebrides. *Watsonia*, **13**, 338–339.

Gilbert, O.L. (1980) Juniper in Upper Teesdale. *Journal of Ecology*, **68**, 1013–1024.

Gilbert, O.L., Marsden, C., Preston, T., Riley, T., Rotherham, I.D. & Smellie, W. (1981) Wildlife Conservation in Sheffield Woodlands. Internal report for the Amenity Woodlands Advisory Group, SCC, Sheffield.

Gilbert, O.L. (1983) The wildlife of Britain's wasteland. *New Scientist*, **97**, 823–829.

Wild, M. & Gilbert, O. (1988) *Sheffield Inner City Habitat Survey*. Sheffield City Wildlife Group, Sheffield.

Gilbert, O.L. (1989, 1991) *The Ecology of Urban Habitats*. London: Chapman and Hall.*[1991, paperback]

Gilbert, O.L. (1990) Wild figs by the River Don, Sheffield. *Watsonia*, **18**, 84–85.

Gilbert, O.L. (1994) *Städtische Ökosysteme*. Neumarm Verlag Radebeul, Stuttgart.*[German translation]

Gilbert, O.L. (1995) Biological Flora of the British Isles: *Symphoricarpos albus* (L) S.F. Blake. *Journal of Ecology*, **83**, 159–166.

Ardron, P.A., Rotherham, I.D. & Gilbert, O.L. (1996) The Influence of Peat-cutting on Upland Landscapes: Case Studies from the South Pennines. Landscapes - Perception, Recognition and Management: reconciling the impossible? Proceeding of the Landscape Conservation Forum Conference, 2-4 April, 1996, Sheffield. *Landscape Archaeology and Ecology*, **2**, 56.

Rotherham, I.D., Ardron, P.A. & Gilbert, O.L. (1997) *Factors determining contemporary upland landscapes.....a re-evaluation of the importance of peat-cutting and associated drainage, and the implications for mire restoration and remediation*. In: *Blanket Mire Degradation. Causes, Consequences and Challenges.* Proceedings of the British Ecological Society Conference in Manchester, 1997. British Ecological Society and the Macaulay Land Use Research Institute, Aberdeen, 38-41.

Ardron, P.A., Rotherham, I.D. & Gilbert, O. (1999) An evaluation of the South Pennines peatlands with reference to the impact of peat cutting. *Peak District Journal of Natural History and Archaeology*, **1**, 67-75.

Gilbert, O. (2000) *Assemblages and assembly rules*. In: Barker, G. (ed.) (2000) *Ecological recombination in urban areas: implications for nature conservation*. Proceedings of a Workshop Held at the Centre for Ecology and Hydrology (Monks Wood), 13th July 2000. UK Man and Biosphere Committee Urban Forum, English Nature, Centre for Ecology and Hydrology. English Nature, Peterborough, 14–16.

Benhouhou, S.S., Dargie, T.C.D. & Gilbert, O.L. (2001) Vegetation associations in the Great Western erg and the Saoura valley, Algeria. *Phytocoenologia*, **31**, 311–324.

Benhouhou S.S., Dargie T.C.D. & Gilbert O.L. (2003) Vegetation associations in the Ougarta Mountains and dayas of the Guir hamada, Algerian Sahara. *Journal of Arid Environments*, **54**, 739–753.

Ardron, P.A. & Gilbert, O.L. (2005) The myxomycetes of the Sheffield area. *Naturalist*, **130**, 13–26.

Gilbert, O.L. (2005) Urban Ecology: Progress And Problems. *Journal of Practical Ecology and Conservation Special Series*, **No. 4**, 5-7.

Chapter 2: Urban Vegetation – a neglected element of British plant community classification

Peter Shepherd
BSG

Introduction

The phrase 'urban vegetation' has been used as a broad catch-all to describe all vegetated land in a town or city area, in other words all vegetation types regardless of origin or age are urban vegetation simply by their physical location within an urban environment. It is true that many of the early surveys of town and cities in the UK took this approach, mapping and classifying (not straight forward given the absence of suitable coverage in standard survey methods) the green spaces of towns and cities covering everything from formal parks and gardens to abandoned land to remnant pieces of countryside encapsulated in urban sprawl. A narrower interpretation of urban vegetation, and one this paper focusses on, is that which focuses on those spontaneous ('natural') plant communities unique to the urban environment that colonise unhindered by human management on derelict sites, buildings, and built forms.

Describing Urban Vegetation

In the 1980's before the publication of the National Vegetation Classification (NVC) there were various attempts to try and develop systems that captured the diversity of vegetation types in towns and cities into a single system. However, these were a combination of habitat types based on semi-natural vegetation of the rural environment, topped up with descriptions of types of formal green space and vegetation that were often no more than stands of single conspicuous (often non-native) species. These attempts at establishing a system classification were not widely adopted and urban green space surveys continued to be based broadly on the Phase 1 habitat survey methodology adapted to accommodate the urban environment as best it could. Inevitably vegetation communities of spontaneuous urgan plant communities were lumped into habitats of ephemeral short perennial vegetation or tall ruderal, neither of which did justicie to the plant communities they encompassed. However, a few urban focussed ecologists recognised the distinctive character of the spontaneuous plant communities of our towns and cities and their value in the urban context and published early descriptions of these vegetation types. Leading the way was Oliver Gilbert who described the spontaneous vegetation of what he called – the 'Urban Commons' in his book *'The Ecology of Urban Habitats'* (1991). Not only did he provide good descriptions of the spontaneous vegetation of urban commons Oliver Gilbert also recognised and accepted the new combinations of plant communities as the natural vegetation of the urban environment.

In 1991 Volume one of the National Vegetation Classification (NVC) - British Plant Communities - Woodland and Scrub was published (Rodwell, 1991). This impressive publication marked a significant change in the British approach to vegetation science and the introduction for many British ecologists to the science of phytosociology, although there had been earlier excellent accounts of the vegetation of Scotland (McVean and Ratcliffe, 1962) and calcareous grasslands (Shimwell, 1971a & b). The arrival of the NVC meant that the vegetation of Britain was now being described and classified in a consistent manner in a system that would allow British vegetation to be placed into the wider European context. The hope in the early 190's was that this would include the spontaneous plant communities of Britain's urban commons, walls and buildings and post-industrial habitats.

Unfortunately, despite the intensive work over many years, it was clear following the publication of the fifth and final volume of the NVC that there remained gaps in the coverage of the description of British plant communities. In 1998 the Joint

Nature Conservation Commission (JNCC) commissioned a review of the coverage of the NVC (Rodwell *et al.,* 2000), which identified known and potential gaps in the NVC. The biggest weaknesses and most numerous gaps were among the freshwater aquatic vegetation of moving and standing waters, shallow or fluctuating pools and water margins and springs. In relation to vegetation of urban and post-industrial habitats it also recognised that a further substantial group of communities comprised of weedy vegetation in urban and post-industrial habitats (Rodwell *et al.*, 2000) was also under represented.

This paper presents an overview of the classification of plant communities that are often considered to be typical of urban areas across Europe and presents descriptions of some plant communities described from urban areas in central England made by the author during his post-doctoral research. It also aims to provide a guide to the character of urban vegetation not described in the NVC to help ecologists working in the urban environment recognise and describe such plant communities and to place them at least within the hierarchical classification system set out in the phytosociological conspectus in volume five of the NVC. This will also enable the relationship of British urban vegetation communities to those described across central Europe to be better understood. Many of the communities described here would have been very familiar to Oliver Gilbert and other urban ecologists of his generation.

The NVC classification hierarchy and nomenclature
Phyotosociological classification systems in Europe utilise a nomenclature and hierarchical classification that traditionally had not been widely used in Britain prior to the publication of the NVC. Whilst Volume 5 of the NVC provides a phytosociaological classification in which the NVC communities are placed British ecologists refer to vegetation types by their English title or letter and number code from the NVC rather than the European phytosociological terminology. The great benefit of the European phytosociological classification set out in Volume 5 of the NVC is seen when a plant community not

described by the NVC is encountered as the community based on its floristics can still be described as belonging to one part of the wider hierarchial classification system.

To use the hierarchial classification system it is important to understand the terminology it uses. The fundamental vegetation unit of European phytoscoiological classification and the NVC is the *Association* or in the NVC the communities described and prefaced by letter and number codes such as MG1, H9 and W14. In the hierarchical classification systems of Europe and the phytosociological conspectus in volume five of the NVC Associations are grouped together to form a higher level in the hierarchy known as an *Alliance*. Above the Alliance is the *Order* and above that the largest grouping of communities or the highest level of the hierarchical classification is the *Class*. The different levels within this hierarchical classification are designated by the use of suffices. At the Association level the suffix – *etum* is added to the radical of the Latin generic name of the character or indicator species of that particular association. Added to this is the specific name in the genitive case (Box 1).

Box 1.

Suffixes used to indicate the hierarchial level in European phytosociological classifications

The following suffices are applied to indicate the various levels within the hierarchy:

RankEndingExample
Class- eteaMolinio-Arrhenather*etea*
Order- etaliaArrhenather*etalia*
Alliance- ionCynosur*ion*
Association- etumCentaureo-cynosur*etum cristati*

The association in this example is synonomous with the MG5 Centaurea nigra – Cynosurus cristatus grassland or the Centaureo-Cynosuretum cristati Br.-BL. & Tx 1952

Sub-associations or sub-communities are identified with the suffix - *etosum*.

Plant communities of urban environments and post-industrial sites

There has been very little description of these communities in Britain and this is reflected in the NVC. In particular, the annual and biennial communities of disturbed waste ground, some scrub and secondary woodland communities and some grassland communities of urban and post-industrial environments, sometimes referred to as synanthropic (with man) vegetation communities, remain undescribed in the NVC.

There are good descriptions of rural weed communities of disturbed natural soils of agricultural and horticultural environments (segetal habitats). These are based on new data collated during the NVC project and to a degree the work of Silverside (1977).

The hierarchical classification of plant community types set out in volume five of the NVC follows the system set out in the European Vegetation Survey (Rodwell, *et al.,* 2000). The classification of plant communities of urban and post-industrial ruderal habitats is presented in Box 2.

Box 2 – NVC classification of plant communities of urban and post-industrial habitats

STELLARIETEA MEDII (Tuxen, Lohmeyer et Preising ex Rochow 1951)
Weed communities of tilled naturl soils of agricultural crops, gardens, ornamental planting beds and waste places. This class is broken down into 3 orders:

Polygono-Chenopodietalia (R.Tx. et Lohmeyer 1950 em J. Tx. 1961) includes arable weed communities on neutral to slightly lime-deficient soils.

Centaureetalia cyani (R.Tx., Lohmeyer et Preising in R.Tx. 1950) includes weed communities of arable crops, gardens and waste places on base-rich soils.

Sisymbrietalia (J.Tuxen in Lohmeyer et al 1962) includes under the alliance *Sisymbrion officinalis (J.Tuxen Lohmeyer et Preising in Tuxen 1950 em Hejny*

---

in Hejny et al 1979) weed communities of compost and dung heaps, disturbed tracksides and recreation areas.

POLYGONO ARENASTRI-POETEA ANNUE (Rivas-Martinez et al. 1991)
Comprises vegetation dominated by rosette forming and creeping hemicryptophytes of disturbed and trampled habitats. The class includes weed and grassy communities of path edges, gateways, tracksides and recreational areas. In the NVC there is one order and two alliances: Lolio-Plantaginion (Sissingh 1960) and Polygonion avicularis (Br.-Bl. Ex Aichinger 1933).

ARTEMISIETEA VULGARIS (Lohmeyer *et al.* ex Rochow 1951)
Perennial and thistle-rich sub-xerophilous communities of temperate and Mediterranean regions. It is shown in the NVC as comprising just one order the ***Onopordetalia acanthii (Br.-Bl. &Tx. ex Klika &Hadac 1944)*** with just one alliance the ***Arction lappae (Tuxen 1937 em. Gutte 1972).***

GALIO-URTICETEA (Passarge ex Kopecky 1969)
Semi-natural and weedy vegetation dominated by perennials on nutrient-rich, relatively stable substrates. In the NVC it comprises two orders, the ***Convolvuletalia sepium (Tuxen 1950)*** and ***Lamio-albi- Chenopodietalia bonus-henrici (Kopecky 1969)***. The latter includes weed and semi-natural communities of tall mesophilious and nitrophilous perennials. Two communities are described, OV24 and OV25 under the alliance ***Galio-Allilarion (Oberdorfer 1957).*** The ***Convoluletalia sepium*** contains natural and semi-natural nitrophilous communities of tall perennial herbs of river banks and shallows and includes under the alliance ***Convolvulion sepium*** the OV26 *Epilobium hirsutum* community.

ASPLENIETEA TRICHOMANIS (Oberdorfer 1977).
Wall vegetation is included within the order ***Tortulo-Cymbalarietalia*** (OV39, OV40 and OV41)

In terms of spontaneous urban plant communities dominated by either annual, biennial and perennial communities there are no vegetation communities described in the phytosociological conspectus of the NVC in the order Sisymbrietalia of the the class Stellarietea medii or the class Artemisietea vulgaris. Yet across central and western Europe these orders and classes include a wide range of annual and biennial plant communities recorded from urban and post-industrial sites. Similar communities occur in Britain, but are awaiting a clear description and classification. It should be noted, however, that descriptions from Europe need to be treated with caution because it is not known the extent to which the integrity of such communities is maintained within the UK with its cooler and wetter climate of the Atlantic biogeographic zone. This is particularly true of many urban weed communities that in central Europe are characterised by a number of more thermophilous species not recorded from the UK. The situation, however, is complicated further by the increasing and often localised colonisation of urban areas by introduced weed species from Europe that find the warmer climates of large urban conurbations to their liking.

Unlike the work of Silverside (1977) on arable weed plant communities there have been few studies of the weed and perennial herb vegetation of urban and post-industrial environments. Very few studies or descriptions have been published and these have not been extensive or based on the NVC. Examples, include Haigh (1980) and Clemens, Bradley and Gilbert (1984) and Sargent (1984). There was also the Conspectus of Urban Vegetation Types prepared by Shimwell (1983) for the Nature Conservancy Council, but this was primarily based on habitats rather than plant communities, although some vegetation types are familiar.

Lunn (1998) undertook studies using the NVC of the vegetation of coal tips in Yorkshire, and Shaw has published descriptions of the natural colonisation of another post-industrial substrate – Pulverised Fuel Ash (Shaw, 1992). There have also been general descriptions of urban plant assemblages in a variety of urban floras such as Derby (Futter and Raynes, 1989), Kings Lynn (Payne, 1995), Sheffield (Shaw, 1988), Nottingham (Shepherd, 1998), Greater London (Burton, 1983) and Glasgow (Dickson, 1991).

The study undertaken by the author as part of his doctoral research (Shepherd, 1991) and survey work since has described British vegetation communities of urban habitats in the main urban centres of the West Midlands, Nottinghamshire, Leicestershire, Derbyshire and Staffordshire. Based on this work and a review of vegetation descriptions from central and western Europe the assemblages of species typically occurring in vegetation communities of the Alliance Sisymbrion of the Class Stellarietea medii and communities of the Class Artemisietea are considered below. In addition, consideration is given to other urban vegetation communities dominated by grasses and scrub that do not appear to fit neatly into the NVC phytosociological conspectus.

Urban communities of the *Sisymbrion officinalis*

This Alliance is classified in the NVC phytosociological conspectus in the Order Sisymbrietalia and the Class Stellarietea medii (Tx, Lohmeyer et Preising ex Rochow 1951) and is described in the NVC as supporting *"weed communities of compost and dung heaps, disturbed tracksides and recreation areas"*. No communities are described in the NVC within the Sisymbrion, yet the majority of weedy communities of the urban environment are likely to fall into the Sisymbrion.

Plant communities of this Alliance are dominated by annual species and develop on a variety of recently disturbed ground including top-soiled planting beds, brick rubble and concrete 'scree', roadside verges and derelict land. They are generally characterised by combinations of goosefoot *Chenopodium album*, hastate orache *Atriplex prostrata*, smooth sowthistle *Sonchus oleraceus*, hedge mustard *Sisymbrium officinale*, other members of the *Sisiymbrium* genus such as, false London rocket *Sisymbrium loeselii* and tall rocket *Sisymbrium altissimum*, Oxford ragwort *Senecio squalidus*, prickly lettuce *Lactuca serriola*, Canadian fleabane *Conyza canadensis*, common orache *Atriplex patula*, barren brome *Anisantha sterilis*, wall barley *Hordeum murinum*, and scentless mayweed *Tripleurospermum inodorum*. They are accompanied by a long list of other plant species that can be locally distinctive reflecting local colonisations, geography and history, but not diagnostic of the communities. The apparently random, mixed assemblage often leads to these communities being described as weedy vegetation with no consistent appearance of structure, but there are constants that characterise these vegetation types.

In the review of gaps in the NVC Rodwell *et al.* (2000) suggested that gallant soldier *Galinsoga parviflora*, flixweed *Descurainia sophia*, and stinking goosefoot *Chenopodium vulvaria* may make distinctive contributions to these communities and certainly these species are regularly recorded in communities of the Sisymbrion in central Europe. However, flixweed and stinking goosefoot were not recorded by Shepherd (1991) from urban areas in central England. Flixweed has a strong distribution in eastern and south-eastern England (Preston *et al.*, 2002) and may have a stronger presence in arable environments than urban wasteland. It is however a characteristic species of communities of the Sisymbrion in plant communities of urban areas in western and central Europe and as such maybe more frequent in urban communities of eastern and south-eastern England. Burton (1983) describes the distribution of flixweed in Greater London as being sporadic and never persisting for long, but that it was recorded from disturbed natural soils such as long new roads and soil tips. Stinking goosefoot has a limited distribution in England being recorded from only 16 10 kilometre grid squares between 1987 and 1999 (Preston, *et al.*, 2002) and as such is unlikely to be widely recorded in urban plant communities at the current time in the UK. It is also a species of nutrient-rich soils often enriched by animal dung, which is more likely to be found in rural locations. Shepherd (1991) more often recorded gallant soldier in central England together with shaggy soldier *Galinsoga quadriradiata* in communities of recently tilled natural soils or deposited light free-draining soils often in gardens and allotments. Such whilst these species may be recorded within communities of the Sisymbrion they may more often be recorded in annual weed communities of the Order Polygono-Chenopodietalia and the Alliance Polygono-Chenopodion polysperm.

Some of the vegetation communities believed to represent the class Stellarietea and the alliance Sisymbrion recorded from urban areas in central England are described below (Shepherd, 1991).

Wall Barley and Barren Brome community *(syn: Hordeetum murini brometosum sterilis (Elias, 1979)*

This is a community dominated by wall barley *Hordeum murinum* which develops on free draining soils at the base of walls, pavement edges, along roadsides and fences, around car parks and paved areas. It has been widely described from continental Europe where at least three different sub-communities have been recognised. Some authors have even proposed a new alliance within the Sisymbrietalia should be recognised to cover the range of vegetation communities characterised by *Hordeum murinum*. In central England, however, these communities do not appear to exhibit such variation. The soils associated with this community are free draining, sandy or stony and base-rich with a pH between 7.8 and 8.2.

A trampled variant of this sub-association has also been recorded in which perennial rye grass *Lolium perenne* and to a lesser extent knot grass *Polygonum aviculare* and annual meadow grass *Poa annua* become more prevalent. The nearest community described in the NVC is OV23 the *Lolium perenne-Dactylis glomerata* community in which *Hordeum murinum* can achieve a high constancy and it is possible that in the absence of further descriptions many stands of *Hordeetum murini brometosum sterilis (Elias 1979)* may be classified as OV23. This community however, develops where the character species have been sown and in areas subject to high trampling pressure. It is similar, but a different plant community and does not fully describe the wall barley communities of stony, free draining, base-rich substrates. A summary of the community as described from central England is presented in Table 1 (Appendix 1).

False London Rocket community *(syn: Sisymbrietum loselii (Gutte, 1969)*

This is an unusual community in that it was only been recorded by Shepherd (1991) in central England from Nottingham where it is one of the commonest yellow crucifer dominated communities in the City. This reflects the distribution of false London rocket *Sisymbrium loeselii*, which has a strong distribution around the towns and cities of central England. It may also be represented further south particularly in London and the East Thames corridor as false London rocket has a stronghold in this area (Preston et al. 2000). Ruderal weed communities can be very dynamic depending on factors such as colonisation and disturbance and some weed communities can be localised. False London rocket was introduced into Nottingham in 1963 and from there is it has spread throughout the City (Shepherd, 1998). Similar communities dominated and characterised by species of *Sisymbrium* or other crucifers such as Hoary mustard *Hirschfeldia incana* are likely to occur. It has been observed by the author that haory mustard has increased singificnatly in weed communitie sin southern and eastern England and south Wales in the last 15 years.

The false London rocket community occurs on a wide range of derelict land on brick rubble and other man-made and natural free-draining substrates. The community is dominated by false London rocket with scentless mayweed *Tripleurospermum inodorum* sbsp. *inodorum* and tall rocket *Sisymbrium altissimum*. It mostly develops on free draining soils with little or no surface organic layer and a pH between 8.0 and 8.5. A sub-community occurs on loamy and slightly compacted soils often where brick rubble and sub-soils have been mixed and crushed. Two sub-communities can be differentiated depending on differences in substrate. One is characterised by the presence of *Senecio squalidus, Artemisia absinthium, Reseda lutea* and *Vulpia myuros*. This sub-community develops on ruderal substrates with a high proportion of brick rubble and concrete. The second sub-community is characterised by *Sisymbrium officinale*,

41

Polygonum aviculare, Capsella bursa-pastoris, Matricaria recutita, Tripleurospermum inodorum sbsp. inodorum, Matricaria matricarioides and *Stellaria media*. It develops on more nutrient-rich substrates with natural soils mixed with rubble and concrete.

A summary of the community as described from central England is presented in Table 2 in Appendix 1.

Oxford Ragwort and Canadian Fleabane community *(syn: Bromo-Erigeretum canadensis* **(Gutte 69).**

This is a widespread ruderal community of brick rubble sites in central England characterised by Canadian fleabane, *Conyza canadensis*, Oxford ragwort *Senecio squalidus* and rat's-tail fescue *Vulpia myuros*. This community typically develops on recently created urban demliton sites or as Oliver Gilbert better describes them, urban commons. These sites are charcaterised by large quantities of brick rubble, accumulated dusts, gravel, concrete, tarmac and cinders. These are often crushed and mixed with fine textured materials. The soils are free draining, have a high sand content with little or no organic matter, but are base-rich with a neutral to calcareous pH range of 7.2 to 8.4.

Similar communities have been described throughout western and central Europe, but they differ substantially from the community described in central England supporting a range of thermopilous species not recorded from England. A similar community described from Europe in terms of the habitat and character species is the *Bromo-Erigeretum canadensis* (Gutte 69). This is a widespread community in central Europe developing in similar circumstances to those in the UK, especially on railway lines, but a key floristic difference is the absence of the grass *Bromus tectorum*. This grass species has a very localised distribution in the UK being recorded from only 25 10 kilometre squares between 1987 and 1999 (Preston, *et al.,* 2002). It is possible that this species is replaced by *Vulpia myuros* or *Vulpia bromoides*. More recently colonisation and spread of introduced species such as narrow-leaved ragwort *Senecio inaequidens* especially in London and the South-east of England as replaced or come to dominate Oxford Ragwort in this community.

Closely related communities characterised by Canadian fleabane and prickly lettuce *Lactuca serriola* are classified in Europe as the Erigeronto canadensis-Lactucetum serriolae (Oberdorfer 57). The relationship with the Oxford ragwort- rat's-tail fescue community is not clear, as character species such as prickly lettuce are rare within this community. Further study of this type of vegetation in particular is required. A summary of the community as described from central England is presented in Table 3 in Appendix 1.

Hedge Mustard and Scentless Mayweed community *(syn: Sisymbrietum officinalis (Hadac, 1978)*

This is a widespread community of mounds of earth, brick and concrete on construction sites and other disturbed areas in central England. It develops on relatively fertile, sandy loams ranging in pH from 7.5 to 8.7 often depending on the amount of concrete and brick in the substrate. The more fertile soils have a higher organic content than other communities recorded from the Sisymbrion and as a consequence have better moisture retaining properties. This is reflected by the high constancy of rough meadow grass *Poa trivialis* and to a lesser extent Shepherd's purse *Capsella bursa-pastoris*. The classification of this community is uncertain at the current time and it may sit more comfortably in the Polygono-Chenopodion polyspermi alliance rather than the Sisymbrion. A summary of the community as described from central England is presented in Table 4 in Appendix 1

Fat Hen and Prostrate Orache community *(syn: Chenopodio rubri-Atriplicetum patulae (Gutte, 1966)*

This is a common community of tilled natural soils in urban areas in central England. It has been recorded from flower beds, allotments and on top-soiled landscaped sites, but more frequently from mounds of earth mixed with brick rubble. The soils are moist, fertile, loamy sands with a pH range between 7.5 and 8.5. There are some similarities between this community and the arable weed communities of root crops and summer cereals (OV7 and OV8). The high constancy of spear-leaved orache *Atriplex prostrata* however, is unusual. Early studies by Clemens *et al.* (1984) of pioneer communities of urban demolition sites in Sheffield described an annual community of disturbed soils characterised by spear-leaved orache. The classification of this community is uncertain at the current time and it may sit more comfortably in the Polygono-Chenopodion polyspermi alliance rather than the Sisymbrion. A summary of the community as described from central England is presented in Table 5 of Appendix 1.

Communities of the Class *Artemisietea vulgaris* (Lohmeyer *et al.* ex Rochow 1951)

The biennial and perennial weed communities of urban areas are characterised by tall vigorous herbs including mugwort *Artemisia vulgaris*, lesser burdock *Arctium minus*, melilot *Melilotus spp.*, tansy *Tanacetum vulgare*, broad-leaved dock *Rumex obtusifolius* and nettle *Urtica dioica*. These communities often replace the annual pioneer communities and can subsequently persist until re-disturbed or colonised by shrubs and trees. In Britain there is a close relationship between these communities and those of the class Galio-Urticetea, in particular, vegetation with a high constancy and cover of nettle (NVC communities - OV 24 and OV 25). Sufficient differences remain, however, especially where mugwort and burdock become more dominant than nettle and creeping thistle *Cirsium arvense* to suggest that they are most likely to be classified in the Class

Artemisietea vulgaris. The NVC phytosociological conspectus currently does not provide descriptions of any plant communtiies that fall into this Class.

Some vegetation communities provisionally assigned to the Artemisietea vulgaris have been described from central England (Shepherd, 1991) and are described in the following section.

Tansy and Mugwort community *(syn: Tanaceto-Artemisietum vulgaris Br.-Bl.1931 corr., 1949)*

This community is characterised by mugwort and tansy, which together with couch grass *Elytrigia repens* and creeping thistle *Cirsium arvense* dominate the vegetation. Nettle *Urtica dioica* is absent or occurs at very low frequency. It has been infrequently recorded from urban areas in central England and is a community of moderately fertile loamy to sandy soils with a pH range of 7 to 7.9 of edges of car parks, roadsides, derelict land and railway sidings. A sub-community characterised by perforate St John's–wort *Hypericum perforatum* occurs on railway sidings.

This community is widespread and frequently recorded in western and central Europe and Herbert Sukopp once referred to it as almost an entirely urbanised vegetation community. In Europe mugwort, tansy, and common toadflax *Linaria vulgaris* are character species and Canadian goldenrod *Solidago canadensis*, black horehound *Ballota nigra* and couch grass are frequent associates. Nettle is conspicuous by its absence or low frequency.

In central England, this community has a restricted or sporadic occurrence, and it may be more widespread in south and eastern England. This community is commonly classified in western and central Europe in the Arction lappae (Tuxen 1937em. Gutte 1972). In the review of the coverage of the NVC, however, Rodwell *et al.* (2002) suggests that this community should be classified under the Dauco-Melilotion (Gors ex Oberdorfer *et al.* 1967). Further study of this community is required to determine its correct classification. A summary of the community is presented in Table 6 in Appendix 1.

Nettle and Mugwort community *(syn: Urtico-Artemisietum vulgaris (Hadac, 1978)*

A closely related and more frequently occurring community is the common nettle and mugwort community. It is perhaps the commonest tall-herb ruderal perennial vegetation community in central England. It develops on loamy sands mixed with brick rubble, cinders and concrete within a pH range of 7.6 to 8.3. It is frequently recorded from earth and rubble mounds on the margins of urban commons, roadside verges, and edges of car parks, derelict land and railway sidings.

Tall perennial herbs dominate the community with mugwort as the only constant species. Near constant species include common nettle and broad-leaved dock *Rumex obtusifolius*. A bryophyte layer also can develop within this community. There is likely to be a sub-community of more ruderal soils with higher pH, but further study would be required. This community is classified in the Arction lappae (Tuxen 1937) alliance largely because of the prominence of mugwort and burdock species over nettle. However, there are similarities with the *Rumex obtusifolius – Artemisia vulgaris* sub-community of the *Urtica dioica – Cirsium arvense* community (OV25b), but this sub-community does not appear to fully reflect the ruderal nature of this community in urban areas and further study is required. A summary of this community recorded from central England is presented in Table 7 in Appendix 1.

White Dead Nettle and Hemlock community *(syn: Lamio-Conietum maculati (Oberdorfer, 1957)*

This tall herb community was infrequently recorded in urban areas in central England. It is characterised by hemlock *Conium maculatum* and white dead nettle *Lamium album*. It is a community of fertile, moist loamy soils on rubbish tips, earth mounds and disturbed ground often close to water. The soils are moist, loamy sands with a pH between 7.1 and 8.1. Where it occurs on drier soils with a higher pH resulting from the high level of contamination by concrete and rubble a sub-community characterised by wormwood *Artemisia absinthium*, sterile brome *Anisantha sterilis* and wild mignonette *Reseda lutea* can be recognised. This community is frequently recorded from western and central Europe on moist loose, humic soils and is classified in the Arction lappae (Tuxen 1937). The dominance of hemlock and the constant occurrence of white dead nettle suggests that it has, like other Arction lappae vegetation, similarities with communities of the Class Galio-Urticeta (Passarge ex Kopecky 1969). A summary of the community recorded in towns and cities in central England is presented in Table 8 in Appendix 1.

Melilot community *(syn: Melilotetum albi-officinalis (Sissingh, 1950)*

This tall herb community is frequently recorded from recently disturbed areas around industrial estates, abandoned clay pits and railway sidings. It has also been recorded from disturbed areas of dry pulverised fuel ash. The soils are alkaline in reaction with a pH between 7.8 and 8.8. They are loamy sands to sandy loams and are frequently mixed with rubble, concrete and other artefacts of dereliction. It is characterised by tall biennial herbs. Wild carrot *Daucus carota* is a frequent associate of the community together with species of clover *Trifolium* spp. and black medick, *Medicago lupulina,* thistles *Cirisum* spp. and scentless mayweed *Tripleurospermum inodorum* sbsp. *inodorum* with creeping bent *Agrostis stolnifera* and Yorkshire fog grass *Holcus lanatus* forming a grass ground layer. In western and central Europe communities dominated by Melilot are classified in the Alliance Dauco-Melilotion (Gors ex Oberdorfer et al 1967), the Order Onopordetalia and the Class Artemisitea. This Alliance is distinguished from communtiies of the supports Arction lappae alliance by a greater preponderance of more xerophilous plant communities. Compared to the descriptions from Europe the stands of this community in central England are lacking some key character species, in particular Viper's bugloss *Echium vulgare* and evening primrose *Oenothera biennis*, although the author has recorded these species as present in Melilot dominated vegetation on the south coast of England givng them a stronger similarity to the communities described from Europe.

Communities of the Dauco-Melilotion are likely to be restricted more southern and eastern parts of Britain where they may better resemble their European counterparts. A summary of the community as described from central England is presented in Table 9 in Appendix 1.

A second alliance of the Onopordetalia is the Onopordion acanthii (Br.-Bl. *et al.* 1936). This alliance supports more xerophilous vegetation communities and no vegetation communities of this alliance were recorded by Shepherd (1991) from central England. Rodwell *et al.* (2002) suggest that communities of this alliance are likely to be fragmentary and form on dry calcareous soils in eastern and south-eastern England, particularly near the sea.

Grassland communities described from urban envrionments in central England

A range of grassland communities is encountered in urban areas. The majority of these occur along roadsides, railways, urban commons, and medium term abandoned land. They comprise tall, unmanaged stands that can typically be assigned to various sub-communities and variants of MG1 - false oat grass grassland (Arrhenatheretum elatioris Br.-Bl. 1919). However, not all grassland communities recorded from central England and other urban areas further to the south-east, are easily assigned to recognised communtiies of the NVC. Perhaps the most distinctive and widespread of these is the rat'-tail fescue community. Less distinctive are the swards dominated by couch grass *Elytrigia repens* and mesotrophic grassland communities dominated by Yorkshire fog grass but lacking the grass species

48

that would classify them as false oat grass communities of managed and unmanaged neutral grassland or communities of meadows or pastures of the Alliance Cynosurion cristati. These communities are considered below.

Rat's-tail Fescue community *(syn: Vulpia myuros community after Brandes, 1983)*

The rat's tail fescue *Vulpia myuros* community typically develops on the hot, dry, cinder beds of railway tracks and sidings. These substrates are low in organic content, free draining and often subject to summer parching. The vegetation is dominated by a uniform fine sward of the annual grass rat's-tail fescue punctuated by taller herbs including evening primrose species *Oenothera* spp., perforate St. John's wort *Hypericum perforatum*, common toadflax *Linaria vulgaris* and wild mignonette *Reseda lutea*. The sward also occurs in a mosaic with bare ground, which often supports procumbent pearlwort *Sagina procumbens*, thyme-leaved sandwort *Arenaria serpyllifolia* ssp. *serpyllifolia* and the moss *Bryum argenteum*. From the study of this community in Central England (Shepherd, 1991) a sub-community charcaterised by silver hari grass *Aira caryophyllea*, and blue fleabane *Erigeron acer* has been recognised where the community occurs on more calcareous substrates.

Similar communities dominated by annual grasses have been described from coal tips in central and northern England by Lunn (1998) and from railway stations across Germany (Brandes, 1983). *Vulpia* dominated communities have also been described from railway land by Shepherd (1991) and other workers in consultancy reports from parts of London and other British cities (R.Carter, pers.comm). The *Vulpia* communities in the East Thames corridor support a high frequency of creeping bent *Agrostis stolonifera*, which may represent a sub-community of these *Vulpia* grasslands. Shaw (pers. comm.) has also recorded a community dominated by *Vulpia myuros* from pulverised fuel ash sites once the early colonising vegetation characterised by halophytes has declined. Here creeping bent also forms a common associate of these grasslands.

The classification of this community is uncertain, but it is suggested that it belongs to the Alliance Thero-Airion (Tuxen ex Oberdorfer, 1957) of the class Koelerio-Corynephoretea (Klika in Klika et Novak, 1941), which according to the NVC includes *"pioneer vegetation of therophytes and hemicryptophyte perennials on dry, infertile sandy soils in the European lowlands"*. The Alliance Thero-Airion supports communities of bare, but stable acid sands. The NVC allocates one community to this Alliance MC5 Arenaria maritima-Cerastium diffusum ssp. diffusum maritime community, which has little or no similarity to this plant community. Rodwell *et al.* (2000) noted that there are inland grass swards rich in ephemerals such as *Vulpia ssp* that may fall into associations such as the Filagini-Vulpietum myuros (Oberdorfer, 1938) or the Aira caryophylleae-Festucetum ovinae &R Tx. 1955). The latter associated with calcareous soils.

Further recording of grasslands characterised by *Vulpia* species is required. A summary of the community described from railway habitats in central England is presented in Table 10 in Appendix 1.

Yorkshire Fog dominated grasslands

In central England Shepherd (1991) described a mesotrophic grassland community dominated by Yorkshire fog grass *Holcus lanatus* from a variety of habitats including urban commons, roadsides and former railway sidings. This community is notable by the absence or low frequency and cover of tall coarse grasses such as false oat grass, which makes classification within existing NVC mesotrophic grasslands difficult. It may be a transitional community to more recogniseable communities of the Arrhenatherion elatioris, although it often persists for a number of years, often succeeding directly to scrub.

Rodwell *et al.* (2002) reported that throughout the UK there are stands of often species-poor and rank swards with frequent red fescue *Festuca rubra*, Yorkshire fog grass *Holcus lanatus*, sweet vernal grass *Anthoxanthum odoratum*, Smooth meadow grass *Poa pratensis*, cock's-foot grass *Dactylis glomerata*, white clover *Trifolium repens* and ribwort plantain *Plantago lanceolata*. The grassland described from urban area by the author appears to be more disturbed than the community described by Rodwell *et al.* (2000) and lacks species such as sweet vernal grass *Anthoxanthum odoratum*.

Couch Grass and Bush Grass dominated communities

Other communities that have been noted from central England but not sufficiently well sampled are those of unmanaged grasslands of urban and post-industrial sites dominated by couch grass *Elytrigia repens* or bush grass *Calamagrostis epigejos*. In both these stand types, species such as false oat grass and other associates of *Arrhenatheretum elatioris* grassland are absent or poorly represented.

Couch grass dominated stands have been recorded in Nottingham from landfill sites capped with sandy soils and also in natural situations on sand and gravel bars along the River Trent. In both cases the more stable grassland areas are dominated by couch with a mixture of associates including tansy.

Rodwell *et al.* (2000) refer to *Elytrigia repens* communities recorded from inland sites on some flood plains (e.g. Derwent Ings) where there are no salt-marsh indicators present that would drive classification towards SM28 Elymus repens salt-marsh community, but no detailed descriptions have been published. Rodwell suggests inland stands may be classified in the Alliance Potentillion anserinae of the Order Agrostetalia stoloniferae. Certainly along rivers *Elytrigia repens* grassland communities are subject to periodic flooding and are also regularly disturbed as a result. In more stable areas such as landfill sites there may be periods of sporadic disturbance, but there is insufficient data and again more studies are required.

Bush grass stands can cover extensive areas of post-industrial sites with varying soils conditions ranging from heavy clays with poor drainage to railway sidings on apparently free draining clinker. In Peterborough and Bedford significant stands have been recorded in consultancy reports on poorly draining clay soils and often associated with former clay workings. In these relatively young grassland communities bush grass can grow to almost the total exclusion of other grasses and even tall herbaceous plants, but in other stands it is mixed with tall herbs such as teasel *Dipsacus fullonum*, creeping thistle *Cirsium arvense* great willowherb *Epilobium hirsutum* and bristly ox-tongue *Helminthotheca echioides*.

In contrast to the stands on clay soils bush grass also forms dense stands on apparently free draining stony soils of railway yards and sidings in Nottingham and Peterborough. Similar stands of vegetation dominated by bush grass with couch grass and tall herbs such Canadian goldenrod *Solidago canadensis* and wild carrot *Daucus carota* have also been recorded in Berlin on derelict brick rubble and former railway sites.

Bush grass appears to have a very diverse ecological range and has been noted on clay soils in ancient woodlands in Britain, and in pine forest clearings, sand dunes, brown coal open cast mine workings, alkali wastes, railway sidings and a range of urban and post-industrial wasteland in Europe (Rebele and Lehmann, 2001).

In the urban and post-industrial locations bush grass is often associated with other clonal grassland and ruderal species, such as *Elytrigia repens*, *Cirsium arvense*, *Solidago canadensis* and *Tanacetum vulgare*. These associates in these circumstances would suggest that bush grass communities should be classified in what was formerly referred to as the Agropyretea, but which is now subsumed into the Class Artemisitea according to the European Vegetation Survey (Mucina, 1997).

These grassland stands are varied and persist for long period of time and require further study before they can be classified.

Scrub of urban derelict habitats

Willow and Buddleja scrub *(syn: Epilobio-Salicetum (Oberdorfer, 1957)*

This is a scrub and tall herb community of stony substrates of derelict buildings and railway land. On some derelict sites the text book succession from annual pioneer communities to scrub is truncated with the rapid colonisation in the first year by tall herbs and shrubs, in particular, grey willow *Salix cinerea*, goat willow *Salix caprea*, rosebay willowherb *Chamaenerion angustifolium*, syacmore *Acer pseudoplatanus* and buddleja *Buddleja*.

This community typically dominates derelict buildings and railway habitats with substrates comprised of clinker, brick rubble and concrete. This is one of the most characteristic scrub communities of ruderal habitats in most British cities. Similar communities have been described from western and central Europe and also from London by Crawley (2011) who describes a Buddleja- Conyza community from similar habitats and with a similar variety of shrub and herbaceous species.

This community is placed by some authors in the association Epilobio-Salicetum (Oberdorfer, 1957) of the alliance Sambuco-Salicion capreae (Tuxen et Neumann 1950). Rodwell *et al.* (2000) identify an elder *Sambucus nigra* – nettle *Urtica dioica* seral scrub community of nutrient –rich mull soils within the order Sambucetalia racemosae (Oberdorfer et Passarge in Scamoni 1963) and the class Rhamno-Prunetea (Rivas Goday et Borja Carbonell 1961). The communities of scrub described from derelict urban envrionments, however, are lacking elder and nettle and have developed on ruderal, stony substrates. As a consequence some authors have classified these ruderal stands of scrub in the class Epilobietea angustifolii (Tuxen et Preising ex van Rochow 1951). It may be that there are sub-communities to be described here or that there are in fact separate plant communities. A summary of the community as described from central England is presented in Table 11 of Appendix 1.

Conclusion

The NVC provides an excellent description of the vegetation communities of the rural, semi-natural and natural environments of the UK and to a lesser extent the built environments of towns and cities. There remain some clear gaps in terms of the vegetation communities of urban and post-industrial habitats, in particular, sub-xerophilous and thermophilous environments. These communities have been widely described from western and central Europe although it is likely that in Britain the more oceanic climate will exclude some of the more extreme xerophilous and thermophilous plants, although this may vary greatly from the enormous urban conurbation that is London in the south-east of the UK to the urban centres of north-western England and Scotland and Northern Ireland. There is a need for a greater focus on such vegetation in the UK and more field data needs to be gathered, collated and reviewed in order to provide a strong basis for the description and classification of these vegetation communities. It is hoped that this paper will be of assistance to those ecologists who like Oliver Gilbert have a fascination for the spontaneous 'rewilded' habitats of urban environments helping them place thes plant communities in the wider range of vegetation types that make up the habitats of the UK.

References

Brandes, D. (1983) Flora und Vegetation der Bahnhofe Mitteleuropas. *Phytoceonologia* **11(1) 31-115**.

Burton, R.M. (1983) *Flora of the London Area. An historical and geographical account of the flowering plants and ferns found wild within 20 miles of St Paul's Cathedral*. London Natural History Society.

Clemens, J., Bradley, C., & Gilbert, O.L. (1984) Early development of vegetation on urban demolition sites in Sheffield, England. *Urban Ecology*, **8**, *139-147*.

Crawley, M.J. (2011) *London*. In: Kelcey, J.G., & Muller, N. (eds) *Plants and Habitats of European Cities*. Springer, Dorlecht, 207-236.

Futter, K., & Raynes, P. (1989) *The Flora of Derby*.

Dickson, J.H. (1991) *The Wild Plants of Glasgow. Conservation in the City and the Countryside*. Aberdeen University Press, Aberdeen.

Gilbert, O.L. (1989) *The Ecology of Urban Habitats*. Chapman and Hall, London.

Haigh, M.J. (1980) Ruderal communities in English cities. *Urban Ecology, **4**, 329-338*.

Lunn, J. (1998) *Ecological and nature conservation aspects of land affected by mining in the Yorkshire Coalfield*. Unpublished MPhil dissertation, Sheffield Hallam University, Sheffield.

Mucina, L. (1997) Conspectus of Classes of European Vegetation. *Folia Geobotanica and Phytotaxonomica*, **32**, 117-172.

McVean, D.N., & Ratcliffe, D.A. (1962) *Plant communities of the Scottish Highlands*. HMSO, London.

Payne, R.M. (1995) The Flora of Kings Lynn. *Transactions of the Norfolk and Norwich Naturalist's Society*, **30** Part 3, 317-342.

Preston, C.D., Pearman, D.A., & Dines, T.D. (2002) *New Atlas of the British and Irish Flora*. Oxford University Press, Oxford.

Rodwell, J.S. (ed.) (1991) *British Plant Communities, Volume 1. Woodlands and Scrub*. Cambridge University Press, Cambridge.

Rodwell, J.S. (ed.) (2000) *British Plant Communities, Volume 5. Maritime communities and vegetation of open habitats*. Cambridge University Press, Cambridge.

Rodwell, J.S., Dring, J.S., Averis, A.B.G., Proctor, M.C.F., Malloch, A.J.C., Schamniee, J.N.J., & Dargie, T.C.D. (2000) *Review of the coverage of the National Vegetation classification*. JNCC Report No. 302, HMSO, London.

Sargent, C. (1984) *Britain's Railway Vegetation*. Institute of Terrestrial Ecology, HMSO, London.

Shaw, M. (ed.) (1988) *A Flora of the Sheffield Area (Two Hundred Years of Plant Records)*. Sorby Record Special Series No. 8, Sorby Natural History Society, Sheffield.

Shaw, P.J.A (1992) A preliminary study of sucessional changes in vegetation and soil development on unamended fly ash (PFA) in southern England. *Journal of Applied Ecology*, **29**, 728-736.

Shepherd, P.A. (1991) *Botanical studies of synanthropic urban vegetation in central England*. Unpublished PhD dissertation, University of Nottingham, Nottingham.

Shepherd, P.A. (1998) *The Plants of Nottingham. A City Flora*. Wildtrack Publishing, Sheffield.

Shimwell, D.W. (1971a) Festuco-Brometea Br.-Bl. & R.Tx 1943 in the British Isles: the phytogeography and phytosociology of limestone grasslands. 1. General introduction; Xerobromion in England. *Vegetatio*, **23**, 1-28.

Shimwell, D.W. (1971b) Festuco-Brometea Br.-Bl. & R.Tx 1943 in the British Isles: the phytogeography and phytosociology of limestone grasslands. Eu-Mesobromion in England. *Vegetatio*, **23**, 29-60.

Shimwell, D.W. (1983) *A conspectus of urban vegetation types*. Urban Ecology Research Unit, No. 2, University of Manchester, Manchester.

Silverside, A.J. (1977) *A phytosociological survey of British arable weeds and related communities*. Unpublished PhD dissertation, University of Durham, Durham.

Appendix 1

Table 1: Summary of Hordeetum murini brometosum sterilis (Elias 1979)

Species	Constancy	
	(a)	(b)
Hordeum murinum	V (4-10)	V
Anisantha sterilis	IV (4-10)	III
Lolium perenne	III (1-5)	V
Poa annua	II (4-5)	II
Polygonum aviculare	I (1-4)	II
Sisymbrium officinale	IV (1-5)	IV
Senecio squalidus	III (1-3)	I
Artemisia vulgaris	III (1-3)	III
Sonchus oleraceus	II (1-4)	II
Artemisia absinthium	II (1-4)	II
Capsella bursa-pastoris	II (1-4)	I
Species with Frequencey I and cover abundance (1-2)		
Galium aparine, Urtica dioica, Vulpia myuros, Bromus hordaeceus sbsp hordaeceus, Geranium pyrenaicum, Matricaria matricoides, Arctium minus, Crepis capillaris, Holcus lanatus, Plantago lanceolata, Poa trivialis, Crepis vesicaria, Rumex crispus, Chamaenerion angustifolium, Cirsium arvense, Dactylis glomerata, Epilobium tetragonum, Lactuca serriola, Rubus fruticosus agg., Rumex obtusifolius, Sisymbrium loeselii, Acer pseudoplatanus (sap), Aegopodium podagraria, Buddleja davidii (sap), Elymus caninus, Epilobium montanum, Euphorbia peplus, Elytrigia repens, Hieracium murorum, Lamium album, Plantago major, Ranunculus repens, Senecio vulgaris, Sisymbrium orientale, Trifolium repens, Hordeum vulgare		
Number of samples	(a) 20	(b) 10
Vegetation Cover: 40-100%.	Vegetation Height: 15-80cm	

(a) Brometosum sub-association
(b) *Lolium perenne* variant

Table 2: Summary of the *Sisymbrietum loeselii* (Gutte 1969)

Species	Constancy		
	(a)	(b)	(c)
Sisymbrium loeselii	V	IV	V
Sisymbrium altissimum	II	V	III
Senecio squalidus	V		III
Artemisia absinthium	IV		III
Cirsium vulgare	III		II
Reseda lutea	II	I	I
Vulpia myuros	II		I
Matricaria recutita	I	V	III
Polygonum aviculare	I	V	III
Capsella bursa-pastoris	I	V	III
Sisymbrium officinale		IV	II
Alliaria petiolata		IV	II
Papaver dubium ssp.*dubium*		IV	II
Matricaria matricarioides		III	II
Stellaria media		III	II
Tripleurospermum inodorum		III	II
Chenopodium album	II	V	III
Cirsium arvense	III	III	III
Artemisia vulgaris	II	V	III
Elytrigia repens	I	IV	II
Atriplex prostrata	II	I	II
Medicago lupulina	II	IV	II
Poa annua	II	III	II
Anisantha sterilis	II	II	II
Fumaria officinalis	II	II	II
Holcus lanatus	II	I	II
Papaver rhoeas	II	I	II

Species with Frequencey (I) and cover abundance (1-2)

Brassica rapa, Fumaria officinalis, Galium aparine, Fallopia convolvulus, Raphanus raphaniastrum, Tussilago farfara, Papaver rhoeas, Lolium perenne, Impatiens glandulifera, Conium maculatum, Galega officinalis, Arabidopsis thaliana, Arrhenatherum elatius, Melilotus officinalis, Urtica dioica, Anagallis arvensis, Arenaria serpyllifolia, Brassica napus Calystegia sepium, Dactylis glomerata, Epilobium hirsutum, Euphorbia peplus, Festuca rubra, Galeopsis tetrahit, Lathryus pratensis, Persicaria maculosa, Silene alba, Solanum dulcamara, Sonchus asper, Taraxacum officinale agg.

Vegetation Cover: 40-90%, Vegetation Height: 60-120cm	Number of samples 16

a) *Senecio squalidus* ruderal sub-community; b) *Matricaria recutita* segetal sub-community; c) *Sisymbrietum loeselii* (Gutte 1969) (total)

Table 3: Summary of the *Senecio squalidus – Conyza canadensis* community

Species	Constancy
Senecio squalidus	IV
Conyza canadensis	IV
Vulpia myuros	III
Artemisia absinthium	III
Holcus lanatus	III
Sonchus oleraceus	III
Epilobium montanum	III
Sonchus asper	II
Sisymbrium officinale	II
Anisantha sterilis	II
Epilobium tetragonum	II
Chamaenerion angustifolium	II
Agrostis stolonifera	II
Poa annua	II
Crepis vesicaria	II
Taraxacum agg	II
Urtica dioica	II
Artemisia vulgaris	II
Cirsium arvense	II
Lolium perenne	II
Medicago lupulina	II
Poa trivialis	II
Trifolium repens	II
Tripleurospermum inodorum	II
Capsella bursa-pastoris	II
Matricaria matricoides	II
Sisymbrium altissimum	II
Crepis capillaris	II
Hordeum murinum	II
Plantago lanceolata	II
Reseda luteola	II
Rubus fruticosus	II
Solidago canadensis	II
Bryum capillaris	II
Antirrhinum majus	II
Arabidopsis thaliana	II
Arrhenatherum elatius	II
Tussilago farfara	II
Senecio jacobaea	II
Melilotus officinalis	II
Carduus acanthoides	II
Desmazeria rigida	II

Lapsana communis	II
Linaria vulgaris	II

Species with Frequencey (I) and cover abundance (1-2)
Poa trivialis, Senecio vulgaris, Arenaria serpyllifolia, Atriplex prostrata, Plantago major, Sisymbrium orientale, Verbascum thapsus, Cirsium vulgare, Salix caprea (sap.), *Veronica arvensis, Digitalis purpurea, Erigeron acer, Festuca rubra, Hypochoeris radicata, Lamium album, Linaria purpurea, Malva neglectam, Poa pratensis, Polygonum aviculare, Rumex crispus, Rumex obtusifolius, Salix viminalis* (sap), *Sedum acre, Sisymbrium loeselii, Tragopogon pratensis, Vicia sepium, Eupatorium cannabinum, Triticum aestivum, Brachythecium rutabulum, Bryum argenteum*

Vegetation Height: 30-90cm, Vegetation Cover: 10-90%	Total Number of samples: 34

Table 4: Summary of the *Sisymbrium officinale – Tripleurospermum inodorum* community

Species	Constancy
Sisymbrium officinale	IV
Tripleurospermum inodorum	IV
Poa trivialis	IV
Capsella bursa-pastoris	IV
Medicago lupulina	III
Sonchus oleraceus	III
Sonchus asper	III
Poa annua	II
Vicia sativa	II
Cerastium fontanum	II
Cirsium arvense	II
Holcus lanatus	II
Trifolium repens	II
Lolium perenne	II
Matricaria matricoides	II
Rumex crispus	II
Barbarea vulgaris	II
Senecio vulgaris	II
Stellaria media	II
Artemisia vulgaris	II
Anisantha sterilis	II
Chenopodium album	II
Cirsium vulgare	II
Galium aparine	II
Plantago major	II
Senecio squalidus	II

Geranium dissectum	II
Lactuca serriola	II
Stellaria media	II
Achillea millefolium	II
Agrostis stolonifera	II
Atriplex prostrata	II
Brassica rapa	II
Festuca rubra	II
Dactylis glomerata	II
Elytrigia repens	II
Plantago lanceolata	II
Poa pratensis	II
Ranunculus repens	II
Tussilago farfara	II
Vulpia myuros	II

Species with Frequencey (I) and cover abundance (1-2)

Artemisia absinthium, Artemisia vulgaris, Crepis vesicaria, Euphorbia peplus, Melilotus officinalis, Taraxacum agg., Veronica arvensis, Bellis perennis, Galium aparine, Cerastium glomeratum, Chamomilla recutita, Conium meculatum, Epilobium montanum, Geranium robertianum, Diplotaxis muralis, Lamium album, Lapsana communis, Rumex obtusifolius, Senecio viscosus, Silene alba, Sisymbrium loeselii, Solanum dulcamara

Vegetation Cover: 40-100%, Vegetation Height: 20-80cm	Total Number of samples: 21

Table 5: Summary of the *Chenopodium album – Atriplex prostrata* community

Species	Constancy
Chenopodium album	V
Atriplex prostrata	V
Polygonum maculosa	III
Polygonum aviculare	III
Capsella bursa-pastoris	III
Stellaria media	III
Tripleurospermum indodorum	III
Sisymbrium officinale	III
Atriplex patula	II
Sonchus oleraceus	II
Polygonum convolvulus	II
Senecio vulgaris	II
Euphorbia peplus	II
Elytrigia repens	II
Senecio squalidus	II
Veronica chamaedrys	II

Fumaria officinalis	II
Sonchus oleraceus	II
Sonchus asper	II
Agrostis stolonifera	II
Galeopsis tetrahit	II
Galium aparine	II
Lamium amplexicaule	II
Lamium album	II
Lamium purpureum	II
Papaver rhoeas	II
Tussilago farfara	II
Poa trivialis	II
Polygonum lapathifolium	II
Galium aparine	II
Impatiens glandulifera	II
Brassica rapa	II
Vicia hirsuta	II
Urtica dioica	II
Arabidopsis thaliana	II
Anchusa arvensis	II
Aethusa cynapium	II
Urtica urens	II

Species with Frequencey (I) and cover abundance (1-2)
Holcus lanatus, Taraxacum officinale agg., *Sisymbrium loeselii, Epilobium montanum, Convolvulus arvensis, Chenopodium rubrum, Chamaenerion angustifolium, Artemisia vulgaris, Allilaria petiolata, Papaver dubium, Raphanus raphaniastrum, Anisantha sterilis, Rumex obtusifolius, Atriplex patula, Rumex crispus, Plantago lanceolata, Artemisia absinthium, Lactuca serriola, Melilotus officinalis, Ranunculus repens, Plantago major, Anagallis arvensis, Brassica napus, Geranium pusillum, Vicia sativa, Achillea millefolium*
Bromus hordeaceus, Chaenorhinum minus, Cirsium vulgare, Conium maculatum, Diplotaxis tennuifolia, Elymus caninus, Epilobium hirsutum, Festuca rubra, Foeniculum vulgare, Galinsoga parviflora, Geranium rotundifolium, Heracleum sphondylium, Papaver somniferum.

Vegetation Cover: 30-100%, Vegetation Height: 30-90cm	Total Number of samples: 35

Table 6: Tanaceto-Artemisietum (Br.-Bl 49)

Species	Constancy
Artemisia vulgaris	V
Tanacetum vulgare	V
Rumex obtusifolius	IV
Arrhenatherum elatius	IV

Dactylis glomerata	IV
Cirsium arvense	IV
Artemisia absinthium	IV
Holcus lanatus	IV
Elytrigia repens	III
Agrostis stolonifera	III
Plantago lanceolata	III
Cirsium vulgare	III
Trifolium repens	III
Carduus nutans	III
Carex hirta	III
Centaurea nigra	III
Taraxacum officinale agg.	III
Festuca rubra	III
Silene alba	II
Foeniculum vulgare	II
Rubus fruticosus	II
Trifolium pratense	II
Lolium perenne	II
Potentilla reptans	II
Senecio jacobaea	II
Stachys sylvatica	II
Achillea millefolium	II
Agrostis capillaris	II
Anisantha sterilis	II
Heracleum sphondylium	II
Poa trivialis	II
Vicia sepium	II
Cytisus scoparius	II
Hypericum perforatum	II
Equisetum arvense	II
Lathyrus pratensis	II
Poa pratensis	II
Symphytum officinale	II

Species with Frequencey (I) and cover abundance (1-2)

Chamaenerion angustifolium, Leucanthemum vulgare, Lotus corniculatus, Lupinus polyphyllus, Rumex crispus, Crepis vesicaria, Solidago Canadensis, Tripleurospermum inodorum, Urtica dioica, Anthriscus sylvestris, Armoracia rusticana, Hypochoeris radicata, Calystegia sepium, Crepis capillaris, Deschampsia cespitosa, Dipsacus fullonum, Galium aparine, Lamium album, Linaria vulgaris, Raphanus raphaniastrum, Reseda luteola, Silene vulgaris, Solanum dulcamara, Tussilago farfara, Vicia hirsuta, Vicia sativa

Vegetation Cover: 100%, Vegetation Height: 100-150cm	Total Number of samples: 10

Table 7: Nettle and Mugwort community (syn: Urtico-Artemisietum vulgaris (Hadac, 1978)

Species	Constancy
Artemisia vulgaris	V
Urtica dioica	IV
Rumex obtusifolius	IV
Cirsium arvense	III
Elytrigia repens	III
Artemisia absinthium	III
Holcus lanatus	III
Anisantha sterilis	III
Malva sylvestris	II
Epilobium hirsutum	II
Arctium minus	II
Cirsium vulgare	II
Arrhenatherum elatius	II
Agrostis stolonifera	II
Epilobium montanum	II
Senecio squalidus	II
Crepis vesicaria	II
Lamium album	II
Medicago lupulina	II
Poa trivialis	II
Trifolium repens	II
Tussilago farfara	II
Calystegia sepium	II
Dactylis golmerata	II
Plantago lanceolata	II
Reseda luteola	II
Rubus fruticosus	II
Taraxacum agg	II
Species with Frequencey (I - II) and cover abundance (1-2)	

Plantago major, Lolium perenne, Tripleurospermum inodorum sbsp inodorum, Sonchus asper, Conium maculatum, Lapsana communis, Sisymbrium officinale, Sonchus oleraceus, Vicia sativa, Carduus acanthoides, Crepis capillaris, Dipsacus fullonum, Heracleum sphodylium, Hypochoeris radicata, Reynoutria japonica juv, Silene alba,Solanum dulcamara, Acer pseudoplatanus juv, Stachys sylvatica, Symphytum orientale, Verbascum thapsus,Vicia hirsuta, Papaver dubium, Papaver rhoeas, Reseda lutea, Sagina procumbens, Senecio jacobaea, Geranium pyrenaicum, Geranium robertianum, Hieracium umbellatum, Sinapsis arvensis, Eurhynchium praelongum, Cytisus scoparius, Bryum argenteum, Buddleja davidii, Chenopodium album, Brachythecium rutabulum, Armoracia rusticana, Galium aparine, Rumex crsipus, Ballota nigra, Chamaenerion angustifolium, Ranunculus repens, Trifolium

pratense, Achillea millefolium, Elymus caninus, Epilobium
tetragonum, Leucanthemum vulgare, Agrostis capillaris, Angelica
sylvestris, Anthriscus sylvestris, Atriplex patula, Bryonia cretica,
Convolvulus arvensis, Digitalis purpurea, Equisetum arvense,
Festuca rubra, Geranium dissectum, Hordeum murinum, Lactuca
serriola, Sherardia arvensis, Silene dioica, Sisymbrium orientale,
Vulpia myuros, Hordeum vulgare

Vegetation Cover: 50-100%, Vegetation Height: 60-150cm	Total Number of samples: 25

Table 8: White Dead Nettle and Hemlock community (syn: Lamio-Conietum maculati (Oberdorfer, 1957)

Species	Constancy	
	(a)	(b)
Conium maculatum	V	V
Lamium album	V	V
Artemisia vulgaris	IV	IV
Cirsium arvense	III	IV
Elytrigia repens	III	IV
Artemisia absinthium	V	III
Anisantha sterilis	IV	II
Plantago lanceolata	IV	II
Holcus lanatus	III	II
Reseda lutea	III	II
Rumex crispus	III	II
Urtica dioica	II	III
Arrhenatherum elatius	IV	III
Galium aparine	III	III
Dactylis gomerata	III	III
Poa trivialis	III	II
Cirsium vulgare	I	II
Festuca rubra	II	II
Rumex obtusifolius		II
Species with Frequencey (I – II) and cover abundance (1-2)		

Anthriscus sylvestris, Silene alba, Heracleum sphodylium,
Hypochoeris radicata, Dipascus, fullonum, Tripleurospermum
inodorum, Ballota nigra, Chamaenerion angustifolium, Ranunculus
repens, Trifolium pratense, Armoracia rusticana, Atriplex patula,
Bryonia cretica, Buddleja davidii, Digitalis purpurea, Eurhynchium
praelongum, Festuca rubra, Geranium pyrenaicum, Geranium
robertianum, Papaver dubium, Papaver rhoeas, Sinapsis
arvensis,Sisymbrium orientaleSonchus asper, Lapsana communis,
Sisynbrium officinale, Sonchus oleraceus, Vicia sativa, Achellea
millefolium, Carduus acanthoides, Crepis capillaris, Elymus caninus
Epilobium tetragonum, Leucanthemum vulgare, Reynoutria

japonica juv, Solanum dulcamar, Acer pseudoplatanus juv Agrostis capillaris, Angelica sylvestris, Brachythecium rutabulum, Bryum argenteum, Geranium dissectum, Chenopodium album, Convolus arvensis, Cytisus scoparius, Equisetum arvense, Hieracium umbellatum, Hordeum murinum, Lactuca serriola, Reseda lutea, Sagina procumbens, Senecio jacobaea, Sherardia arvensis, Silene dioica, Stachys sylvatica, Verbascum thapsus, Vicia hirsuta, Vulpia myuros, Hordeum vulgare	
Vegetation Cover: 90-100%, Vegetation Height: 80-200cm	Total Number of samples: 10

    (a)   Artemisia absinthium ruderal sub-community

    (b)   White Dead Nettle and Hemlock community (Total)

Table 9: Melilot community (syn: Melilotetum albi-officinalis (Sissingh, 1950)

Species	Constancy
Melilotus alba	V
Melilotus officinalis	III
Medicago lupulina	IV
Eolcus lanatus	IV
Trifolium repens	IV
Cirsium arvense	III
Trifolium pratense	III
Tripleurospermum inodorum	III
Agrostis stonlonifera	III
Cirsium vulgare	III
Plantago lanceolata	III
Artemisia absinthium	III
Melilotus altissima	III
Elymus rapens	III
Poa trivialis	II
Artemisia vulgaris	II
Crepis vesicaria	II
Sonchus oleraceus	II
Vulpia myuros	II
Lolium perenne	II
Laucanthemum vulgare	II
Sonchus asper	II
Tussilago farfara	II
Vicia sativa	II
Arrhenatherum elatius	II
Epilobium tetragonum	II
Ranunculus repens	II
Reseda luteola	II

Species	Constancy
Dactylis glomerata	II
Festuca rubra	II
Malva sylvestris	II
Senecio squalidus	II
Rubus fruticosus	II
Deschampsia cespitosa	II
Geranium dissectum	II
Vicia sepium	II
Anthyllis vulneraria	II
Poa pratensis	II
Bryum nigra	II
Hieracium pilsella	II
Lotus corniculatus	II
Hieracium pilosella	II
Malva neglecta	II
Oenothera erythrosepala	II
Carduus acanthoides	II
Elymus caninus	II
Tanacetum vulgare	II

Species with Frequencey (I) and cover abundance (1-2)

Poa annua, Cerastium fontanum, Chamaenerion angustifolium, Epilobium montanum, Rumex obtusifoliusk Senecio jacobaea, Senecio vulgaris, Achillea millefolium, Vicia cracca, Equisetum arvense, Potentilla reptans, Anisantha sterilis, Silene alba, Cynosurus cristatus, Resdea lutea, Lotus corniculatus, Hypericum perforatum, Carduus mutans, Chenopodium album, Atriplex patula, Carex hirta, Cichorium intybus, Centaurium erythraea, Conium maculatum, Cymbalaria muralis, Erigeron acer, Foeniculum vulgare, Linaria vulgaris, Lupinus polypyllus, Solidago canadensis, Salix caprea juv, Matricaria matricoides, Trifolium arvense, Polygonum aviculare, Torilis japonica, Aethusa cynapium, Anagallis arvensis, Anchusa arvensis, Anthriscus sylvestris, Arctium minus.

Table 10 Rat's-tail Fescue community (syn: Vulpia myuros community after Brandes, 1983)

Species		Constancy
	(a)	(b)
Vulpia myuros	V	V
Hypericum perforatum	I	III
Epilobium montanum		III
Reseda lutea	III	III
Linaria vulgaris	I	II
Aira caryophyllea	V	I
Erigeron acer	IV	II
Oenothera erythrosepala	IV	III

Plantago lanceolata	V	II
Crepis vesicaria	V	IV
Hypochoeris radicata	IV	IV
Holcus lanatus	IV	IV
Bryum argenteum	III	III
Artemisia absinthium	III	III
Cerastium fontanum	IV	III
Cirsium arvense	III	III
Chamaenerion angustifolium	I	III
Medicago lupulina	V	III
Rubus fruticosus	III	III
Ceratodon purpureus		III
Sagina procumbens	III	II
Arenaria serpyllifolia	II	II
Artemisia vulgaris		II
Senecio squalidus	I	II
Species with Frequencey (I - II) and cover abundance (1-2)		
Agrostis capillaris, Trifolium repens, Dactylis glomerata, Trifolium pratense, Achillea millefolium, Arrhenatherum elatius, Equisetum arvense, Tanacetum vulgare, Diplotaxis tenuifolia, Matricaria matricoides, Sonchus oleraceus, Trifolium arvense, Verbascum thapsus, Bryum capillare, Aster nove-belgii, Anisantha sterilis, Chaenorhinum minus, Leucanthemum vulgare, Poa annua , Trifolium campestre, Trisetum flavescens, Festuca rubra, Funaria hygrometrica, Cirsium vulgare, Rumex acetosella, Senecio jacobaea, Silene alba, Epilobium tetragonum, Acer pseudoplatanus juv, Hieracium murorum, Hieracium pilosella, Plantago major, Prunella vulgaris, Sonchus asper, Taraxacum agg., Urtica dioica, Carduus acanthiodes, Geranium robertianum, Poa pratensis, Poa trivialis, Potentilla reptans, Rumex crispus, Silene vulgaris, Arctium lappa,Centaurium erythraea, Crepis capillaris, Lolium perenne, Lotus corniculatus, Melilotus alba, Melilotus officinalis, Reseda luteola, Polygonum aviculare, Salix caprea juv, Epilobium parviflorum		
Vegetation Cover: 50-100%, Vegetation Height: 25-70cm	Total Number of samples: 21	

(a) *Aira caryophyllea* sub-community
(b) Rat's-tail Fescue community (Total)

Table11 Willow and Buddleja scrub (syn: Epilobio-Salicetum (Oberdorfer, 1957)

Species	Constancy
Chamaenerion angustifolium	V
Salix caprea juv	III
Buddleja davidii	III
Artemisia vulgaris	V
Senecio squalidus	V
Holcus lanatus	IV
Tussilago farfara	IV
Epilobium hirsutum	IV
Agrostis stolonifera	III
Ceratodon purpureus	III
Cirsium arvense	III
Epilobium montanum	II
Hieracium murorum	II
Poa trivialis	II
Sagina procumbens	II
Sonchus oleraceus	II
Taraxaum agg.	II
Anisantha sterilis	II
Epilobium tetragonum	II
Hordeum murinum	II
Sisymbrium loeselii	II
Rumex crispus	II
Species with Frequencey (I) and cover abundance (1-2)	
Acer pseudoplatanus, Alopecurus mysuroides, Arrhenatherum elatius, Artemisia absinthium, Artemisia vulgaris juv., Betula pendula, Carduus acanthoides, Cerastium fontanum, Cirsium vulgare, Crepis vesicaria, Hieracium pilosella, Lapsana communis, Tanacetum parthenium	
Vegetation Cover: 50-90%, Herb Height: 100-125cm, Shrub Height: 300-500cm	Total Number of samples: 6

The Lower Don Valley by Ian Rotherham

Chapter 3: 'Square bashing' – lichens over time and space

Mark R. D. Seaward

Emeritus Professor, School of Archaeological & Forensic Sciences, University of Bradford, Bradford BD7 1DP

Summary: The Mapping Scheme has undoubtedly been one of the British Lichen Society's success stories: not only has it contributed to our knowledge of the distribution, ecology and status (and thereby conservation) of lichens in Britain and Ireland, but it has also involved a very large proportion of our membership as well as non-members, particularly ecologists and environmentalists, in fieldwork – affectionately known as 'square bashing'. The history of the BLS Mapping Scheme is traced from its inception in September 1963 to show the development of data retrieval, access and output. Particular attention is paid to the evolution of the mapping cards, the improvement in computer facilities, and the elaboration of chorological material, site and red data lists. Reference is also made to the importance of using historical data and herbaria to provide a dynamic dimension to maps. Tribute is paid to the many lichenologists particularly Oliver Gilbert, who have made the BLS's Mapping Scheme and subsequent development of a BLS Database such an on-going success.

Introduction: As one gets older, one becomes more interested in those who made the subject, rather than the subject itself. It is to one of these, Oliver Gilbert, that I based my oral presentation at an Urban Environments Conference dedicated to him at Hallam University in 2005, components of which appear here in print in a more permanent form to recognise some of his many lichenological achievements.

During 45 years of my career I shared the friendship of Oliver Gilbert in my home, in the field and on the lecture platform in Britain and abroad, and through voluminous correspondence. We were of a similar age with similar academic backgrounds, possessed an undoubted passion for lichenology, particularly pollution monitoring (Gilbert, 1970 – the forerunner of the widely accepted scale of Hawksworth & Rose, 1970; Seaward 1973), urban ecology (Seaward, 1982; Gilbert, 1989) and conservation (Gilbert, 1977; Seaward, 1982a), and were former Presidents of the British Lichen Society and recipients of its Ursula Duncan Award.

In September 1963, Jack Laundon, John Sheard and I met at the Natural History Museum to consider implementing a mapping scheme for the British Lichen Society, only five years after its foundation. At that time, field meetings were a major part of the Society's programme, as they still are today, but other than meagre reports in *The Lichenologist* highlighting the rare and interesting finds, no attempt had been made to regularize field recording or to consider a national database similar to that of the Botanical Society of the British Isles. It should also be noted that at that time the BLS membership was composed mainly of academics in universities and museums, as well as college and school teachers, and that the enthusiasm of the amateur had not been fully catered for. Although those at the AGM of the BLS in January 1964 recognised other areas in need of attention, such as providing a *Flora*, there was unanimous support for a Mapping Scheme as outlined by the three of us to demonstrate an opportunity to fuse the professional and amateur membership.

The British Lichen Society Mapping Scheme: The Mapping Scheme has undoubtedly been one of the Society's success stories: not only did it contribute significantly to our knowledge of the distribution, ecology and status (and thereby conservation) of lichens in Britain and Ireland, but it also involved a very large proportion of our membership as well as non-members, particularly ecologists and environmentalists, in fieldwork – affectionately known as "square bashing". Prior to this, the only distribution data for lichens had relied upon Hewett Cottrell Watson's vice-county system established in the mid-19th century, which had been adopted by Walter Watson for his *Census Catalogue of British Lichens* in 1953; composed originally of 112 recording units for England, Scotland and Wales, plus one for the Channel Islands, it was expanded by a further 40 units to embrace Ireland by Robert Praeger in 1901. The new system adopted by the BLS was based on the BSBI's 10 x 10 km grid square units. Such artificality came as a shock to some members since the parochial approach (parishes & counties) was transcended; however, although the grid system for England, Scotland and Wales fitted neatly into the Ordnance Survey of Britain, it was necessary to extended these grid lines into Ireland since the Ordnance Survey of Ireland was at an angle of 15° to the former and the very basic technology available at this time could not cope with this variation from the norm (e.g. Hawksworth et al. 1973, 1974, Coppins 1976). Furthermore, the c. 3500 grid square units for the BSBI for both Britain and Ireland had to be expanded to c. 3800 units to accomodate the needs of lichenologists who investigated rocky seashores exposed by tidal movements. Our objective, as it says on the label of the tin, was "a mapping scheme"; to achieve this, we had to develop a system "fit for purpose" which recognised that computer technology 50 years ago was very basic, so data retrieval would often rely heavily on a back-of-envelope approach and on members adopting particular species; Oliver Gilbert, for example, chose species of the genus *Solorina*, early maps of which appeared in *The Lichenologist* in 1975 and eventually in the *Lichen Atlas* (Gilbert, 1998).

We set the ball rolling with a mapping card in 1964; unfortunately this was short-lived since it listed only 154 taxa, reflecting the ability to actually name species in the field, and the reverse blank side was used to list other taxa – sad to say, the standard of recorders' handwriting frequently came under scrutiny. Our revised mapping card in 1968 (listing 728 taxa) stood the test of time when one considers that the taxa listed had to represent those lichens likely to be found in the field at that time (Figure 1) there were 1,530 British taxa (including a few lichenicolous & allied fungi).

It was also apparent that a numbering system for all taxa was essential – even abbreviations for names generated ambiguity. Over the years, further revisions of the database, with the card needing to cater for the increasing number of British and Irish taxa, have been constantly applied; in 2004, for example, 403 lichenicolous fungi (to coincide with David Hawksworth's 2003 checklist) were imported into the database. The enormous number of new taxa to be added and the nomenclatural revisions to be made is relentless: currently (May 2019) there are BLS numbers for 2,663 taxa (1,928 lichens, 520 lichenicolous fungi, and 215 allied fungi and nomenclaturally unresolved taxa).

In the mid-1970s, it was clear from the volume of data coming in, and improvements in computer technology, that it was necessary to take on extra help. Thankfully, a post-doctoral NERC fellowship awarded to Chris Hitch enabled the Mapping Scheme to establish a credible database. In-house computer software was developed at Bradford University and punch-card operators in its Computer Centre inputted completed record cards; to achieve this, we developed an intermediary stage by translating card annotations onto A3 data transfer sheets. Such data transfer was necessarily only for the purpose of creating basic lists and maps.

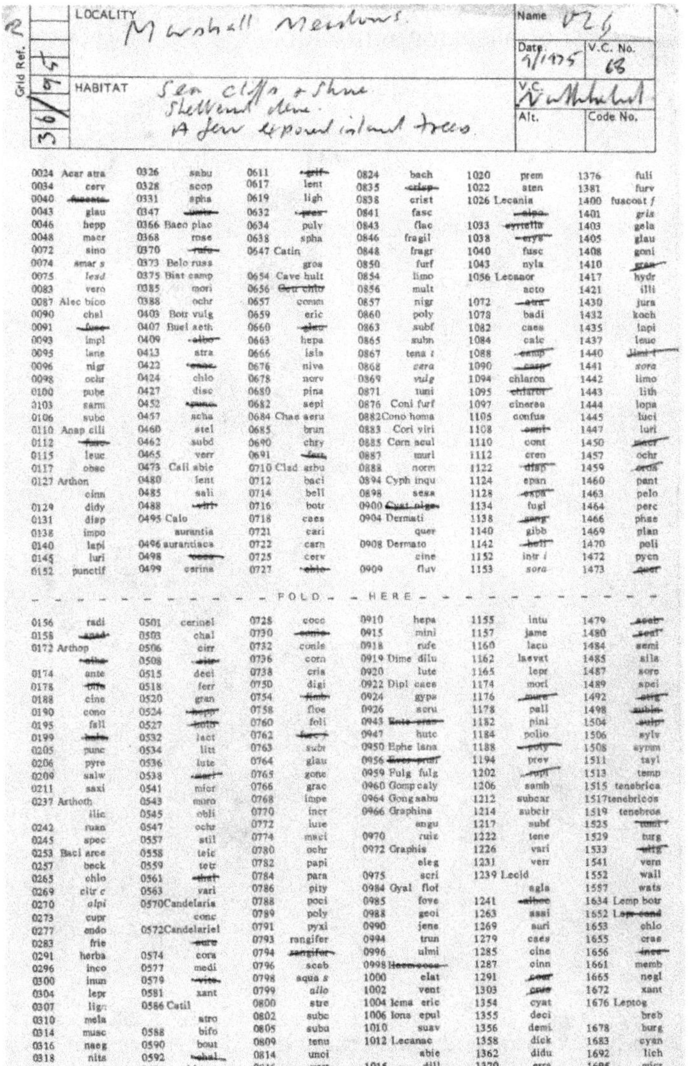

Figure 1. 1968 mapping card completed by Oliver Gilbert in 1975 for a single site in a Northumbrian 10 x 10 km grid square

Early trial runs had shown that elaborations of such basic information could not be achieved by the main-frame computer. Even so, punched card errors ensued and it was necessary to validate data by "chatter" print-outs/sheets (Figure 2), and confirmed by maps on screen which were duly printed, albeit in an elongated format; any disjunct distribution spots required qualification by the recorders. The "elongated" maps were sent out to lichen specialists for annotation.

Figure 2. Early 10 x 10 km grid square computer 'chatter' printout to validate punch card data

To introduce a dynamic into the maps, to show, for example, past and present distributions, various symbols and colours were trialled for the 10 x 10 km grid square spots. It was clear that a single map could only demonstrate three things: where a lichen was, where it had been, and where it had not been recorded; any variation of this, such as where a lichen had been, then disappeared and subsequently returned, or distributions according to particular date-lines, could not be adequately portrayed or indeed captured/interpreted by the observer. After these trials it was decided to use just two symbols, a solid black spot to denote 1960 onwards records and an open circle to denote pre-1960 records; it should be noted that the latter represented a large proportion of late nineteenth-century records mainly due to the declining interest in lichenology during the first half of the twentieth century.

As the completed cards came into us, it was clear that we knew more about more remote areas, such as the Highlands and Islands, than what was on our doorsteps, sometimes a reflection of a holiday and in one case a honeymoon. Furthermore, one could discern the trails of specialists and those that had their eye-in for particular taxa: it would appear, for example, that only Oliver Gilbert knew how to identify *Physcia dubia* in the field. In consequence, the biased maps generated were of limited biogeographical value. Such work provided a firm basis for exploring our country's flora irrespective of where one lives – namely a platform for national rather than parochial activities – but it should also be noted that some of us paid particular attention to urban and industrial environments at a time when they had been side-lined as 'lichen deserts' due to atmospheric pollution (Gilbert, 1965; Seaward, 1975). Such areas often supported limited but interesting lichen assemblages, and even negative recording, that established base-lines that have proved to be of immense value in evaluating the success or otherwise of programmes aimed at ameliorating our environment in recent decades. Since field meetings were an important feature of the Society's programme, the results of which at that time were regularly published in *The Lichenologist*, attention was frequently paid to holding them in underworked areas (Seaward, 1988), the objective being to provide essential distributional data for the Mapping Scheme. It was, however, pleasing to note that by the early 1980s BLS members had taken the Mapping Scheme to heart and completed mapping cards were being returned to the Mapping Recorder on an almost daily basis (Seaward, 1988); this is also reflected in the progress maps published in a variety of sources, particularly in *The Lichenologist* between 1972 and 1992.

At this stage it was thought desirable to publish some maps. Although Chris Hitch and I knew that such maps would be far from complete, they would nevertheless provide a reasonable picture of what could be achieved from existing data derived from the Mapping Scheme and from the abstraction of reliable records from published and herbarium sources. So, in the late 1970s, computer-derived maps of what were thought to be reasonably well-known species in terms of their taxonomy, ecology and distribution, were distributed to colleagues, several of whom had a specialised knowledge of the particular species. The printed versions of such maps at that time were elongated and lacked coastal lines, being constructed from basic symbols designated to show old (pre-1960) and new (1960 onwards) records. The response was magnificent. It is a well-recognised fact that if you want to obtain more detailed / accurate maps then this can be achieved by sending out preliminary versions so that the recipients can criticise the output by saying "it occurs there and here, and I am sure it grows there..." (Figure 3)!

Once the revised maps had been retrieved and problematic "spots" resolved, 176 species were selected as being suitable for publication. However, since the computer technology to produce such maps did not exist, these had to be manually constructed and to this end we employed undergraduates over the summer of 1980 to laboriously enter data spot-by-spot by means of Letraset onto large-scale maps (Figure 4). Two years later, we witnessed the results of our labours when volume 1 of *Atlas of the Lichens of the British Isles*, published by the Institute of Terrestrial Ecology, appeared (Seaward & Hitch, 1982). This was warmly received, more particularly as the large format maps provided yet another opportunity for BLS members to infill gaps with further spots to make good some of the deficiencies (Seaward, 1983).

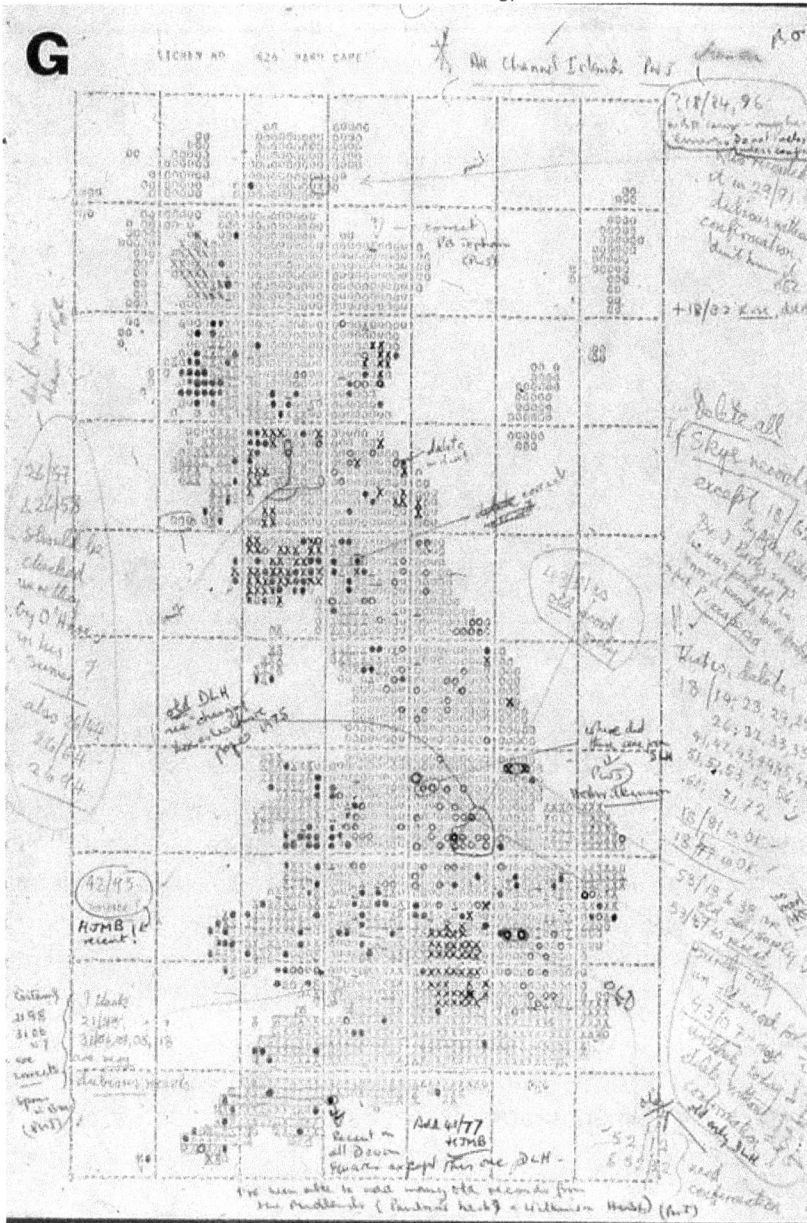

Figure 3. Early computer-derived elongated map of *Flavoparmelia caperata* annotated by numerous lichenologists, particularly Francis Rose and Peter James

Figure 4. Letraset map laboriously prepared by students in 1980 for the first *Atlas* published in 1982

However, Volume 2 never proved necessary since, with the improvement in the technology, software was developed in Bradford University's Computer Centre (by Stan Houghton and myself) to generate maps which were to stand the test of time, being very much akin to those used by other mapping programmes, and solving, for example, the problem of amalgamating the different grid systems of Britain and Ireland (Seaward, 1988; Hawksworth & Seaward, 1990). In consequence, in 1984, 1985 and 1991, *Provisional Atlases* were produced in-house and circulated to interested persons for comments; the annotated copies returned provided a natural development of the Mapping Scheme, namely the publication of *Atlas* fascicles. Since our knowledge of the distributions of many species was still far from complete, the intention of the fascicles was to provide updated replacements in due course; although six fascicles were published (Seaward 1995, 1996, 1998-2001), this intention was only realized for one species. The texts to the maps were provided by numerous authors, including Oliver Gilbert, who contributed the section on Aquatic Lichens in Fascicle 5 based on extensive fieldwork (Figure 5) that involved a 3-year survey of 25 English rivers (Gilbert & Giavarini, 1997), as well as entries for several other taxa in Fascicles 3 and 6. Of particular merit is the detailed information on the ecology, biogeography, status and conservation provided for each species mapped, thus making good the deficiences of such information in the British and Irish Lichen Floras (Purvis *et al.*, 1992; Smith *et al.*, 2009) where, due to lack of space, only abbreviated notes on such topics could be provided.

Figure 5. Oliver Gilbert's quest for aquatic lichens (source: BLS Archive)

In due course, a wealth of records came into the Mapping Scheme from a wide variety of sources, such as the important surveys of selected habitats initiated by the BLS Conservation Committee and the churchyard survey initiated by Tom Chester (Figure 6), as well as from important analyses of herbarium collections, often in association with the preparation of taxonomic monographs (e.g. Sheard, 1967, Gilbert, 1978, Coppins, 1983) and local and indeed national floras. By 1994, one or more distribution maps had been published for 350 lichen taxa in Britain and Ireland (Seaward, 1996). Such work was invaluable in the construction of Red Data Lists (e.g. Church *et al.*, 1996), the inclusion of species not only reliant upon knowing in how many squares a particular lichen was currently present, but from how many squares it had disappeared. However, it is pleasing to note that earlier work, which often demonstrated the disappearance of major lichen assemblages from much of England and Wales, largely due to air pollution, has been superceded in recent years by the reinvasion of the lichens (Seaward, 1997, Coppins *et al.*, 2001), but not necessarily those which formerly dominated our landscape – a more recent factor dictating lichen assemblages over wide areas being nitrification, often to excessive levels (hypertrophication – Seaward & Coppins, 2004), and most probably climatic changes, such as global warming. Such interpretations are only only possible through detailed time and space analyses of distribution patterns of biomonitors (Seaward, 1992, 1998a).

Figure 6. Tom Chester and Ivan Pedley assisting Oliver Gilbert to reach an *Acarospora* sp. on the windowsill of a Shropshire church in 2000 (source: BLS Archive)

The maps incorporating past and present distributions have proved of immense value, but it has often proved difficult to portray this on a single map, as for example where a lichen was once found, subsequently disappeared, and has now returned (Seaward, 1998a). Even portraying past and present distributions can be fraught with difficulties; for example, in the case of the potentially useful maps included in earlier editions of Dobson's *Lichens* it is impossible to differentiate between the open circles and solid spots – in fact the former appear 'more solid' than the latter (Seaward, 2015), and in the latest edition (Dobson, 2018) the red/green colour scheme is not only a problem for those suffering from colour blindness, but is also unhelpful for determining changes in distribution patterns.

Conclusions: It is clear from the mapping work that it is of paramount importance to conserve certain archival material, including of course herbarium specimens. Such sources contain invaluable information to provide a dynamic element to our biogeographical and ecological studies, being essential in interpreting our past, present and indeed future environment. British lichenologists are singularly fortunate in having access to a very considerable amount of data, in the form of publications (e.g. Hawksworth & Seaward, 1977), archival material and herbarium collections amassed over the past 300 years by a succession of enthusiasts, many of whom worked tirelessly to promote the subject both locally and nationally. Many of them dedicated their time, energy and indeed wealth to establishing nationwide links through voluminous and helpful correspondence, the naming and exchange of specimens, and the publication of invaluable guides to lichen identification. Oliver Gilbert was one such person, his herbarium material has been accessed into local and national collections, and much of his correspondence and notes has been accumulated in the BLS Archives. In so doing, such enthusiasts have united kindred spirits and provided the basis for the establishment of national goals achieved in the first instance by a variety of projects.

Recent advances in computer technology have necessitated a rethink on various aspects of the mapping and related programmes; to this end, Janet Simkin and the Data Committee accepted the challenge and computer software and systems have been adapted or developed to furnish the Society's needs. However, although such work should be applauded, its complexity can exceed the needs of some members and, furthermore, the elaborate collection of data and their manipulation on personal computers can detract from good honest fieldwork by enthusiasts such as Oliver Gilbert. Added complications arise from the dissemination of this information to a wide range of databases, publications, personal requirements etc. in a variety of formats. It should be noted that in the early years of the mapping scheme, before it was necessary to go public, I was highly protective of the data, particularly in respect of the conservation of rare species and sensitive sites. However, most data were freely supplied to *bona fide* researchers, with no question of charging for supplying maps for publication provided the BLS source was duly acknowledged.

The invaluable databases assembled for England, Scotland, Wales and Ireland in recent years have been achieved in no small measure from the effective use of field data derived from many sources which has raised awareness of lichens in both the scientific and wider community, as well as providing training for beginners in lichenology; such projects are vital in promoting lichenology at a time when the number of institutional-based lichenologists is pitifully low. Information technology, mainly via the internet, has also been important in promoting a wide range of the Society's activities, including its taxonomic, mapping and biomonitoring work.

In conclusion, I quote the profound words of William Lauder Lindsay in his remarkable book *A Popular History of British Lichens* published in 1856:

> "We may now be said to be entering on a new era in lichenology; it is now being studied in a more philosophic spirit, and with all the aids which modern discoveries in science ... can furnish. Facts are being earnestly and patiently sought after; generalization and theory avoided until a sufficiency of data be accumulated ... volunteers are coming forward ... eager for the work solely on account of its difficulty ... But the labours of the student must equally begin and terminate on

the spot where the Lichens grow ... there he [& she] must watch patiently and note accurately – it may be for a series of years – the stages of origin, growth, and decay of species under all the influences, terrestrial and aerial, by which these are so liable to be affected."

Acknowledgements: The first 50 years of the British Lichen Society's Mapping Scheme would have been impossible without the enthusiasm and devotion of many of its members such as Oliver Gilbert, and the sponsorship it received from a wide variety of governmental, commercial and industrial sources such as NERC, WWF, CEGB and Control Data, but more particularly from the University of Bradford, which placed no financial burden on the Society. While it is hard for me to single out the work of individuals, I must officially recognise the two years of postdoctoral work of Christopher Hitch and the Director of Bradford University's Computer Centre, Stanley Houghton, for their unstinting contribution at a critical stage of the project. It was a privilege to front the BLS Mapping Scheme for a very major part of my life.

References:

Church, J.M., Coppins, B.J., Gilbert, O.L., James, P.W., & Stewart, N.F. (1996) *Red Data Books of Britain and Ireland: Lichens. Volume 1: Britain.* Joint Nature Conservation Committee, Peterborough.
Coppins, B.J. (1976) *Distribution patterns shown by epiphytic lichens in the British Isles.* In: D.H. Brown, D.L. Hawksworth & R.H. Bailey (eds) *Lichenology: progress and problems.* Academic Press, London, 249-278.
Coppins, B.J. (1983) A taxonomic study of the lichen genus *Micarea* in Europe. *Bulletin of the British Museum of Natural History (Botany),* **11** (2), 17-214.
Coppins, B.J., Hawksworth, D.L., & Rose, F. (2001) Lichens. In: D.L. Hawksworth (ed.) *The Changing Wildlife of Great Britain and Ireland.* Taylor & Francis, London, 126-147.

Dobson, F.S. (2018) *Lichens. An illustrated guide to the British and Irish species.* Richmond Publishing, East Burnham Park.

Gilbert, O.L. (1965) Lichens as indicators of air pollution in the Tyne Valley. In: G.T. Goodman, R.W. Edwards & J.M. Lambert (eds) *Ecology and the Industrial Society.* Oxford University Press, London, 35-47.

Gilbert, O.L. (1970) A biological scale for the estimation of sulphur dioxide pollution. *New Phytologist,* **69**, 629-634.

Gilbert, O.L. (1977) Lichen conservation in Britain. In: M.R.D. Seaward (ed.) *Lichen Ecology.* Academic Press, London, 415-436.

Gilbert, O.L. (1978) *Fulgensia* in the British Isles. *The Lichenologist,* **10**, 33-45.

Gilbert, O.L. (1989) *The Ecology of Urban Habitats.* Chapman & Hall, London.

Gilbert, O.L. (1998) *Solorina.* In: *Lichen Atlas of the British Isles.* Fascicle 3. M.R.D.Seaward (ed.) British Lichen Society, London.

Gilbert, O.L. (2000) Aquatic Lichens. In: M.R.D. Seaward (ed.) *Lichen Atlas of the British Isles.* Fascicle 5. British Lichen Society, London.

Gilbert, O.L., & Giavarini, V.J. (1997) The lichen vegetation of acid water-courses in England. *The Lichenologist,* **29**, 347-367.

Hawksworth, D.L. (2003) The lichenicolous fungi of Great Britain and Ireland: an overview and annotated checklist. *Lichenologist,* **35**, 191-232.

Hawksworth, D.L., Coppins, B.J., & Rose, F. (1974) Changes in the British lichen flora. In: D.L. Hawksworth (ed.) *The Changing Flora and Fauna of Britain.* Academic Press, London, 47-78.

Hawksworth, D.L., & Rose, F. (1970) Qualitative scale for estimating sulphur dioxide air pollution in England and Wales using epiphytic lichens. *Nature, London,* **227**, 145-148.

Hawksworth, D.L., Rose, F., & Coppins, B.J. (1973) Changes in the lichen flora of England and Wales attributable to pollution of the air by sulphur dioxide. In: B.W. Ferry, M.S. Baddeley, & D.L. Hawksworth (eds) *Air Pollution and Lichens.* Athlone Press, London, 330-367.

Hawksworth, D.L., & Seaward, M.R.D. (1977) *Lichenology in the British Isles 1568 - 1975. An historical and bibliographical survey.* Richmond Publishing, Richmond.

Hawksworth, D.L. & Seaward, M.R.D. (1990) Twenty-five years of lichen mapping in Great Britain and Ireland. *Stuttgarter Beiträge zur Naturkunde*, ser. A, **456**, 5-10.

Lindsay, W.L. (1856) *A Popular History of British Lichens.* L. Reeve, London.

Purvis, O.W., Coppins, B.J., Hawksworth, D.L., James, P.W., & Moore, D.M. (eds) (1992) *The Lichen Flora of Great Britain and Ireland.* Natural History Museum / British Lichen Society, London.

Seaward, M.R.D. (1973) Lichen ecology of the Scunthorpe heathlands. 1. Mineral accumulation. *Lichenologist*, **5**, 423-433.

Seaward, M.R.D. (1975) Lichen flora of the West Yorkshire conurbation. *Proceedings of the Leeds Philosophical and Literary Society*, sci.sect., **10**, 141-208.

Seaward, M.R.D. (1982) Lichen ecology of changing urban environments. In: R. Bornkamm, J.A. Lee, & M.R.D. Seaward (eds) *Urban Ecology.* Blackwell Scientific Publications, Oxford, 181-180.

Seaward, M.R.D. (1982a) Principles and priorities of lichen conservation. *Journal of the Hattori Botanical Laboratory*, **52**, 401-406.

Seaward, M.R.D. (1983) The Atlas at last. *British Lichen Society Bulletin*, **52**, 1-6.

Seaward, M.R.D. (1988) Progress in the study of the lichen flora of the British Isles. *Botanical Journal of the Linnean Society*, **96**, 81-95.

Seaward. M.R.D. (1992) Large-scale air pollution monitoring using lichens. *Geojournal,* **28**, 403-411.

Seaward, M.R.D. (ed.) (1995) *Lichen Atlas of the British Isles.* Fascicle 1. [Introduction & *Parmelia*]. British Lichen Society, London.

Seaward, M.R.D. (ed.) (1996) *Lichen Atlas of the British Isles.* Fascicle 2. [*Cladonia* part 1 & List of Published Maps]. British Lichen Society, London.

Seaward, M.R.D. (1997) Urban deserts bloom: a lichen renaissance. *Bibliotheca Lichenologica*, **67**, 297-309.

Seaward, M.R.D. (ed.) (1998) *Lichen Atlas of the British Isles*. Fascicle 3. [Physciaceae, *Arctomia, Lobaria, Massalongia, Pseudocyphellaria, Psoroma, Solorina, Sticta* & *Teloschistes*]. British Lichen Society, London.

Seaward, M.R.D. (1998a) Time-space analyses of the British lichen flora, with particular reference to air quality surveys. *Folia Cryptogamica Estonica*, **32**, 85-96.

Seaward, M.R.D. (ed.) (1999) *Lichen Atlas of the British Isles*. Fascicle 4. [*Cavernularia, Degelia, Lepraria, Moelleropsis* & Pannariaceae]. British Lichen Society, London.

Seaward, M.R.D. (ed.) (2000) *Lichen Atlas of the British Isles*. Fascicle 5. [Aquatic Lichens & *Cladonia* part 2]. British Lichen Society, London.

Seaward, M.R.D. (ed.) (2001) *Lichen Atlas of the British Isles*. Fascicle 6. [*Caloplaca*]. British Lichen Society, London.

Seaward, M.R.D. (2015) Spots before the eyes. *British Lichen Society Bulletin*, **116**, 144-152.

Seaward, M.R.D., & Coppins, B.J. (2004) Lichens and hypertrophication. *Bibliotheca Lichenologica*, **88**, 561-572.

Seaward, M.R.D. & Hitch, C.J.B. (ed.) (1982) *Atlas of the Lichens of the British Isles*. Volume 1. Institute of Terrestrial Ecology, Natural Environment Research Council, Cambridge.

Sheard, J.W. (1967) A revision of the lichen genus *Rinodina* (Ach.) Gray in the British Isles. *The Lichenologist*, **3**, 328-367.

Smith, C.W., Aptroot, A., Coppins, B.J., Fletcher, A., Gilbert, O.L., James, P.W., & Wolseley, P.A. (eds) (2009) *The Lichens of Great Britain and Ireland*. British Lichen Society, London.

Watson, W. (1953) *Census Catalogue of British Lichens*. Cambridge University Press, London.

Chapter 4: Oliver Gilbert, pioneer of urban woodland management – and what happened next in Sheffield...

Melvyn Jones

Summary: Oliver Gilbert had a deep and long-lasting interest in urban woodlands including semi-natural ancient woodland. His research interests embraced the identification of small fragments of ancient woodland surviving in urban areas, the impacts of urbanisation on ancient woodlands particularly the introduction of non-native species and the negative effects of inappropriate management. And because he was a member of staff in the Department of Landscape Architecture at the University of Sheffield, the city was the locale of important research, writing and practical experiments on urban woodlands. Through Sheffield City Council's Moorland and Amenity Woodland Advisory Group, Oliver conducted a series of experimental management projects in Ecclesall Woods and Bowden Housteads Wood. These experiments took the form of the creation of half- to one-acre glades to increase habitat diversity. Oliver's experiments in the two woods resulted in the vigorous re-growth of shrubs and trees, and a great increase in spring flowers, previously suppressed by low light intensities. The strong re-growth in the experimental glades re-assured the members of the Council staff and councillors who had previously been unconvinced by the concept of 'active' management and very worried about the expected strong critical response from members of the public. Oliver's pioneering efforts marked the beginning of more than thirty years of successful management and interpretation in Sheffield's council-owned ancient woods which are described and analysed.

Keywords: glade and coppicing experiments, active woodland management, Fuelling a Revolution Project, special interest groups, South Yorkshire Forest Partnership, Woodland Heritage Champions Project

Introduction: Oliver Gilbert had an abiding interest in urban woodlands, including semi-natural ancient woodland (Gilbert, 1991). Among his research interests were the identification of small fragments of ancient woodland surviving in urban areas, the effects of urbanisation on ancient woodlands particularly the ingress of alien plants, the positive impacts of glade creation and thinning on ground flora and the negative effects of inappropriate management including the planting of exotics and the removal of decaying and dead trees (Gilbert, 1992). Oliver's pioneering efforts marked the beginning of a long period of successful active management and interpretation in Sheffield's council-owned ancient woods, and Sheffield-based Oliver was in on it at the very beginning. Let me explain.

Coppicing in Sheffield's woods and the associated crafts had gradually come to an end during the second half of the nineteenth century and many of the woods were sold to or presented as gifts to the City Council mostly for recreational purposes. Then for almost a century, these publicly-owned woods were neglected and unmanaged except where dead and dying trees were judged to be a danger to the public. The benign neglect of the woods made them much less attractive than in the past. On top of that in the early 1970s, the biggest publicly-owned block of ancient woodland, Ecclesall Woods, covering 150 ha, was the subject of a survey by Southern Tree Surgeons Ltd who made recommendations for its future management including the introduction of exotic species, the clearance of 'weeds', bramble and bracken, the drainage of wet areas and the provision of car parks and picnic areas. The public who used the woodland opposed the proposed management prescription and the City Council decided not to proceed and instead set up a 'Moorland and Amenity Woodlands Advisory Group' (MAWAG), whose members included independent local environmental experts (e.g. MJ, OG, Harold Smith, Ian Rotherham, Stephen Morton) and senior local authority officers (e.g. Arroll Winning, Roger Kite, Dan Lewis, John Shaw, Len Carr and others), to advise the local authority on woodland management and to avoid future conflicts of interest. Oliver was an influential member of the group.

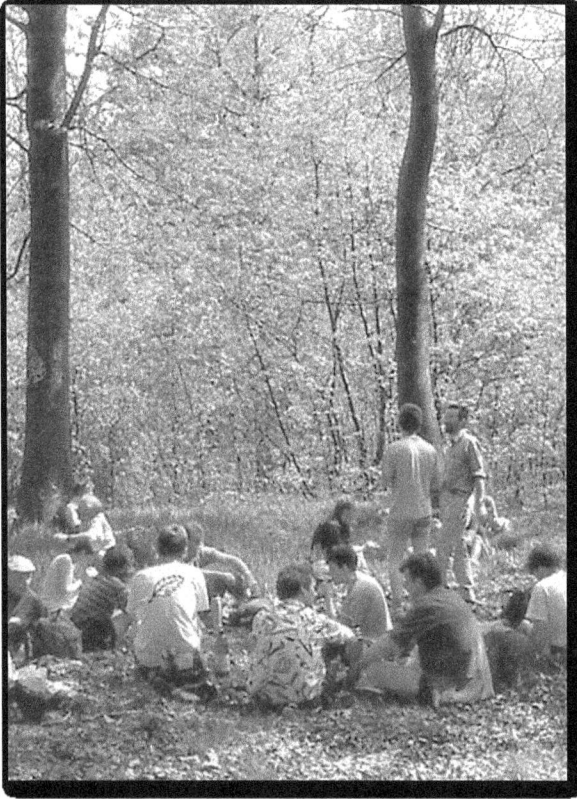

Figure 1: One of Oliver Gilbert's experimental glades in Bowden Housteads Wood 1995, fifteen years after its creation

Through MAWAG Oliver conducted a series of experimental management projects in Ecclesall Woods and Bowden Housteads Wood. These experiments took the form of the creation of half to one acre glades to increase habitat diversity (Gilbert, 1982). Although created as conservation areas they also soon became activity spaces for children visiting the woods. However the play activity did not excessively affect the glades. Between 60 and 90 per cent of the cut trees sprouted vigorously, a great increase in spring flowers including bluebell, slender St John's wort, greater stitchwort and common cow-wheat, took place and honeysuckle and guelder rose, previously suppressed by low light intensities, also started to flower. The rapidity of re-growth in the experimental glades re-assured the members of the Council staff and councillors who were sceptical about 'active' management and fearful of the critical reaction of local residents.

Through his publications and his work with MAWAG Oliver Gilbert was a crucial influence on the decision to begin to actively manage Sheffield's ancient woodlands. The rest of this paper summarises the almost complete turn-around in attitudes to council-owned broad-leaved amenity woodland in Sheffield from the early 1980s and the active management and interpretation programmes that followed.

Surviving, but neglected and unmanaged

None of the known late medieval coppice woods in Sheffield disappeared through the wanton behaviour of woodmen and other exploiters of wood and timber. Woods disappeared or were reduced in size over a long period of time as a result of clearance for quarrying and mining operations, through agricultural expansion, industrial development, the spread of settlement, and road building. For example, a large part of the great pasture wood recorded in 1161 that stretched from the Birley Stone at Grenoside down to the River Don between Wardsend and Oughtibridge was cleared in the medieval period and early modern period for agriculture, leaving only the narrow wooded common on Birley Edge in the west, Wilson Spring halfway down the slope, and Beeley Wood beside the River Don. Much later Hall Carr Wood in Brightside, Sheffield, completely disappeared in the nineteenth century as a result of industrial development; as did most of Tinsley Park, this time mostly because of coal mining. Burngreave Wood disappeared as a result of the population explosion in Sheffield in the second half of the nineteenth century and the need to create a cemetery. A few sessile oaks and a few ancient woodland indicators still survive in the cemetery (and were brought to the attention of local naturalists by Oliver Gilbert). A great swathe was cut through Smithy Wood near Chapeltown as a result of the construction of the M1 motorway at the end of the 1960s, and two swathes were cut through Bowden Housteads Wood through the construction of the Sheffield Parkway in 1970 and the Mosbrough Parkway in 1990.

Nevertheless, the survival rate of ancient woodland sites, although heavily planted, is surprisingly high considering the rapid population growth and expansion of housing and industry in the nineteenth century. For example the population of the parish of Sheffield was about 20,000 in 1750 but by 1900 the borough population was approaching 400,000. Of the known documented coppice woods within the present city boundaries that were in existence in 1600, only two had been lost by 1850. Altogether, present research, based on location, site, shape and ground flora suggests that there are more than eighty ancient woods or fragments of ancient woodland within the present city boundaries of which sixty-seven are publicly-owned woods. For thirty-five of these publicly-owned woods, we have unequivocal documentary evidence that they were in existence before 1600 (Jones, 1986a; Jones 1986b; Jones, 2009).

However, for almost a century, until the 1980s, the city's ancient broadleaved woods, excepting the minority still in private hands, and which were often coniferised, were neglected and unmanaged except where dead or dying trees were judged to be a danger to the public. They were increasingly even-aged with dense canopies and poorly developed shrub layer. They contained much poorer displays of spring flowers, some breeding birds and butterflies had been reduced in number or were no longer found in woods where they were once common, and local residents were increasingly afraid of walking in the woods because they were dark and gloomy and engendered a fear of personal attack. The more accessible woods were also sometimes heavily vandalised and full of litter. Having survived for hundreds and in some cases for thousands of years, there was a real danger that Sheffield's woodland heritage would be squandered. Our ancestors quite deliberately protected the woods by actively managing them; until lately, the twentieth century attitude in urban areas like Sheffield seems to have been at best, to let them take care of themselves, and at worst, to abuse them unmercifully.

Figure 2: A view into Buck Wood in the mid-1980s, showing its even-aged structure and absence of a shrub layer and ground flora

Having said that, one ill-judged attempt to introduce active management at Little Matlock Wood in the Loxley valley in Sheffield, caused much unease, and correspondents to local newspapers criticised what was seen as 'council vandalism', going on to say that once it came to the attention of the Sheffield Countryside Management Team 'the wood was doomed'. It became all too clear that managing public woods in a heavily-populated area in the late twentieth century was as much about public relations as woodmanship and ecological principles.

A new woodland policy: Despite the many ancient woods, their outstanding natural history and heritage importance, their immense value was not fully recognised as late as the 1980s by Sheffield's political leaders or by many of the salaried officers who ought to have known better. In 1986, for example, a large label in the new wildlife gallery at Weston Park Museum proclaimed that there were two ancient woods in Sheffield – Ecclesall Woods and Wharncliffe Woods. Wharncliffe Woods are in fact partly in Barnsley. And the other almost eighty ancient woods and ancient woodland fragments were not recognized.

In 1985, the City Council Recreation Department's Moorland and Amenity Woodland Advisory Group commissioned a study from the author to determine the status and management history of the major woods in the city and the ensuing report presented in 1986 (Jones, 1986b) made it clear that there was documentary proof that more than thirty of the woods in the City Council's ownership were ancient (i.e. in existence before the year 1600). The City Council then approved a Woodland Policy, put together by MAWAG, in 1987 (Sheffield City Council, 1987). Its primary aim was to ensure the protection and perpetuation of the ancient woodlands surviving in the city and to realise their potential in as many ways as possible. The policy sought to maintain the ancient woods in a healthy state, to protect, conserve and encourage their rich flora and fauna, and to preserve their important historical and archaeological value. In all this the public were to be encouraged to play a full part by expressing their views, becoming involved in management, and monitoring effects and consequences. It is worth quoting from the policy directly to show the major change in attitudes that had taken place:

Most of the City's broadleaved woodlands are ancient and have existed for centuries if not for thousands of years. It is because our predecessors protected and preserved these woodlands that we are able to enjoy their many benefits today. We have a similar obligation to future generations, and the development of healthy woodlands and their perpetuation is, therefore, of primary importance and must take precedence over all other considerations. It would be both tragic and irresponsible for us to allow our woodland heritage to be lost. It is beyond human ability to create ancient woodland. Once it is destroyed, it is destroyed forever. (Sheffield City Council, 1987, p. 4).

This policy was largely enshrined in the City Council's *Nature Conservation Strategy* document published in 1991 (Bownes *et al.*, 1991).

Renewed management of Bowden Housteads Wood after a century of neglect: The Woodland Policy was put into action in Bowden Housteads Wood in the early spring of 1988 (Jones & Rotherham, 2011; Jones & Rotherham, 2012). Bowden Housteads is one of the earliest recorded ancient woods in South Yorkshire, being recorded as early as 1332 as a wood pasture. By 1600, it was a coppice-with-standards and was coppiced continuously until almost the end of the nineteenth century. It is typical of ancient woods in that it lies on an ancient parish boundary, and its boundaries, sinuous and zig-zagging, had remained largely intact for at least two hundred years. It was heavily planted in the late nineteenth century. In 1916 the Duke of Norfolk sold the wood to Sheffield Corporation for £6,000 for use as a place of recreation. Since then, not only was it left virtually unmanaged for more than seventy years, but also a large section of the wood was lost through open-cast coal mining in the 1940s.

It was also bisected by the construction of the Sheffield Parkway (A630) in 1970 and the southern part of the wood was further sub-divided by the creation of the Mosborough Parkway in 1990. The wood became increasingly even-aged, with a dense canopy resulting from the closely-planted trees, especially in those areas dominated by beech, causing suppression of ground flora and erosion of bare soils on steep slopes. Because it was gloomy and monotonous it was much less attractive to insects, mammals and birds, and visitors felt less safe walking there. Its ancient boundary walls were also in a state of great disrepair and it was heavily littered in places. A further potential problem was concern that the woodland was becoming drier because the water catchment had been reduced in size and the water table had fallen due to the gradual urbanization of the surrounding area with a potential negative impact on the woodland's ecology.

But it was still a heavily used public open space. In June 1986 a user survey of the wood had been conducted among a random selection of adult respondents in 236 households living in those parts of Richmond, Handsworth, Darnall, Manor and Woodthorpe lying adjacent to the wood (Jones, 1986c). In answer to the question 'If you visited a local wood which one it be?', 228 answered 'Bowden Housteads'. Eighty-one per cent of these 228 respondents said they visited the wood on a daily, regular or occasional basis. One hundred and fifteen of these respondents took walks there, seventy-six walked a dog, twenty-nine explored with young members of their family and forty-two used it as a short cut. Eighty-seven of the users said that when they visited the wood they went alone. Respondents cited chopping down trees, dumping rubbish, starting fires, using airguns and off-road motorbiking as serious problems. At the end of the questionnaire survey respondents were asked to offer any other comments about the wood. Complimentary comments included 'important for wildlife and relaxation', 'a precious place for children to go and come in contact with nature', 'we need woodlands, need bits of green' and 'somewhere different to walk in – best thing in the area'. But these were balanced by critical comments that emphasised the lack of management such as: 'once meant a lot; now it has deteriorated', 'very dark and gloomy', 'wants cleaning up', 'an unsafe place to walk in or for children to play in', and 'needs supervising by a ranger'.

This then was the situation after nearly three-quarters of a century of public ownership: Bowden Housteads was still heavily used but in great need of sympathetic management.

This major improvement project was funded jointly by the City Council and the Countryside Commission (Sheffield City Council, 1987b). The main operation was thinning, to provide more space for the native trees to develop, and to help diversify the woodland by encouraging the regeneration of the shrub layer and the flowering of the ground flora. The thinning was irregular and several glades were created. It was fitting that the first active management in a Sheffield wood was in Bowden Housteads

Wood, one of the two locations where Oliver had conducted his glade creation experiments.

Figure 3: A streamside glade in Bowden Housteads Wood

The project involved a major public relations campaign. Before the commencement of operations, public meetings were held and guided walks around the wood were undertaken. Four hundred letters were posted to local residents about the project, notices about what was to be done and why were posted in and around the wood, news items appeared in the local press, and a broadcast was made on local radio. One important aspect of this campaign was to reassure local residents that felling trees did not mean the destruction of a well-loved wood. The point was made that the sound of a chainsaw should be taken to be a sign of good woodland management practice and not council vandalism.

An article appeared in *The Star*, the local evening newspaper, under the title 'Massacre in a good cause' based on an interview with Dan Lewis, the Council's woodland officer. It began by stating that Dan Lewis wanted to convince the public that his 'chain saw massacre' would have a happy ending, and went on to make the point that the public must accept that trees must be felled if they wanted 'to save their woodland from becoming a tree and flower graveyard' (Pleat, 1988). The project was a major new departure in woodland management in the city. It was an 'active' rather than a 'care and maintenance' approach, and it was sympathetic both to the origins and history of the wood and to the local residents who were its users.

In the early 1990s, woodland management was extended to other sites, and the winters of 1991-92 and 1992-93 saw management activity in Roe Wood and Woolley Wood. But what had taken place at Bowden Housteads Wood, Roe Wood and Woolley Wood was just a beginning. Further management at short intervals over a long period would be necessary in order to achieve and maintain the sought-after uneven structure and the beauty and interest that it brings in its train.

Re-introduction of small-scale coppicing

On a much smaller scale in the spring of 1994 a multi-purpose feasibility study began, in which four experimental areas were re-coppiced with 0.3- to 0.4-ha areas in four Sheffield woods: Ecclesall Woods, Great Roe Wood, Shirtcliff Wood and Buck Wood (Jones and Talbot, 1995). This was part of the Local Agenda 21 action involving the principal local authorities throughout the UK to carry forward the action proposed in the government's Sustainable Development Strategy in response to the Rio Declaration on Environment and Development. Local Agenda 21 was about people taking action in their local environment for the benefit of themselves, for wildlife and for the planet as a whole. The idea behind the feasibility study, which was jointly supported by Sheffield City Council and the

South Yorkshire Forest Project (see below), was to find out whether re-coppiced woodland would provide a limited number of woodland craft jobs, create products for which there was a local demand, improve the structural and species diversity of the woodlands and enhance their amenity value.

The experiments created much initial interest: on one weekend in the winter of 1994-95, for example, when the experimental area in Ecclesall Woods was being extended, two guided walks through the woods to explore the history of the site, examine the re-coppicing experiments and to see demonstrations of pole-lathing, charcoal making and hurdle making, attracted more than 300 people. Observations by the author found that eighteen months after the creation of the experimental coppiced area in Ecclesall Woods, twelve botanical indicators had appeared that were absent in the surrounding un-coppiced high forest woodland. The project in Buck Wood won a British Telecom/World Wide Fund for Nature partnership award for its efforts in providing an example of sustainable woodland management. Following these experiments, at the end of the decade, as described below, active woodland management in the city's ancient woodlands with environmental, economic, educational and social objectives in mind, would take a giant step forward.

Special interest groups and partnerships: Such groups have added new impetus to professional and community involvement in the sustainable management of ancient woodlands across the region. For example, the Gleadless Valley Wildlife Group, founded in 1987 (and now Gleadless Valley Wildife Trust), has been particularly influential in managing and interpreting the important ancient woodlands in the Gleadless Valley in Sheffield. The Friends of Ecclesall Woods, which was formed in 1993 and has a membership varying between 120 and 140, has been a model of community involvement in woodland conservation and management. Members of the group have been involved in practical conservation tasks, particularly the resurfacing of footpaths, and they have also successfully bid for lottery grants to help them in their work. In 2001, for example, they secured an 'Awards for All' grant from the Heritage Lottery Fund which enabled them to fund the undertaking of an archaeological survey of the woods and the creation of an archaeological trail with an accompanying leaflet. This leaflet has recently been re-designed and reprinted. In 2002 they obtained a Local Heritage Initiative grant which has led to the construction of a footpath to

Figure 4: A scene at an events day connected to the Ecclesall Woods experimental coppicing in the winter of 1994-95

the woodcollier's grave, the production of a full-colour leaflet (*A Seasonal Walk around Ecclesall Woods*), and an archaeological survey of the hill-top enclosure and whitecoal pits. More ambitiously they have produced an 85-page book, *Ecclesall Woods, Sheffield: a Flora* (Smyllie, 2006), illustrated in colour, again generously supported by the Local Heritage Initiative.

The newest 'Friends of' group is the Friends of Gillfield Wood formed in 2011. With the help of the Heritage Lottery Fund they have produced a detailed history of the wood and an illustrated leaflet. They organise monthly committee meetings, organise meetings with invited speakers and on the last Sunday of every month in collaboration with the Countryside & Parks ranger service they organise conservation work days, typical tasks including thinning, repair of gates and walls and maintenance of footpaths.

The Working Woodlands Trust, formed in 1997 by a group of local professional woodland workers, has also been a welcome influence in promoting sustainable woodland management in the city's woods until its demise in 2015. The Trust aimed to provide innovative and enjoyable educational woodland events, provide advice and support for community-based woodland initiatives, promote the use of locally-produced woodland products and provide support for sustainable wood-based businesses. The Working Woodlands Gallery at Ecclesall Woods Sawmill, opened in 2008, was a shop window for Working Woodlands members. On the same site in 2011 the City Council opened a new woodland activity centre, the J. G. Graves Woodland Discovery Centre, including an education room and outdoor classroom with display and exhibition space. Woodland craft courses are an important feature at the Centre.

Figure 5: The J.G. Graves Woodland Discovery Centre in Ecclesall Woods

The South Yorkshire Biodiversity Research Group (SYBRG) with the Biodiversity and Landscape History Research Institute, in conjunction with Sheffield Hallam University, has, since 1994 been conducting research on woodland ecology, history, archaeology and management, organising seminars, conferences and workshops. Through Wildtrack Publishing they have been producing conference proceedings and books. Much of their activity has had a local focus. In 2003, for example, a major international conference took place, *Walking and Working in the Footsteps of Ghosts*, which was concerned with the history, ecology, archaeology and management of woodlands with contributors from France, Holland, Spain, Hungary and Sweden as well as from Great Britain (Rotherham, Jones and Handley, 2012). But there were also local contributions and delegates visited local ancient woods. In 2008, a major publication took place in the form of *The Woodland Heritage Manual: a guide to investigating wooded landscapes* (Rotherham, Jones, Smith, & Handley, 2008). This publication was the culmination of a project called *The Woodland Heritage Champions Project* organised by members of the SYBRG and funded by the Heritage Lottery Fund, the Woodland Trust, the Forestry Commission and English Heritage. The project took the form of workshops for volunteers during which the main elements of the guide would be presented and trialled and feedback would be received from group members. The project was a country-wide project with workshops held in nine different regions of England from Cumbria and North Yorkshire in the north to East Devon and Surrey/East Sussex in the south. The South Yorkshire workshop involved members of three woodland groups: the Gleadless Valley Wildlife Trust, the Friends of Ecclesall Woods and the Steel Valley Project based in Stocksbridge. Then in 2011, SYBRG organised a series of workshops funded by the Heritage Lottery Awards for All scheme and the South Yorkshire Community Foundation entitled *Discovering Neighbourhood Woodlands*. The workshops introduced local enthusiasts to the ways they could uncover the secrets of the history, archaeology and wildlife of their local woodland. Six short guides, in leaflet form, were published in connection with the workshops on subjects such as documentary research, identifying an ancient woodland, woodland archaeology and botanical indicators of ancient woodland. In 2011 and 2012, SYBRG organised a series of workshops and field visits in and around Stocksbridge, Silkstone and Birds Edge investigating the history and archaeology of the industrial uses of their local woodlands under the heading *Industrial Treescapes*. A free survey pack was produced (Handley, Jones, Rotherham, & Spode, 2012) which is also available free to download from the internet.

Figure 6: An outdoor workshop at a meeting of the SYBRG Discovering Neighbourhood Woodlands Project

A major influence on local attitudes to woodland management in the last three decades was the South Yorkshire Forest Partnership. This project, established in 1991 and closed in 2016, was a partnership between Barnsley, Rotherham and Sheffield Councils, the Countryside Agency and the Forestry Commission. Its aim was to develop multi-purpose forests which would create better environments for people to use, cherish and enjoy. The South Yorkshire Forest area covered most of the Coal Measure country in the three metropolitan districts of Sheffield, Barnsley and Rotherham. Although not just concerned with ancient woodlands, among its objectives were commitments to protect areas of historical, archaeological and ecological interest (i.e. the existing ancient woodlands), to increase opportunities for access and recreation, and to encourage the development of timber-based industries, employment opportunities and woodland products. Following a year of public consultation, the South Yorkshire Forest's first Plan was published in August 1994 (South Yorkshire Forest, 1994). This established a policy framework and a strategic approach to woodland management throughout the South Yorkshire Forest area – for private as well as publicly-owned woods – and guided developments into the twenty-first century.

The Fuelling a Revolution Project: In 1997, the South Yorkshire Forest Team put together a £1½ m bid to the Heritage Lottery Fund for a five-year action plan to restore 35 Coal Measure woodlands in Sheffield, Rotherham and Barnsley – called *Fuelling a Revolution - The Woods that founded the Steel Country* (South Yorkshire Forest, 1997). In February 1999, it was announced that the bid had been successful and a five-year Heritage Woodlands Project was launched in September 1999. Twenty-two of the thirty-five woodlands within the project were in the ownership of Sheffield City Council, eleven in Rotherham and two in Barnsley.

The project also helped Rotherham MBC buy Canklow Wood from the Duke of Norfolk for £135,000, £101,000 of which was provided by the Heritage Lottery Fund. There was much activity on a broad front connected with the project – archaeological surveys, development of management plans, active woodland management programmes, interpretation for local communities, the development of educational materials and activities and the commissioning of public art works.

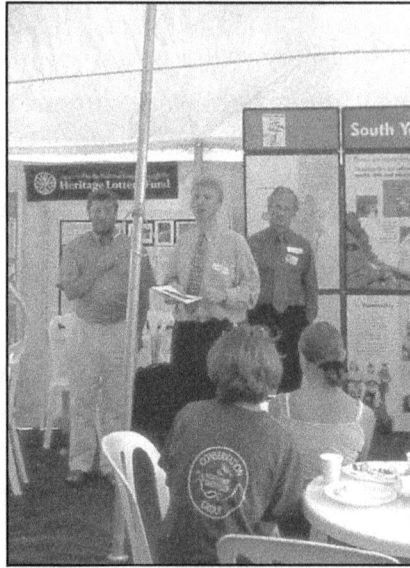

Figure 7: The launch of the Fuelling a Revolution Project in September 1997

Active management took place in all 35 of the *Fuelling a Revolution* woodlands, usually a combination of group felling, thinning and coppicing. The aims of the management were to maintain or reinstate the semi-natural characteristics of the woodlands by promoting a diverse woodland structure. This, it was hoped, would encourage a rich and diverse ground flora and birdlife and at the same time promote the woodlands as places for safe and accessible recreation and as educational resources. In order to safeguard the ground flora and the archaeology, where the ground is steep or particularly sensitive, working horses rather than wheeled vehicles were used to remove felled trees.

A second management plan for Bowden Housteads, to build on the work undertaken between 1987 and 1991, was compiled as part of the *Fuelling a Revolution* Project. This covered the period from 2000 to 2005 (Sheffield City Council, 2000). In 1999, prior to the plan being put together a small-scale household questionnaire survey was undertaken (100 persons) and a visitor survey (50 persons). Results of the surveys very much echoed those of the 1986 survey. People said they used the site because of the peace and quiet away from traffic, the wildlife and for exercise. They disliked the continued vandalism, litter, motorbikers and the feeling that it was not an altogether safe place. The improvements most frequently requested were a nature trail, information boards and guided walks, a staff presence and more wild flowers. A small 'Friends of Bowden Housteads' group had been formed in 1996, and this small group of enthusiasts also funnelled local concerns to the woodland managers.

The management plan for 2000 to 2005 reflected the desire of the city's woodland team to try to solve the problems raised and the requests made by the public. The vegetation management objectives of the plan were to restore natural species composition by continued selective thinning of sycamore, whitebeam and beech and so encouraging natural regeneration. Willow would be encouraged in selected wet areas and the age diversity of the woodland would be further encouraged through the reintroduction of group felling. It was also promised that surveys would be undertaken to monitor ecological change. Additionally access would be improved through upgrading the path system (the Trans-Pennine Trail and the National Cycle Route (Sustrans) now pass through the site) and educational and interpretive materials would be produced.

The most recent plan for Bowden Housteads Wood covered the period 2009 to 2013 (Sheffield City Council, 2013) and aimed to build on the work undertaken as part of the plans for 1987 to 1991 and 2000 to 2005. The vegetation management consisted of continued small-scale thinning to promote uneven-aged woodland and diversity of species, structure and habitats. This, of course, was thirty years after Oliver Gilbert's first experimental glades in the wood had prompted the first active management in Sheffield's woods for almost a century.

Native tree and shrub species were favoured and natural regeneration was used wherever possible to provide new trees. During thinning operations a proportion of trees were allowed to develop to over-maturity and natural senescence, and, where

107

not a danger to the public, dead wood, standing and fallen, was left to undergo natural decay processes.

The programmes of interpretation and education developed for schools and the general public connected with the *Fuelling a Revolution* project, were particularly impressive. For schools, 'school weeks' were organised in Sheffield, for example, in Wheata Wood (a bodger's camp), Gleadless Valley woods and Bowden Housteads Wood, and woodland play schemes were also successfully run. In May 2002, a 'big book' for the literacy hour for Sheffield schools pitched at Year 3 pupils, *Sheffield Woodland Detectives* (Jones and Jones, 2002) was launched and has been used in 23 of the City's primary schools. For the general public a series of woodland craft courses, run in partnership with The Working Woodlands Trust, were fully booked. A series of eight woodland leaflets were also produced. Guided walks and other events, such as bluebell wood walks were features of the project. A *Fuelling a Revolution* website – www.heritagewoodsonline.co.uk – which provides general and site-by-site information for people of all ages about the heritage woodlands and their restoration was also set up. An unusual aspect of the project was the commissioning of public works of art to be placed in woods. These ranged from a colourful entrance to Rollestone Wood in the Gleadless Valley in Sheffield by artist Karen Gillan in collaboration with local school children; the carving of the face of 'the Wildman of the Woods' into a tree in Hinde Common Wood, Sheffield, by Jason Thomson; and a large sculpture of a steel giant with a hammer in his hand by the same sculptor at the side of the Sheffield Parkway in Bowden Housteads Wood, reflecting the close connection between South Yorkshire's ancient woods and the development of the steel industry.

An exciting new development was the purchase, completed in 2013 through a grant of £273,000 from the Heritage Lottery Fund, of Greno Woods (i.e. Greno Wood and the adjacent Hall Wood), by Sheffield and Rotherham Wildlife Trust. This large area of ancient woodland (it covers 169 ha) was managed as coppice-with-standards from the late medieval period until the late nineteenth century. It was then converted to high forest through the planting of beech, sweet chestnut, sycamore and conifers and managed as a commercial plantation by its private owner. Following a detailed study of the history of the woods (Jones, 2012) and an archaeological survey in 2014, the Trust removed a large area of conifers and began to manage large areas of the woods sustainably as broadleaf woods through thinning, coppicing and planting. It intends to continue to harvest the remaining conifer cover to provide income for further management projects. Interpretation of the site takes place through interpretation boards, leaflets and guided walks (including phone apps). Unfortunately, some accidental damge to industrial archaeology such as very early charcoal hearths occurred because they were unrecognied when site work commenced.

Figure 8: The Steel Giant in Bowden Housteads Wood

Conclusions: With all these positive woodland initiatives, Sheffield's woodlands look much better now than they did four decades ago. Awareness of the cultural importance of local ancient woods has been raised to a much higher level than hitherto and interest in their critical importance for wildlife as well as their educational and recreational potential has been re-awakened. And it cannot be emphasized enough that all this active management work started with those experimental glades created by Oliver Gilbert that played such an important role in changing the attitudes to the city's woodland resource.

There has been much public support for the City Council's approach to conserving and restoring the city's ancient woodland heritage. But it cannot be emphasised enough that tree and woodland management is not a one-off event; it needs to be continuous and long-term. All the progress that has been made could be lost if management is not continued at the same level into the future. National government policies since 2010 have eroded local public services, and look likely to continue to do so into the foreseeable future. The work that has taken place since the early 1980s is very encouraging, but it is just the beginning; the challenge, as everyone knows only too well, is to sustain it in the medium- and long-term.

Figure 9: Woolley Wood in early May 2018.

110

References

Bownes, J.S., Riley, T.H., Rotherham, I.D., & Vincent, S. M. (1991) *Sheffield Nature Conservation Strategy*. Sheffield City Council, Sheffield.

Gilbert, O.L. (1982) The management of urban woodland in Sheffield. *ECOS*, **3**(2), 31-34.

Gilbert, O.L. (1991) *The Ecology of Urban Habitat.* Chapman & Hall, London.

Gilbert, O.L. (1992) The urban influence and its implications for the management of Ecclesall Woods. *Ecclesall Woods – Past, Present and Future*, report by Sheffield City Ecology Unit, I.D. Rotherham (ed.), Sheffield City Ecology Unit, Sheffield, 4-6.

Gilbert, O.L. (1997) The effect of urbanisation on ancient woodland. *British Wildlife*, **8**, (4), 213-218.

Handley, C., Jones, M., Rotherham, I.D., & Spode, F. (2012) *Industrial Treescapes Project, Survey Pack*, South Yorkshire Biodiversity Research Group, Sheffield (free to download at www.ukeconet.org).

Jones, M. (1986a) Ancient woods in the Sheffield area: the documentary evidence. *Sorby Record,* **24**, 7-18.

Jones, M. (1986b) *Sheffield's ancient woods: some notes on their history and past management*. Sheffield City Polytechnic, Sheffield.

Jones, M. (1986c) *Bowden Housteads Wood: Household Survey*. Sheffield City Polytechnic, Sheffield.

Jones, M. (2009) *Sheffield's Woodland Heritage*, 4th edition, Wildtrack Publishing, Sheffield.

Jones, M. (2012) *A History of Greno Woods*, report for Sheffield and Rotherham Wildlife Trust.

Jones, M. and Jones, J. (2002) *Sheffield Woodland Detectives*. Sheffield City Council, Sheffield.

Jones, M., & Rotherham, I.D. (2011) Management issues in urban woodlands: a case study of Bowden Housteads Wood, Sheffield. *Aspects of Applied Biology*, **108**, 113-121.

Jones, M., & Rotherham, I.D. (2012) Managing urban ancient woodlands: A case study of Bowden Housteads Wood. Sheffield. *Arboricultural Journal*, **34**, 4, 215-233.

Jones, M., & Talbot, E. (1995) Coppicing in urban woodlands: a progress report on a multi-purpose feasibility study in the City of Sheffield. *The Journal of Practical Ecology and Conservation*, **1** (1), 46-52.

Pleat, J. (1988) Massacre in a good cause. *Sheffield Star*, 2 February.

Rotherham, I.D., Jones, M., Smith, L., & Handley, C. (2008) *The Woodland Heritage Manual: a guide to investigating wooded landscapes*. Wildtrack Publishing, Sheffield.

Rotherham, I.D., Jones, M., & Handley, C. (eds) (2012) *Working & Walking in the Footsteps of Ghosts, Volume 1: the Wooded Landscape*. Wildtrack Publishing, Sheffield.

Sheffield City Council (1987a) *Sheffield Woodland Policy*. Sheffield City Council, Sheffield.

Sheffield City Council (1987b) *Bowden Housteads/ Corker Bottoms 'Greenlink' Management Plan*. Department of Land and Planning, Sheffield City Council, Sheffield.

Sheffield City Council (2000) *Bowden Housteads and Spring Wood, Management Plan, 2000-2005*. Sheffield Leisure Services, Sheffield City Council, Sheffield.

Sheffield City Council (2009) *Bowden Housteads Wood: Draft Management Plan 2009-2013*, Sheffield Leisure Services. Sheffield City Council, Sheffield.

Smyllie, B. (2006) *Ecclesall Woods, Sheffield: a Flora*. Friends of Ecclesall Woods, Sheffield.

South Yorkshire Forest (1994) *South Yorkshire Forest: Forest Plan*. South Yorkshire Forest, Sheffield.

South Yorkshire Forest (1997) *Fuelling a Revolution – the woods that founded the Steel country, application to the Heritage Lottery Fund (No 6-00700)*. South Yorkshire Forest Partnership, Sheffield.

Chapter 5: Species inclusion and exclusion in the biodiverse city

Robert A. Francis
King's College London

Summary: The utopian ideal of the biodiverse city is growing in popularity, and it is clear that there is increasing desire to accommodate biodiversity in cities, partly because of the ecosystem services it provides. New concepts and techniques for increasing biodiversity in cities have developed over recent years. However, there has been limited consideration of how we actively include and exclude different species within urban environments, the tensions inherent in the different approaches, and the implications this may have for the emergence of the biodiverse city. In this chapter, I consider that a spectrum of largely unrecognised species desirability exists that shapes our approaches to urban biodiversity, and which contains both compositionalist and functionalist elements.

Species inclusion focuses on species that may have existed in pre-urban ecosystems, but that do not easily persist in cities under their own agency ('anturbic' species), alongside species that thrive in cities ('synurbic' species), in situations where exurban populations are in decline. Species exclusion focuses on pests (of which many are synurbic) and non-native species, due to the societal impacts they may cause. And a third category exists: species which are neither encouraged nor discouraged (or even acknowledged) and occupy urban ecological niches spontaneously, ignored or disregarded by most citizens. I explore these approaches here, noting that all types of species have value, and that a renegotiation of how we interact and share the city with such species will be important for the ultimate realisation of the biodiverse city.

Keywords: urban ecology, biodiversity, reconciliation ecology, recombinant communities, non-native species, anturbic, synurbic, nescience

Introduction: The city has become a spontaneous experimental frontier for exploration into how our species and the many others we share the Earth with might coexist (Braun, 2005; Francis *et al.*, 2012). Certainly the notion of a biodiverse city – a biophilic, co-constructed landscape comprised of enmeshed green space and biodiversinesque architecture – has become self-evidently desirable and increasingly portrayed in utopian terms across the sciences, social sciences, and arts (Ignatiena and Ahrné, 2013; Beatley, 2014; Shaffer, 2018). Driven in part by the recognition of the value of biodiversity in underpinning urban ecosystem services, increasing focus on maximising the *space* available to nonhuman species, in the form of habitat area and connectivity, has emerged in the ecological literature (Goddard *et al.*, 2010; Francis, & Lorimer, 2011; Beninde *et al.*, 2015).

Yet biodiversity is a complex and contested concept (Zimmerer, 2009), and making space for nonhumans is only part of the story of the biodiverse city. Understanding different conceptualisations of real and idealised *place* that nonhuman species occupy in cities represents a fundamental concern necessary for both reimagining and actively managing current and future urban ecosystems; a concern that ultimately lies at the heart of both the utopian aspiration for ecologically sustainable urbanisation, and in the achievement of whatever form of 'good Anthropocene' (Bennett *et al.*, 2016) humanity might ultimately be able to attain.

Recent scientific advances in the study of urban ecology and urban biodiversity have established ways in which both individual species and functioning ecological communities (Gaston *et al.*, 2005; Alvey, 2006; Tratalos *et al.*, 2007; Beninde *et al.*, 2015) might be best encouraged within cities, as well as demonstrating the importance of nonhuman species and various configurations of urban nature for all citizens (REFS). This developing body of research has led to a drive for urban biodiversity conservation and enhancement, primarily involving the adoption of 'urban greening' principles and methodologies that combine elements of spatial (landscape) ecology with urban planning, to increase area and connectivity of green infrastructure that will ideally provide more and better habitat for an idealised but relatively unexplored 'urban biodiversity', and species of conservation concern (Beninde, 2015). Such efforts embed ecological habitat within the city in proximity to humans; particularly where emergent ecological engineering techniques are utilised, such as the construction of living roofs and walls (Oberndorfer *et al.*, 2007; Francis, & Lorimer, 2011). It is in this proximity and the 'situating' of species within the city that some of the more interesting questions of the appropriate place of urban nonhumans lie.

Urban biodiversity is complex, and both spatially and socially transgressive. It is spatially transgressive because 'wild', undomesticated and uncultivated organisms and spontaneously-formed ecological assemblages are distributed across the city. They encompass all forms of social space, from public to domestic. Socially transgressive, because (1) humans and the species they privilege by intentionally cultivating and installing them into public and private space, are discomforted, compromised and threatened by other successful urban species (e.g. those that become pests); and (2) because societal expectations of 'appropriate' ecological communities are confounded by 'recombinant' assemblages (e.g. Rotherham, 2017), wherein organisms of different evolutionary and geographical origins, as well as different habitat requirements, coexist in assemblages that are not found in more natural ecosystems; so that traditional ecological and nature conservation values based around typological ecological communities (e.g. the National Vegetation Classification in the UK) and 'nativeness' can become violated and problematic (Coates, 2007; Fortwangler, 2013).

Indeed, approaches to urban biodiversity and habitat creation have largely been functionalist, in that they have often been concerned less with the individual species or community types that are present than with the ecological roles they may play; for example, encouraging pollinators or avian apex predators such as raptors (Hall *et al.*, 2016; Bird *et al.*, 2018). Ideologically, this is more in line with rewilding efforts, which likewise emphasise functionality and more flexible adaptive management with no specific endpoint rather than trying to create or preserve specific communities; although they do not subscribe to rewilding's general focus on megafauna (Lorimer *et al.*, 2015). A compositionalist approach, wherein ecological communities are viewed in terms of what is there and what 'should' be there, what *belongs* – and which is the primary philosophy behind traditional conservation approaches and attempts to prevent species invasions (Callicott *et al.*, 1999) – is less appropriate to urban ecosystems, in which nothing intrinsically belongs. And yet, there are expectations and desirability around particular species or communities, which can be centred on function (services and disservices), characteristics (charisma) or typologies (e.g. native or non-native). Navigating these tensions is a challenge for the emerging biodiverse city.

Despite this complexity, there has been relatively little reflection on what a biodiverse city would look like, or with regards to the types of species or ecological communities that are the desired beneficiaries of urban greening or ecological engineering interventions; nor acknowledgement of the tensions that exist in encouraging (both functionally and compositionally) 'desirable' species to the city on the one hand and discouraging 'undesirable' species on the other. Such tensions inevitably confound the real or perceived success of ecological enhancements and will shape how and why we share our current and future cities with other members of the living world, whether acknowledged or not.

In this chapter, I explore this tension in our differential approach to nonhuman species in cities. The central conflicts exists between the (often unacknowledged) desire to (1) encourage those species that may have existed in pre-urban ecosystems, but that do not easily persist in cities under their own agency ('anturbic' species); (2) encourage those species that thrive in cities ('synurbic' species), in situations where exurban populations are in decline, so that the city acts as a refuge for such species; and (3) exclude those synurbic species that become 'pests' or otherwise problematic due to their large populations, close proximity to humans, and societal impacts. Alongside these broad categorisations, there are a range of species that exhibit more neutral or differential responses to the urban environment, and which are neither encouraged nor discouraged (or even acknowledged) and occupy urban ecological niches spontaneously, ignored or disregarded by most citizens. Our approach to them is perhaps best described as 'nescient'.

I suggest that a spectrum of subjective, largely unrecognised species desirability therefore exists that shapes our approaches to urban biodiversity. Recognising and confronting such tensions is necessary for reconceptualising urban ecological assemblages, their place in the city, and our relationship with them; thereby facilitating a dialogue of 'desirability' of species and how this feeds into the principles and objectives of urban greening efforts. Without such reflections, the observation made several decades ago by pioneering urban ecologist Oliver Gilbert that 'the most appropriate method of accommodating wildlife [in cities] is still undecided...' (Gilbert, 1991) will remain a perennial issue.

I now consider three broad approaches to urban biodiversity, focusing on inclusion, exclusion and nescience towards nonhumans in urban ecosystems, and how these may shape our relationships with other species and the emergence of the biodiverse city.

Species inclusion through urban reconciliation ecology: Reconciliation ecology is the reconciling of human and nonhuman use of space (Rosenzweig, 2003; Francis and Lorimer, 2011). In an urban context, it is essentially the ecological engineering or sympathetic management of human public and domestic spaces (e.g. buildings, parks, gardens, transport infrastructure) in ways that do not compromise societal use but allow coexistence between humans and nonhumans.

Reconciliation efforts that enhance biodiversity in cities are usually performed to achieve co-benefits in terms of broader ecosystem services, for example planting vegetation to ameliorate urban runoff and reduce heat island effects as well as provide habitat for plants and insects (Tratalos *et al.*, 2007; Lovell, & Taylor, 2013). Techniques usually focus on (1) the creation and ecological management of green infrastructure, including public and private green spaces such as parks and gardens; and (2) ecological engineering of the built environment to create 'biodiversinesque' architecture (Ignatieva, & Ahrné, 2013), using technology such as living roofs and walls (Francis, & Lorimer, 2011). Where the intention of such interventions is to improve 'biodiversity' in general, this is often expressed in vague terms, i.e. the creation of habitat that allows 'more' species/individuals, or a greater functional range of species, to persist. But the logical ideal of ecological enhancements is to allow sustainable populations of those species that are typically *unable* to survive in the city to do so; to 'soften' the urban environment sufficiently to allow their persistence within urban ecological communities, rather than provision of 'more of the same'. This would be important for the emergence of the biodiverse city. To achieve this, reconciliation efforts need to be sympathetic to those species that are more sensitive to urbanisation.

Differential responses of species to urban conditions are well-documented, though both variable and complex (Kark *et al.*, 2006; Francis, & Chadwick, 2012; Garcia *et al.*, 2017). Those species that struggle most to survive in cities (anturbic) are amongst the first to be lost when urbanisation occurs, and are likely to be (1) organisms that rely on ecosystems that are often lost with urbanisation or preceding land use change, such as wetlands or climax-sere woodland (Pauchard *et al.*, 2006; Forman, 2008); (2) organisms that require large areas of intact 'interior' habitat (i.e. sheltered, away from 'edge' conditions and their associated disturbances; Fernández-Juricic, 2001), which are lost as landscape fragmentation occurs; and/or (3) those that are sensitive to urban-specific impacts such as noise pollution or the urban heat island effect (Newport et al. 2014). Such species have sometimes been termed 'urban avoiders' (Gering, & Blair, 1999; Kark *et al.*, 2006), and are characterised by either absence from urban areas, or greatly reduced population densities or fitness.

Encouraging anturbic species to cities is challenging. Engineering or restoring ecosystems, or their ecological conditions, that do not 'urbanise well' is problematic. Species that require climax/ancient (long-standing) woodland, heathland, chalk grassland, wetlands and so on, are hard to create suitable and sustainable conditions for. Although there are efforts to recreate some of these ecosystems in the urban environment (e.g. wetlands; Kim *et al.*, 2011), achieving sufficient area and quality of habitat to allow species populations of urban avoiders to persist indefinitely remains to be realised. Where ecosystems are successfully created, provision of 'interior' habitat (e.g. dense, shaded woodland, or deep water) for species that need less disturbance is even more problematic. This is perhaps the main limitation of reconciliation efforts, as these create an abundance of 'edge' habitat – there is no interior on a living roof or garden and most urban green space is limited in size and/or complex in shape (exacerbating edge effects), or frequently disturbed by humans. Ecological engineering or adaptive management of the urban environment to reduce disturbance or stress from light, noise and heat is possible, but again in its infancy (Gaston *et al.*, 2012; Santamouris, 2014). Nonetheless, these possibilities should be more robustly explored as we consider both the ideological and practical emergence of the biodiverse city.

It should also be noted that some reconciliation efforts may in effect create ecological traps. For example, Williams et al. (2014) note that although the biodiversity benefits of green roofs are often lauded, they support few rare taxa and their long-term habitat restoration/replacement potential is untested; they may, in effect, be sink habitats, where species and communities exist only temporarily. Likewise, urban stormwater wetlands may represent a useful habitat, but will also accumulate pollutants, ultimately compromising those species and communities that may establish (Hale *et al.*, 2015). The significance of potential ecological traps remains to be more comprehensively investigated.

As noted, most reconciliation efforts are aimed at 'biodiversity' in general. Some, however, actively target synurbic species (those that maintain higher densities in urban areas than in their natural habitat (Francis, & Chadwick, 2012)) in those situations where species are in decline more broadly outside the city, or where there are compelling reasons. For example, in the UK, hedgehog species are of priority conservation concern due to declining populations, but are showing some signs of recovery in urban areas (Wilson, & Wembridge, 2018) and feature in several local (urban) Biodiversity Action Plans. In many cases (such as the hedgehog), these tend to me more charismatic species, encouraged compositionally rather than functionally. However, some species are encouraged for more functional reasons, such as some species of pollinator (e.g. bumble bees), which can also do well in cities (Hernandez *et al.*, 2009).

However, reconciliation efforts may provide habitat for both desired and undesired species. MacIvor, & Ksiazek (2015) note that garden and domestic pests such as aphids and ants are common on green roofs and that, although outbreaks are not widely reported in the literature, the proliferation of such ecosystems will increase cases of reported infestations. In one anecdotal example, a green roof installed on a school in Barrow-in-Furness was suggested as the source of a harvest mite infestation, which led to several students being bitten and indications that the roof would need to be treated or removed (Prior, 2013). Vegetation on buildings or in gardens, along with standing water features such as ponds, may harbour undesirable pests such as mosquitoes (Gaston *et al.*, 2005; Song *et al.*, 2013); though they may be no more amenable to such species than the built environment in general (Wong & Jim, 2016).

Reconciliation ecology is therefore important for achieving the biodiverse city, but there has so far been relatively little consideration of how to bring back anturbic species – those elusive urban avoiders – and there has generally been more focus on biodiversity more broadly conceived, selected charismatic species, and those which already have an affinity for the urban and are therefore more easily encouraged.

Species exclusion through population control, ecosystem restoration and hostile architecture: Some urban species are regarded by citizens as pests, as they are "species that interfere with human activities (e.g. recreation), negatively affect human health, or cause negative impacts to industry" (Hassan, & Ricciardi, 2014, p.219). Pests are often, though not always, human commensals that have reached high densities in the urban environment (and so are often 'synurbic'), thereby becoming increasing problematic due to the disservices they cause, their proximity to people, and the sheer number of individuals. This definition of pests reflects a functionalist view, in that those species that have negative agency on humans are those that are persecuted, not those that simply 'don't belong'.

Non-native (alien/exotic) species are also often excluded or considered undesirable, though the categorisation and treatment of non-natives is complex, and especially so in urban areas. There has been criticism of approaches to non-natives that determine the value or appropriateness of species based on a compositional approach, i.e. that such species do not comprise members of the 'original' or native communities. This is especially problematic for urban areas, which represent novel ecosystems and do not have typical communities unmediated by human agency (see below) – arguably, no species (or indeed all species) belong to the city.

However, this compositional approach underlines one of functionality and pragmatism: non-native species generally present a significant risk for invasion and ecological, economic or societal harm (Hassan, & Ricciardi, 2014); though this can be hard to predict for individual species. The compositional approach of excluding species based on provenance is therefore one of precaution. The biological extension of Douglas's (1966) assertion that dirt is "matter out of place" is that non-native species are 'species out of place' and that in this case the organism/species represents a form of biological pollution or hazard (see e.g. Ricciardi *et al.*, 2011). Non-native and invasive species therefore tread a line somewhere between benign presence and malignant harm that is spatially and temporally fluid, with impacts dependent on local environmental characteristics, time since introduction, and population size, amongst other things (e.g. Ricciardi *et al.*, 2013).

Certainly, some non-native species are desired by people and various industries (e.g. for horticulture, domestic pets or recreation), and the majority are benign (though this too is depending on environment and timescale). Some species provide notable ecosystem services (alongside disservices), including food sources and habitat for pollinators – an observation made for Japanese knotweed (*Fallopia japonica*) by Gilbert (1989) – and regulation of water pollution (Pejchar, & Mooney, 2009). Regardless of the complexity of our understanding and approach to non-native species, it is clear that urban areas are sources for non-native spread (Padayachee *et al.*, 2017; Franci, & Chadwick, 2015), just as they are areas that concentrate pest populations and impacts (Bonnefoy *et al.*, 2008).

As a result of this, cities are subject to extensive, though often heterogeneous and disorganised, efforts to control and remove pests and non-natives. A multi-billion dollar urban pest control industry exists globally (Dhang, 2014), while annual economic losses from urban invasive species would also rank in the billions of dollars, even based on conservative estimates (Pimentel *et al.*, 2005).

Prevention of introduction and establishment is the most common form of control, though this is especially difficult in urban areas, which tend to be transportation hubs containing multiple vectors for species movement (both aquatic and terrestrial); especially global cities that are at the centre of shipping, trade, industry and tourism (Padayachee *et al.*, 2017). With limited capacity for prevention of movement, both legislation and awareness-raising initiatives are put in place to try to stop spread, with an example of the latter being the Check-Clean-Dry campaign in the UK (NNSS, 2019); though rates of invasion continue to increase (e.g. Jackson, & Grey, 2013).

Removal of established non-natives is exceptionally difficult. Control usually focuses on physical, chemical and biological measures (Francis, & Pyšek, 2012; Francis, & Chadwick, 2015), with physical and chemical control being most prevalent. Such efforts can be effective in the short term: for example Cockel *et al.* (2014) reported some success in reducing populations of Himalayan balsam along an urban river (*Impatiens glandulifera*) by weeding; while Ruiz-Avila, & Klemm (1996) found that physical removal of mats of floating pennywort (*Hydrocotyle ranunculoides*), followed by application of glyphosate, to be an effective short to medium term control strategy. Long-term control successes are more elusive and management is often not well configured for urban environments (Gaertner *et al.*, 2016); a situation further complicated by high disturbance and introduction effort in cities, meaning that any extirpations are often temporary.

Sometimes entire ecosystems are restored with non-native exclusion as a key objective. For example, river restoration efforts also act as a form of physical control, by removing non-native species or their habitat; though so far such interventions have had limited success. In many cases, non-natives are well suited to urban river conditions; sometimes more so than the extirpated natives that are the desired beneficiaries of the restoration efforts. For example, Arango *et al.* (2015) examined post-restoration responses in an urbanised stream in the Pacific Northwest (USA) and found that less than a year after restoration, the fish community retained its dominance by non-native eastern brook trout (*Salvelinus fontinalis*). Suren (2009) planted a native macrophyte (*Myriophyllum triphyllum*) into urban streams dominated by non-natives, following weeding to reduce non-native populations, but these efforts were ultimately unsuccessful. Even with significant effort and extensive ecosystem transformation, the desired removal of non-natives is very difficult to achieve. Instead of eradication, adaptive management and increased tolerance of non-native species is perhaps pragmatic and necessary – though much debate rages about societal perceptions and approaches to non-native and invasive species (e.g. Russell, & Blackburn, 2017).

Cities and citizens have a history of adaptation to exclude undesirable species, ranging from changes in bed design and domestic practices to reduce populations of commensal bed bugs (Potter, 2011) to more recent attempts to prevent birds resting or nesting on buildings or trees using spikes or gels that have an offensive odour and contain ultraviolet light that birds perceive as flame (Dillon, 2018); a form of hostile architecture. Exclusion can also be indirect, such as the tendency to clean plants from the walls of buildings, despite them often presenting no problem or even providing benefits (Viles *et al.*, 2011). Sometimes exclusion is unintentional, for example the design of more integral concrete, steel or glass walls that do not offer opportunities for plants to colonise (Francis, 2011). The ways in which we exclude species, intentional and unintentional, direct and indirect, are myriad and complex, and their implications for urban biodiversity need further exploration.

Functional (rather than compositional) exclusion is the most logical approach to problematic or undesirable urban species. But there is also an argument to be made around the value of the disservices that species and biodiversity more broadly, may provide. Even the act of being exposed to other species, problematic or not, helps us to learn how to respect, value and interact with nonhumans. Miller's (2005) assertion that each successive generation has lower expectations of environmental quality, biodiversity and interactions with other species – variously termed 'extinction of experience' or 'generational amnesia' (e.g. Khan, 2002) – also applies to the frequency, quality and type of interactions that people may have with *undesirable* nonhumans. Pests like bed bugs for instance, that were once commonplace and an accepted part of everyday domestic life for most people, are now regarded as an unacceptable threat at odds with modern living standards (Eddy, & Jones, 2011). However, the absence of such pests has created an 'extinction of exposure' to the disservices that such species create, leading to a lack of tolerance towards less desirable species, even in situations where the disservices are relatively minor; for example proximity to relatively harmless insects that are important for pollination or food webs, such as bees and spiders. As we recognise the need for multispecies conviviality in the biodiverse city, increasing engagement with less desirable species should help to build up emotional and psychological resilience to the full spectrum of species such a city would support.

Nescience, spontaneous species assemblages and novel ecosystems: Most species in the city exist largely unrecognised and unacknowledged by the majority of citizens, who go through their daily lives generally unaware of the communities they live amongst, unless they are present in domestic space or designated public spaces such as parks. Many urban species, particularly plants, emerge spontaneously in many habitats, from disturbed areas to roadsides, railway tracks, walls and so on (Francis, & Chadwick, 2013). In many cases they are appreciated only as background scenery, attracting little interest or recognition -a tendency known as 'plant blindness' for floral communities (Balding, & Williams, 2016). The diversity of such habitats can be relatively high, but the urban (and recombinant) context means that it is often considered as lacking in value. In many cases, diversity is associated with heterogeneity and complexity, which can be perceived by people as messy or untidy, and therefore undesirable (Ignatieva, 2010).

In reality, these are exciting habitats and communities. The habitats themselves cover a spectrum from analogue – replicating conditions that exist elsewhere in nature, such as building walls being similar to cliff faces – to novel, creating habitat conditions that have no natural equivalent (Lundholm, & Richardson, 2010). The communities that assemble are recombinant, compiled from various habitat, geographical and evolutionary backgrounds (Rotherham, 2017), their persistence supported by their sheer abundance within the urban environment. They can display a range of behavioural and adaptive responses to urban conditions, with some showing evidence of rapid evolutionary adaptation (Schilthuizen, 2018).

Importantly, the spontaneous emergence of recombinant communities shows that ecosystem processes are intact within the city, and that a form of rewilding is happening by itself. Embracing the biodiverse city means we must have a greater understanding of these processes and be open to the assemblages that form naturally within the city. They are, after all, a key educational resource, both for ecologists and for citizens, and are useful for encouraging wider engagement with biodiversity in all of its forms. As Dunn *et al.* (2006) note, urban nature is, and will increasingly be, central to people maintaining contact with, and appreciation for, the honhuman world.

Towards the biodiverse, reconciled city: The city has utopian aspirations to be biodiverse, 'urbanised' and 'biodiverse' need not necessary be oxymorons, and cities will certainly continue to play an important role in the story of biodiversity in the Anthropocene (Shaffer, 2018). How we might cohabit with other species in the habitat that we have made for ourselves is a central question; importantly, there should be no expectation that the arrangement should necessarily be a happy one. We need, and are a component of, the nonhuman world, and cannot be apart from it. Instead, the issue is one of necessity and pragmatism: which species can we coexist with, and still maintain essential ecological and societal functions and services?

For the biodiverse city to be realised, new approaches are needed. Recognition of the heterogenous, spontaneous and complex nature of recombinant species, and the novelty of urban environments, is important, as is the need to more fully appreciate – and tolerate – a wider range of species and the ecosystem services and disservices they provide.

The biodiverse city is potentially a rewilded city. This may not be the same as rewilding elsewhere – the potential for introducing large mammals and keystone predators to the city is after all limited (for the present) – but should embrace rewilding's principles of no proscribed end state and adaptive management as conditions change. This would, for example, include active management where there are notable threats (such as disease vectors), but overall efforts should be made to encourage both spontaneous emergence of ecological communities, as well as those anturbic species that struggle to persist in contemporary urban environments. Urban environmental education should, drawing on elements of environmental and conservation psychology (Clayton, & Myers, 2009), equip citizens to live in the rewilded city.

These ideas contribute to a new and emerging phase in the history of urbanisation. The privileging of species in the past (for example garden plants, domestic pets and charismatic 'wild' animals) is now shifting to greater acceptance of species, and their active encouragement. Traditional conservation values tied to compositionality of natural or semi-natural ecological communities are being unpicked and replaced with functionalist approaches that are concerned more with functioning assemblages of species.

Reconciliation of human and nonhuman is possible in the biodiverse city, but more work is needed on developing an ecological evidence base for which techniques are most appropriate for encouraging biodiversity, alongside societal change to encourage greater engagement of citizens with urban nature. This is indeed a key frontier of urban ecology.

References

Alvey, A.A. (2006) Promoting and preserving biodiversity in the urban forest. *Urban Forestry & Urban Greening*, **5**(4), 195-201.

Arango, C.P., James, P.W. & Hatch, K.B. (2015) Rapid ecosystem response to restoration in an urban stream. *Hydrobiologia*, **749**(1), 197–211.

Balding, M. & Williams, K.J.H. (2016) Plant blindness and the implications for plant conservation. *Conservation Biology,* **30**(6), 1192-1199.

Beatley, T. (2014) *Imagining biophilic cities.* In: Lehmann, S. (ed.) *Low Carbon Cities: Transforming Urban Systems.* Routledge, London, 123– 134.

Beninde, J., Veith, M., & Hochkirch, A. (2015) Biodiversity in cities needs space: a meta-analysis of factors determining intra-urban biodiversity variation. *Ecology Letters*, **18**(6), 581-592.

Bird, D.M., Rosenfield, R.N., Septon, G., Gahbauer, M.A., Barclay, J.H., & Lincer, J.L. (2018) *Management and conservation of urban raptors.* In: Boal, C.W., & Dykstra, C.R. (eds) *Urban Raptors: Ecology and Conservation of Birds of Prey in Cities.* Springer, 258-272.

Bonnefoy, X., Kampen, H., & Sweeney, K. (eds) (2008) *Public Health Significance of Urban Pests.* World Health Organisation, Copenhagen.

Braun, B. (2005) Environmental issues: writing a more-than-human urban geography. *Progress in Human Geography*, **29**(5), 635-650.

Callicott, J.B., Crowder, L.B., & Mumford, K. (1999) Current normative concepts in conservation. *Conservation Biology*, **13**(1), 22-35.

Clayton, S., & Myers, G. (2009) *Conservation Psychology: Understanding and Promoting Human Care for Nature*. Wiley Blackwell, Oxford.

Coates, P. (2007) *American Perceptions of Immigrant and Invasive Species: Strangers on the Land.* University of California Press, Berkeley.

Cockel, C.P., Gurnell, A.M., & Gurnell, J. (2014) Consequences of the physical management of an invasive alien plant for riparian plant species richness and diversity. *River Research and Applications*, **30**(2), 217-229.

Dhang, P. (ed.) (2014) *Urban Insect Pests: Sustainable Management Strategies*. CABI, Wallingford.

Dillon, T. (2018) AMHARC [Creative work: general category] Available from: http://eprints.uwe.ac.uk/38073

Douglas, M. (1966) *Purity and Danger: An Analysis of Concepts of Pollution and Taboo*. Routledge, London.

Dunn, R.R., Gavin, M.C., Sanchez, M.C. & Solomon, J.N. (2006) The pigeon paradox: dependence of global conservation on urban nature. *Conservation Biology*, **20**(6), 1814-1816.

Eddy, C. & Jones, S.C. (2011) Bed bugs, public health, and social justice: part 1, a call to action. *Journal of Environmental Health*, **73**(8), 8-14.

Fernández-Juricic, E. (2001) Avian spatial segregation at edges and interiors of urban parks in Madrid, Spain. *Biodiversity & Conservation*, **10**(8), 1303–1316.

Fortwangler, C. (2013) Untangling introduced and invasive animals. *Environment & Society*, **4**(1), 41-59.

Forman, R.T.T. (2008) *Urban Regions: Ecology and Planning Beyond the City*. Cambridge University Press, Cambridge.

Francis, R.A. (2011) Wall ecology: a frontier for urban biodiversity and ecological engineering. *Progress in Physical Geography*, **35**(1), 43-63.

Francis, R.A., & Chadwick, M.A. (2012) What makes a species synurbic? *Applied Geography*, **32**(2), 514-521.

Francis, R.A., & Chadwick, M.A. (2013) *Urban Ecosystems: Understanding the Human Environment*. Routledge, London.

Francis, R.A. & Chadwick, M.A. (2015) Urban invasions: non-native and invasive species in cities. *Geography*, **100**(3), 144-151.

Francis, R.A., & Lorimer, J. (2011) Urban reconciliation ecology: the potential of living roofs and walls. *Journal of Environmental Management*, **92**, 1429-1437.

Francis, R.A., Lorimer, J. & Raco, M. (2012) Urban ecosystems as 'natural' homes for biogeographical boundary crossings. *Transactions of the Institute of British Geographers,* **37**(2), 183-190.

Francis, R.A., & Pyšek, P. (2012) *Management of freshwater invasive alien species.* In: Francis, R.A. (ed.) *A Handbook of Global Freshwater Invasive Species*, Routledge, London, 435-446.

Gaertner, M., Larson, B.H.M., Irlich, U.M., Holmes, P.M., Stafford, L., van Wilgen, B.W., & Richardson, D.M. (2016) Managing invasive species in cities: A framework from Cape Town, South Africa. *Landscape and Urban Planning*, **151**, 1-9.

Garcia, C.M., Suárez-Rodríguez, M. & López-Rull, I. (2017) *Becoming citizens: avian adaptations to urban life.* In: Murgui, E. & Hedblom, M. (eds.) *Ecology and Conservation of Birds in Urban Environments*. Springer, Dortrecht, 91-112.

Gaston, K.J., Smith, R.M., Thompson, K. & Warren, P.H. (2005) Urban domestic gardens (II): experimental tests of methods for increasing biodiversity. *Biodiversity & Conservation*, 14, 395.

Gaston, K.J., Davies, T.W., Bennie, J., & Hopkins, J. (2012) Reducing the ecological consequences of night-time light pollution: options and developments. *Journal of Applied Ecology*, **49**(6), 1256-1266.

Gering, J.C., & Blair, R.B. (1999) Predation on artificial bird nests along an urban gradient: predatory risk or relaxation in urban environments? *Ecography*, **22**(5), 532-541.

Gilbert, O.L. (1989) *The Ecology of Urban Habitats*. Chapman and Hall, London.

Goddard, M.A., Dougill, A.J., & Benton, T.G. (2010) Scaling up from gardens: biodiversity conservation in urban environments. *Trends in Ecology & Evolution*, **25**(2), 90-98.

Hale, R., Coleman, R., Pettigrove, V., & Swearer, S.E. (2015) Identifying, preventing and mitigating ecological traps to improve the management of urban aquatic ecosystems. *Journal of Applied Ecology*, **52**(4), 928-939.

Hall, D.M., Camilo, G.R., Tonietto, R.K., Ollerton, J., Ahrné, K., Arduser, M., Ascher, J.S., Baldock, K.C.R., Fowler, R., Frankie, G., Goulson, D., Gunnarsson, B., Hanley, M.E., Jackson, J.I., Langellotto, G., Lowenstein, D., Minor, E.S., Philpott, S.M., Potts, S.G., Sirohi, M.H., Spevak, E.M., Stone, G.N., & Threlfall, C.G. (2016) The city as a refuge for insect pollinators. *Conservation Biology*, **31**(1), 24-29.

Hassan, A., & Ricciardi, A. (2014) Are non-native species more likely to become pests? Influence of biogeographic origin on the impacts of freshwater organisms. *Frontiers in Ecology and the Environment*, **12**(4), 218–223.

Hernandez, J.L., Frankie, G.W., & Thorp, R.W. (2009) Ecology of urban bees: a review of current knowledge and directions for future study. *Cities and the Environment*, **2**(1), 3.

Ignatieva, M. (2010) *Design and future of urban biodiversity*. In: Müller, N., Werner, P., & Kelcey, J.C. (eds) *Urban Biodiversity and Design*, Blackwell, London.

Ignatieva, M., & Ahrné, K. (2013) Biodiverse green infrastructure for the 21st century: from "green desert" of lawns to biophilic cities. *Journal of Architecture and Urbanism*, **37**(1), 1-9.

Jackson, M.C. & Grey, J. (2013) Accelerating rates of freshwater invasions in the catchment of the River Thames. *Biological Invasions,* **15**(5), 945–951.

Kahn, P.H., Jr. (2002) *Children's affiliations with nature: structure, development and the problem of environmental generational amnesia*. In: Kahn, P.H., Jr, & Kellert, S.R. (eds) *Children and Nature: Psychological, Sociocultural, and Evolutionary Investigations*, MIT Press, Massachusetts, 93-116.

Kark, S., Iwaniuk, A., Schalimtzek, A., & Banker, E. (2006) Living in the city: can anyone become an 'urban exploiter'? *Journal of Biogeography*, **34**(4), 638-651.

Kim, K-G., Lee, H., & Lee, D-H. (2001) Wetland restoration to enhance biodiversity in urban areas: a comparative analysis. *Landscape and Ecological Engineering*, **7**(1), 27–32.

Lorimer, J., Sandom, C., Jepson, P., Doughty, C., Barua, M., & Kirby, K.J. (2015) Rewilding: science, practice, and politics. *Annual Review of Environment and Resources*, **40**, 39-62.

Lovell, S.T., & Taylor, J.R. (2013) Supplying urban ecosystem services through multifunctional green infrastructure in the United States. *Landscape Ecology*, **28**(8), 1447–1463.

Lundholm, J.T., & Richardson, P.J. (2010) Habitat analogues for reconciliation ecology in urban and industrial environments. *Journal of Applied Ecology*, **47**(5), 966-975.

MacIvor, J.S., & Ksiazek, K. (2015) *Invertebrates on green roofs*. In: Sutton, R.K. (ed.) *Green Roof Ecosystems*. Springer, 333-355.

Miller, J.R. (2005) Biodiversity conservation and the extinction of experience. *Trends in Ecology & Evolution*, **20**(8), 430-434.

Newport, J., Shorthouse, D.J., & Manning, A.D. (2014) The effects of light and noise from urban development on biodiversity: Implications for protected areas in Australia. *Ecological Management & Restoration*, **15**(3), 204-214.

Non-Native Species Secretariat (NNSS) (2019) Check, Clean, Dry. Available at: http://www.nonnativespecies.org/checkcleandry/

Oberndorfer, E., Lundholm, J., Bass, B., Coffman, R.R., Doshi, H., Dunnett, N., Gaffin, S., Köhler, M., Liu, K.K.Y., & Rowe, B. (2007) Green roofs as urban ecosystems: ecological structures, functions, and services. *BioScience*, **57**(10), 823–833.

Padayachee, A.L., Irlich, U.M., Faulkner, K.T., Gaertner, M., Procheş, S., Wilson, J.R.U., & Rouget, M. (2017) How do invasive species travel to and through urban environments? *Biological Invasions*, **19**(12), 3557–3570.

Pauchard, A., Aguayo, M., Peña, E., & Urrutia, R. (2006) Multiple effects of urbanization on the biodiversity of developing countries: The case of a fast-growing metropolitan area (Concepción, Chile). *Biological Conservation*, **127**(3), 272-281.

Pejchar, L., & Mooney, H.A. (2009) Invasive species, ecosystem services and human well-being. *Trends in Ecology & Evolution*, **24**(9), 497-504.

Pimentel, D., Zuniga, R., & Morrison, D. (2005) Update on the environmental and economic costs associated with alien-invasive species in the United States. *Ecological Economics*, **52**(3), 273-288.

Potter, M.F. (2011) The history of bed bug management – with lessons from the past. *American Entomologist*, **57**(1), 14-25.

Prior (2013) Insects in green roof close Cumbria school. Available from: http://www.constructionenquirer.com/2013/10/08/insects-in-green-roof-close-cumbria-school/

Ricciardi, A., Palmer, M.E., & Yan, N.D. (2011) Should biological invasions be managed as natural disasters? *BioScience*, **61**(4), 312–317.

Ricciardi, A., Hoopes, M.F., Marchetti, M.P. & Lockwood, J.L. (2013) Progress toward understanding the ecological impacts of nonnative species. *Ecological Monographs*, **83**(3), 263-282.

Rotherham, I.D. (2017) *Recombinant Ecology - A Hybrid Future?* Springer.

Rosenzweig, M.L. (2003) Reconciliation ecology and the future of species diversity. *Oryx*, **37**(2), 194-205.

Ruiz-Avila, R.J. & Klemm, V.V. (1996) Management of *Hydrocotyle ranunculoides* L.f., an aquatic invasive weed of urban waterways in Western Australia. *Hydrobiologia*, **340**, 187-190.

Russell, J.C. & Blackburn, T.M. (2017) The rise of invasive species denialism. *Trends in Ecology & Evolution*, **32**(1), 3-6.

Santamouris, M. (2014) Cooling the cities – A review of reflective and green roof mitigation technologies to fight heat island and improve comfort in urban environments. *Solar Energy*, **103**, 682-703.

Schilthuizen, M. (2018) *Darwin Comes to Town: How the Urban Jungle Drives Evolution*. Picador.

Shaffer, H.B. (2018) Urban biodiversity arks. *Nature Sustainability*, **1**, 725–727.

Song, U., Kim, E., Bang, J.H., Son, D.J., Waldman, B. & Lee, E.J. (2013) Wetlands are an effective green roof system. *Building and Environment*, **66**, 141-147.

Suren, A.M. (2009) Using macrophytes in urban stream rehabilitation: a cautionary tale. *Restoration Ecology*, **17**(6), 873-883.

Tratalos, J., Fuller, R.A., Warren, P.H., Davies, R.G., & Gaston, K.J. (2007) Urban form, biodiversity potential and ecosystem services. *Landscape and Urban Planning* **83**(4), 308-317.

Viles, H., Sternberg, T., & Cathersides, A. (2011) Is ivy good or bad for historic walls? *Journal of Architectural Conservation,* **17**(2), 25-41.

Williams, N.S.G., Lundholm, J., & MacIvor, J.S. (2014) Do green roofs help urban biodiversity conservation? *Journal of Applied Ecology,* **51**(6), 1643-1649.

Wilson, E., & Wembridge, D. (2018) The State of Britain's Hedgehogs 2018. Available at: https://www.britishhedgehogs.org.uk/pdf/sobh-2018.pdf

Wong, G.K.L., & Jim, C.Y. (2016) Do vegetated rooftops attract more mosquitoes? Monitoring disease vector abundance on urban green roofs. *Science of the Total Environment,* **573**, 222-232.

Zimmerer, K.S. (2009) *Biodiversity.* In: Castree, N., Demeritt, D., Liverman, D., & Rhoads, B. (eds) *A Companion to Environmental Geography,* Blackwell, London, 50-65.

Chapter 6: The ecology of post-industrial sites and the Oliver Gilbert legacy

Peter J.A. Shaw

University of Roehampton

Summary: The aim of this review is to assemble Oliver Gilbert's studies on urban/brownfeld floral diversity, set them into a wider context, and explore the extent these have bequeathed us a coherent intellectual legacy that informs current policy-making. He came early to the understanding that the mixes of self-sown natives and escaped garden floras form valid ecosystems as worthy of study as anything in pristine habitats, often with a high aesthetic and biodiversity value. Even now these ideas remain unconventional, but evidence is accumulating that these "recombinant" communities support native biodiversity (e.g. pollinators) as well as wholly native assemblages.

Introduction – flowers in cities: Although Oliver Gilbert was best known for his research on UK lichens (elsewhere in this volume), he also dedicated research effort to the ecology of urban ecosystems. Much of this was focussed on the flora colonising abandoned land in the ex-industrial north of England, finding many interesting examples in his native Sheffield, but he collected data from towns around the UK (including in Scotland and Wales), and the findings and results generalised to a wide range of anthropogenic systems. The aim of this review is to explore how his observations and ideas have shaped current thought and practice in conservation practices in human-impacted environments.

The best known, and arguably most significant work that Oliver produced on urban flora was a report to Natural England "The flowering of the cities" (Gilbert, 1993), which celebrated the diversity of floras associated with urban settings. His key observation was that although urban/brownfield sites are wholly artificial, they colonise with plant species in patterns that resemble 'natural' ecosystems, and often contain unusual mixes of species that merit academic study, maybe conservation. This was innovative at the time (though also advocated by Ray Gemmell (Gemmell, 1977; Greenwood, & Gemmell, 1978) and Tony Bradshaw (Bradshaw, 1989) – as he commented "As many [urban plant communities] are normally regarded as falling outside conventional ecology, their study has been largely neglected" (Gilbert, 1993). He introduced the notion of the "Urban Commons", the mix of plants (typically ruderal) which appear unsown on neglected land. At the time these were denigrated as "weeds", more out of familiarity than because they caused anyone any problems, and significant effort and resources were (and are) invested into destroying them. (They often produce highly visible displays of showy flowers that, in other circumstances, could have been seen as a visual enhancement).

Oliver noted that urban sites are characterised by high levels of disturbance, but also often high pH (from cement etc) and nutrients, making them ideal for colonisation by plants such as *Chenopodium* spp, *Senecio squalidus* and *Epilobium hirstutum*. Although climate is the primary determiner of recombinant plant communities, with wetter towns (Manchester, Glasgow) having more grasses / reeds (Gilbert, 1993) than drier towns, there are also sometimes patterns relating to local history or social characteristic. Examples include a predominance of Golden Rod *Solidago canadense* in urban sites in Birmingham, attributed to a long history of "Guinea gardens" (allotments) in that city, where Goldenrod was often grown, or Alexanders *Smyrnium olasutrum* in Norwich may be a legacy of its extensive cultivation by monks there (Gilbert, 1983, 1989). Areas associated with the wool trade had "Shoddy aliens" where shoddy (waste from imported wool, often with non-native seeds caught in the wool) has been dumped on fields. Plants associated with the wool trade this way include *Amaranthus* spp and *Erodium moschatum* (Gilbert, 1989, Shimwell, 2006). Oliver noted how native species could form natural-looking communities with escaped garden plants, an observation that lead to the notion of "Recombinant plant communities" (Meurk, 2010). Meurk documents similar observations of native/alien species characterising urban areas in New Zealand and California. In their handbook on ecological restoration, Gilbert & Andersen (1998) listed categories of restoration approaches including (rather cynically) the creation of "Political habitats" defined as colourful habitats created for people in urban areas, whose roles include education and propaganda but which do not aim to recreate natural communities.

Oliver did not just study urban floras on standard common lands. An unusual observation of his was that badly maintained walls supported a remarkably diverse array of plants, mainly non-native (Gilbert, 1992b). The proportion of self-sown adventives in this manmade habitat seems to be higher than any other he studied.

Brownfield floras: Another "urban" habitat that interested Oliver comes under the general post-industrial heading of "brownfield sites". He observed that in areas where industrial wastes had been left outdoors to weather down naturally the floral assemblages often held unusual species or combinations. Thus, where the blocks of slag from blast furnaces (effectively a man-made lava) had been dumped on land near Wigan, the artificial boulders had self-sown plants dominated by *Festuca rubra* (Gemmell, 1977 p. 30). The species that established best on these blocks of slag were typical of calcareous grassland (Ash *et al.*, 1994). This presumably reflected the low fertility and high pH of the substrate.

While Oliver started as a researcher, the north of England still held substantial areas of land covered in legacy substrates from heavy industrial processes. One typical such material was "Leblanc process waste", the heterogenous and strongly alkaline residue from the obsolete Leblanc process once used to create washing soda (sodium carbonate) from sea salt, coal, limestone and sulphuric acid. In summary, the salt was heated with sulphuric acid to release fumes of HCl. The resulting sludge was mixed with limestone and coal and burned, releasing carbon monoxide and leaving a mix of (water-soluble) sodium carbonate and insoluble wastes, mainly calcium sulphide, along with unburned residues. This mix was washed with water and evaporated to collect the sodium carbonate, leaving a waste (locally called "galligu") which was highly alkaline, infertile, and with high levels of free sulphides (giving an odour of bad eggs). It was also produced in large amounts – roughly 1 ton of sodium carbonate generated 10 tons of galligu (Shaw, & Halton, 1998). During the early phase of the industrial revolution in northern England the cotton mills needed sodium carbonate to wash the cotton, supplied by the Leblanc process. The resulting galligu was generally just dumped onto the land surface, leaving the site barren unsightly and smelly. Relatively large areas of land were blighted this way, especially in the area north of Manchester. Leblanc waste is almost entirely a Victorian legacy since the Leblanc process was superseded by the Solvay process (more efficient and less polluting) about 1900.

The natural colonisation of Galligu went through several phases, each explicable by the changes in substrate chemistry (Shaw & Halton 1998). The initial alkalinity settled down as the material absorbed CO_2, while the sulphides slowly oxidised away to sulphate (by the action of bacteria, probably dominated by *Thiobaccillus* spp). This left a red/brown substrate with high levels of free calcium carbonate (40 to 60%, Gilbert, 1989) which allowed colonisation by calcicoles. Since the industrial north-west of England has almost entirely acid soils, Leblanc process waste generated local patches of calcareous grassland in an otherwise acid matrix. Typical plants on leblanc process waste included yellowwort *Blackstonia perfoliata*, purging flax *Linum catharticum* and orchids in the genus *Dactylorhiza* including northern marsh orchid *D. purpurella*.

Most Leblanc process waste sites have now been "restored", generating a paradox the Oliver hinted at (Gilbert, 1989). From being a widespread and deeply unwelcome pollutant, Leblanc process waste has declined to the point that it could be argued as being one of our most endangered habitats (Shaw, 2011). The last Leblanc site in Newcastle was destroyed/"restored" in the 1990s, as a safety measure, leaving just five patches in the world of this industrial revolution legacy (Shaw 2011), all showing themselves as this red soils supporting marsh orchids and calcicoles. The largest such patch is outside Bolton, now protected by the Moses Gate Country Park, where the 10 hectares of former galligu support fourteen species of orchid including a rare inland population of the brick-red early marsh orchid *Dactylorhiza incarnata coccinea*, normally a species of dune slacks. This site was mapped in detail by Burrows (1995), who could identify residual patches of acidic boiler slag which had developed heath-like acidophilic flora, contrasting sharply with the calcicoles growing on the process waste. (An informal survey by the author found that this boiler slag also held the acidophilic Collembolan *Protaphorura armata*, common in acid woodland litter but not found elsewhere on the site). This well-known Leblanc site comes with an anecdote, which is that the orchids were first discovered when school children nearby were asked collect a bouquet of wild flowers to decorate the school, and a teacher queried whether the orchids had been stolen from a garden display! The oxidation of sulphides in the soil profile is a slow process. A metre down into the red Leblanc waste in Bolton the deeper strata still contain free sulphides – blue from reduced iron (Fe II). If this subsoil is reacted with acid it generates alarming quantities of (toxic) H_2S gas (Shaw & Halton, 1998).

Oliver observed that other industrial solid wastes underwent interesting patterns of floral colonisation, whose details depended crucially on the substrate chemistry. A simple example of this is on colliery spoil, an inherently acidic material (due to sulphide oxidation) which is still a widespread landscape-forming material in much of the north-west of England. Initially recalcitrant to plant growth, it colonises with acidophilic grasses, giving way to secondary birch (*Betula pendula*) woods with hawthorn (Hall, 1957), probably leading to oak woodland

Quercus robur after many decades. Dark-coloured steep-sided mounds covered in young birch woodland are characteristic features of the landscape in ex-coal mining areas, and Oliver saw these as valid ecosystems that enhanced local ecological diversity. This mindset has yet to receive official approval, with considerable sums of money being spent to bulldoze spoil mounds such as the "Wigan alps" (Wigan Park Services, 2018). These expensive landscaping exercises, aimed at restoring "natural" landscapes, almost certainly reduced biodiversity and certainly reduced habitat heterogeneity (a key prerequisite for diversity). Box (1993) suggested that a key test of whether a brownfield site has habitat value is whether children can play hide and seek there!

Gilbert noted that a key characteristic of urban/brownfield communities is the process of ecological succession (Gilbert, 1993). They act as a simulacrum of conditions where a natural disturbance tears open a soil profile exposing new bare and infertile substrata (glacial retreat, cliff slides, sand dune blow-outs etc). Like most successions these progress through short-lived low growing plants through to woodland. He described a typical urban succession (based on observations especially in and around Sheffield) as starting with the "Oxford Ragwort" phase 0 to 3 years after abandonment, so called due to the dominance of *Senecio squalidus* (itself a garden escape), along with many other species notably *Epilobium angustifolium*, *Salix* spp. and *Buddleia*. The native plants at this stage include species known from pollen records to have been post-glacial colonists. Adapted to bare base-rich soil with no grazing and little competition, Oliver suggested that "a number of species have not had it so good [since the end of the ice age]. After 3 to 6 years the taller herbs dominate – e.g *Epilobobium* spp, *Solidao canadensis*, *Lupinus* spp, Michaelmas daisy *Aster nova-belgii*, Goat's Rue *Galega officinalis*. (All garden escapes except *Epilobium*.) After 8 to 10 years these are supplanted by native tussocky grasses, typically *Arrhenatherum elatius*, *Elymus repens*, *Dactylis glomerata*. A common pattern is for herbs to persist in species-rich pockets among the grass tussocks. This is replaced by scrub woodland dominated by trees with windblown seeds – *Salix, Buddleia* birches. (Oddly, oak rarely does well at this stage). Oliver noted that the composition of these urban woods is quite unlike any natural woodland, with ash hawthorn and willows alongside laburnum, orchard apples, and whitebeams.

Gilbert took a particular interest in the waste sites associated with coal-fired power stations, which generate copious volumes of rather homogenous, chemically distinctive solid and semi-solid waste. Foremost here is the powdery dust left after burning coal dust at 1,500°C, which by law must be removed from stack emissions to minimise public nuisance. This powder (henceforth pfa, the acronym for Pulverised Fuel Ash) can be used for making cement or breezeblocks but traditionally was simply dumped onto the land surface in mounds or lagoons. Approximately 10% the mass of coal used for combustion ends up as pfa (Shaw, 1974) so the volumes created are considerable. Pfa lagoons cover many tens of hectares of land near many present or former power stations, eg at Radley (from Didcot PS), Gale Common (from Eggborough and Ferrybridge), Tilbury (Tilbury PS), the Barlow mound (Drax), Wakefield (Wakefield PS) and many more (Shaw 2011). Gale Common alone handle 49 million m^3 of waste annually (www1), Oliver observed that such sites underwent a classic ecological succession in which nitrogen fixing plants (mainly in the fabacea) play an important role early on, attributed to pfa having minimal fixed nitrogen but high levels of phosphate and molybdenum. At a British Ecological Society meeting in Liverpool, discussing local field visits, Oliver was heard saying "Let's visit a pfa site – lots of legumes". He could also have said "to see marsh orchids" since mature, unimproved pfa sites habitually harbour dense populations of *Dactylorhiza* orchids, usually hybrid swarms including *D. fuschsii*, *D. praetermissa* and *D. incarnata* plus hybrids (Shaw, 1998). Unamended pfa undergoes a surprisingly consistent, well-defined successional sequence associated with changes in its chemistry (Shaw 1992, 1994). When fresh it is saline and high in boron salts, and is toxic to most plants – this stage is mainly colonised by halophytes, notably *Atriplex prostrata* but also *Pucinellia* spp and *Spergularia* spp. As salts weather out the salinity falls and halophytes are replaced by ruderals, grasses and fabacea, followed by *Dactylorhiza* orchids and birch/willow seedlings. Orchid numbers can explode to dominate the site for a few years (e.g. Shaw, 2009), but these inevitably decline again. A recurring theme of old pfa sites is for local conservationists to highlight the spectacular displays of orchids just as they start to decline (Shaw, 1994, 2015). Meaford PS in Staffordshire invited visitors to their ash lagoons around 2000, just as the orchid population crashed. The Lee Valley ran a dedicated river cruise to showcase their orchid boardwalks, the year that the numbers plummeted!

Legacy? Although Oliver gave us the phrase "Urban Commons", it is hard to find a direct legacy from Gilbert's work on urban flora into the current planning system. This still has a strong presumption in favour of building on "brownfield sites". The mainstream mindset remains as described by Oliver in 1993 *"Officially such sites are looked at as undesirable, unsightly and depressing. The aim of many local authorities is to convert them into conventional landscape of mown grass and trees once money becomes available"* (Gilbert, 1993 p. 5). By way of example, current guidelines on colliery spoil disposal warn of the need to avoid damaging sensitive habitats (or archaeological sites) but do not mention that the spoil mound itself may become a site of ecological interest, or of industrial archaeological value (ODPM, 2019). If one searches on "Planning guidance" on the government web pages one finds this about "Brownfield registers": "Part 1 of a brownfield land register will comprise all brownfield sites that a local planning authority has assessed as appropriate for residential development, having carried out any procedures such as consultation which they consider appropriate. This will include sites with extant full planning permission, outline planning permission and permission in principle as well as sites without planning permission" (WW2). In 2009, a "brownfield" site in West Thurrock marshes was approved for destruction by development, despite it housing seventeen protected species, and intended to be part of the Thames Gateway park system (NBN, 2019). In fact classic "brownfield" sites in the UK are home to some of our rarest species, especially in the Hymenoptera and especially in the Thames gateway (Gibson, 1998; Harvey 2007.)

There have been some glimmerings of official attitudinal shifts. Mabey (2010) celebrated the "weeds" the colonisers of our derelict land. Natural England has defined Open Mosaic Habitats on Previously Developed Land as a BAP priority habitat, citing in particular its invertebrates (JNCC 2010). Similarly, the UK's first brownfield nature reserve has been opened on Canvey Island (English Nature, 2005). Some mining spoil "bings" in Scotland became briefly famous, and suggested as worthy of conservation, because they appeared to be the home of a new endemic orchid *Epipactis youngii* (Richards, & Porter, 1982; Scott, 1993), until the species was invalidated (Harris, & Abbot, 1997).

One of Oliver's characteristic attitudes that seems rather out of tune with current policy frameworks, was his insouciance about the establishment of non-native species. Long-standing official caution has been intensified by newly emerging pathogens, notably the arrival of "oak death" (though more a disease of larch) *Phytophthora ramorum* (Grünwald *et al.*, 2008) and ash dieback (*Chalara fraxinea*) in the UK from imported stock (Heuch, 2014), and fears over *Xylella* arriving similarly (Mabbett, 2018). By contrast, Oliver confined his studies to plants and described as natural-looking the recombinant communities formed in urban waste ground when garden escapes ("aliens") establish alongside native flora (Gilbert, 1993). We know from more recent work that non-native garden flowers can well support native insect communities (Salisbury *et al.*, 2017) but the general attitude among UK land managers is that arrival of non-native species is a nuisance to be minimised. An exemplar of the difficulty in establishing a consistent policy comes from the well known invasive garden escape Himalayan balsam *Impatiens glandulifera* (Beerling, & Perrins, 1993). This smothers the banks of waterways so that its deliberate release is contravention of Schedule 9 of the 1981 Wildlife and Countryside Act. Set against this it produces masses of nectar-rich flowers that benefit bees (Starý, & Tkalcú 1998; Bartomeus *et al.*, 2014).

Oliver was unusual in his appreciation of self-sown sycamore *Acer pseudoplatanus*, which has gained notoriety for the ease with which its windblown seeds establish on bare ground. The leaves being large and flat certainly smother ornamental lawns, and are thought to suppress establishment of native plants. Because it forms dense populations of seedlings in suitable soil, one tends to assume it will develop into monocultural secondary woodland, and being non-native it should feed few invertebrates. In fact Oliver observed few problems with native species being excluded by sycamore litter (though some mosses were suppressed), that sycamore seedlings almost never develop into pure sycamore woodland, and that its invertebrate species list is similar to the closely related native field maple *Acer campestre*. More importantly, the biomass of insects on sycamore is higher than almost any UK native tree due to it supporting infestations of the sycamore aphid, meaning that this "invasive alien" is a valuable food resource for native insectivores, supporting hoverflies and lacewings, in turn attracting parties of tits *Parus* and *Cyanistes* (Gilbert, 1989 p. 304). In other words, Oliver saw that sycamore saplings are a biodiversity resource not a management problem.

Oliver even managed to be positive about Japanese knotweed *Reynoutria* (=*Fallopia*) *japonica*, (one female clone from volcanic slopes in Japan, arrived in London in 1850 – Connolly, 1977), despite this being perhaps our most notorious invasive plant. It is described as "a late nectar source for a variety of insects" (Gilbert, 1993, photograph 13). He observed a stand of *Reynoutria* in Sheffield by the River Don where the floodwaters had washed in seeds of Celandine *Ranunculus ficaria* and wood anemone *Anemone nemoralis* (Gilbert, 1989, 1993). The latter, an ancient woodland indicator, flourished under the intermittent shade of the knotweed, whose leaf phenology matched the woodland conditions *Anemone* was evolved to share. (He also noted garden-escape daffodils growing in the same habitat, exploiting the same phenology). This stable, arguably attractive, combination of an arch-invasive garden escape and a quintessentially native woodland indicator epitomised what Oliver found fascinating and satisfying about urban ecology. It seems likely that – under the twin influences of increasing urbanisation and anthropogenic climatic disruption – future ecosystems will increasingly be mixtures of "aliens" and "natives", as observed and documented in Gilbert' work (Pierce, 2015), so that his enthusiasm for mixed communities looks far-sightedly futuristic.

A useful concept introduced by Oliver that informs many aspects of urban ecology is the "palimpsest" (Gilbert, 1989, 1993). This term which is widely used by landscape historians, comes from the ancient practice of re-using parchment, so that one document may have several older ones hidden away under the newest text. Similarly, the plant assemblages in urban sites often contain traces of previous land uses (especially gardens) mixed in with more recent colonists. The notion recurs in more recent papers on urban geography e.g. Crang (1996). If one had to choose a single legacy to epitomise Oliver's contribution to urban ecology, a strong candidate would be the "Sheffield Figs", a unique aspect of the urban woodland succession in Sheffield (Gilbert, & Pearman, 1988; Gilbert, 1992a). These date from the days when Sheffield made a lot of steel in big, rather open factories, and of fig biscuits! In the absence of regulation of water pollution, all the steel works just dumped waste heat into the River Don, making it run warm enough for figs to germinate and young plants to survive the winters. (Untreated sewage also ran there, a known vector for fig seeds.) There is no longer the thermal pollution, but in the 1980s, two local naturalists noted the figs and passed on the observation. Oliver identified a population of well-grown fig trees along the Don which no longer need the heat. His experiments showed that the warm, sewage-polluted Don was a plausible vector for fig seeds (even finding viable fig seeds in the mud), and that winter warmth was the critical parameter for seedling fig survival (Gilbert, 1992a). These trees look likely to stand testament to the steel industry, and to Oliver's studies, for decades if not centuries to come, and have acquired a near-cult status (eg Rotherham, 2016; Mabey, 1996) among Sheffield naturalists. They have formal protection as industrial heritage by Sheffield City Council, perhaps the only case where a non-native species is afforded heritage status?

References

Ash, H.J. Gemmell, R.P., & Bradshaw, A.D. (1994) The introduction of native plant species on industrial waste heaps: a test of immigration and other factors affecting primary succession. *Journal of Applied Ecology*, **31**, 74-84

Barber, E.C. (1972) *Win Back the Acres: The Treatment and Cultivation of DFA Surfaces*. CEGB Paper, Central Electricity Geneating Board, London.

Bartomeus, I., Vilà, M., & Steffan-Dewenter, I. (2010) Combined effects of *Impatiens glandulifera* invasion and landscape structure on native plant pollination. *Journal of Ecology*, **98**, 440-450.

Beerling, D.J., & Perrins, J.M. (1993) Biological flora of the British Isles: *Impatiens glandulifera* Royle (Impatiens Roylei Walp.). *Journal of Ecology, 81*, 367-82.

Box, J. (1993) Conservation or greening – the challenge of post-industrial landscapes. *British Wildlife*, **5**, 273-279.

Bradshaw, A. (1989) Wasteland management and restoration in northern Europe. *Journal of Applied Ecology*, **26**, 775-786.

Burrows, C. (1995) *An investigation into the flora of Nob End*. Unpublished MSc thesis, Lancaster University, Lancaster.

Connolly, A.P. (1977) The distribution and history in the British Isles of some alien species of *Polygonum* and *Roynoutria*. *Watsonia*, **11**, 291-311.

Crang, M. (1996) Envisioning Urban Histories: Bristol as Palimpsest, Postcards, and Snapshots. *Environment and Planning A, 28*, 429-452

English Nature (2005) Canvey Wick SSSI: citation available at htps:// necmsi.esdm.co.uk/PDFsforWebCitation/2000497.pdf

Gemmell, R. (1977) *The colonisation of industrial wasteland.* Studies in Biology, **80**, Institute of Biology, London.

Gibson, C.W.D. (1998) *Brownfield, red data. The value of artificial habitats for invertebrates.* English Nature Research Report, **273**, Peterborough.

Gilbert, O.L. (1983) The Wildlife of British wasteland. *New Scientist*, **67**, 824-829.

Gilbert, O.L. (1989) *The Ecology of urban habitats.* Chapman & Hall, London.

Gilbert, O.L. (1992) The Ecology of an urban river. *British Wildlife*, **2**, 129-136.

Gilbert, O.L. (1992) *Rooted in Stone – the natural flora of urban walls.* English Nature, Peterborough.

Gilbert, O.L. (1993) *The Flowering of the Cities. The natural flora of urban commons.* Report to English Nature, Peterborough.

Gilbert, O.L., & Pearman, M. (1988) Wild figs by the Don. *Sorby Record*, **25**, 31-33.

Gilbert, O.L., & Anderson, P. (1998) *Habitat creation and repair.* OUP, Oxford.

Greenwood, E.F., & Gemmill, R. (1978) Derelict industrial land as a habitat for rare plants in S. Lancs (VC 59) and W. Lancs (VC60). *Watsonia*, **12**, 33-40.

Grünwald, N.J., Goss, E.M., & Pres, C.M. (2008) *Phytophthora ramorum*: a pathogen with a remarkably wide host range causing sudden oak death on oaks and ramorum blight on woody ornamentals. *Molecular plant pathology*, **9**, 729-740.

Hall, I.G. (1957) The ecology of disused pit heaps in England. *Journal of Ecology*, **45**, 689-720.

Harris, S.A., & Abbott, R.J. (1997) Isozyme analysis of the reported origin of a new hybrid orchid species, *Epipactis youngiana* (Young's helleborine), in the British Isles. *Heredity*, **79**, 402-407.

Harvey, P. (2007) The 2007 AGM address: Brownfield invertebrates in Essex - nationally important and under threat. *Essex Naturalist*, **24**, 8-14.

Heuch, J. (2014) What lessons need to be learned from the outbreak of ash dieback *Chalara fraxinea* in the UK? *Arboricultural Journal*, **36**, 32-44.

JNCC (2010) *UK BAP priority habitats description. (Inland rock). Open Mosaic- Habitats on Previously Developed Land* (updated 2010).

Mabey, R. (1996) *Flora Britannica*. Random House, London.

Mabey, R. (2010) *Weeds – how vagabond plants gatecrashed civilisation and changed how we think about nature.* Profile Books Ltd, London.

ODPM (2019) *Minerals planning guidance 3: Coal mining and colliery spoil disposal.* HMG https://www.northyorks.gov.uk/sites/default/files/fileroot/Pla nning%20and%20development/Minerals%20and%20waste%20 planning/Examination%20Library/LPA%20Docs/LPA42%20MPG 3%20Coal%20mining%20and%20colliery%20spoil%20disposal.p df

Mabbett, T. (2018) What happens when *Xylella f.* arrives in the UK? *International Pest control*, **60**, 232-236.

Meurk, C.D. (2010) *Recombinant ecology of urban areas.* In: Eds. Douglas, I., Goode, D., Houck, M., & Maddox, D. *The Routledge Handbook of Urban Ecology*, Chapter 17, Routledge, London.

NBN (2019) "Appeal lost". https://nbn.org.uk/news/buglife-loses-appeal/. Accessed 22-11-19

Niemela, J. (1999) Ecology and urban planning. *Biodiversity and Conservation*, **8**, 119-131.

Pierce, F. (2016) *The New Wild: Why Invasive Species Will be Nature's Salvation.* Beacon Press, London.

Richards, A.J., & Porter, A.F. (1982) On the identity of a Northumberland *Epipactis. Watsonia*, **14**, 121-128.

Rotherham, I.D. (2016) River Don Fig Forest. https://ianswalkonthewildside.wordpress.com/2016/01/08/riv er-don-fig-forest/

Salisbury, A., Al-Beidh, S., Armitage, J., Bird, S., Bostock, H., Platoni, A., Tatchell, M., Thompson, K., & Perry, J., (2017) Enhancing gardens as habitats for plant-associated invertebrates: should we plant native or exotic species? *Biodiversity and Conservation*, **26**, 2657-2673.

Scott, M. (1993) Save that spoil, and Glasgow's orchid. *BBC Wildlife*, **11**, 11.

Shaw, P.J.A. (1992) Successional changes in vegetation and soil development on unamended fly ash (PFA) in southern England. *Journal of Applied Ecology*, **29**, 728-736.

Shaw, P.J.A. (1994) Orchid woods and floating islands - the ecology of fly ash. *British Wildlife*, **5**, 149-157.

Shaw, P.J.A. (2009) Succession on the PFA/Gypsum Trial Mounds at Drax Power Station: The First Fifteen Years. *Journal of Practical Ecology and Conservation*, **8**, 1 – 13.

Shaw P.J.A. (2011) Management of brownfield sites for biodiversity. *Aspects of Applied Biology,* **108**, 179-192.

Shaw, P.J.A. (1998) Morphometric analyses of mixed *Dactylorhiza* colonies (Orchidaceae) on industrial waste sites in England. *Botanical Journal of the Linnean Society*, **128**, 385 – 401.

Shaw, P.J.A., & Halton W. (1998) Classic sites: Nob End, Bolton. *British Wildlife*, **10**, 13-17.

Shaw, P.J.A. (2015) Nature reserves, orchids and fly ash. *Urban Ecology Review*, **5**, 89-90.

Shimwell, D.W. (2006) A shoddy tale – perspectives on the wool alien flora of West Yorkshire in the 21st century. *Watsonia*, **26**, 127-137.

Starý, P., & Tkalcú, B. (1998) Bumble-bees (Hym., bombidae) associated with the expansive touch-me-not, *Impatiens glandulifera* in wetland biocorridors. *Anzeiger für Schädlingskunde*, **71**, 85-87.

Wigan Park Services (2018) The three sisters recreation area. https://www.thehamletwigan.co.uk/wp-content/uploads/2018/03/Binder1.pdf Accessed 27 November 2019

WW1 (2019) http://www.powerstations.uk/gale-common-ash-disposal-site/ Accessed 27 November 2019

WW2 (2019). https://www.gov.uk/guidance/brownfield-land-registers Accessed 27 November 2019

Himalayan balsam by Ian Rotherham

Chapter 7: An overview of the processes of recombinant ecology

Ian D. Rotherham

Summary: This chapter presents ideas and models relating to the establishment and functioning of recombinant ecological systems as a part of 'novel' ecology. Issues of invasive and exotic species have long been of interest to ecologists and natural historians (for example Salisbury, 1961; Fitter, 1945; and Lever, 1977); and in recent decades have risen to a high point on conservation agendas. However, the ecological effects, beyond the immediacy of invasion and species displacement are rarely considered. However, in the UK with the work of Gilbert (1989, 1992a, 1992b), and of Barker (2000), this began to change. Furthermore, around the world, as communities become increasingly urbanised and rates of urbanisation grow the emergence of distinctive and novel ecologies is more obvious. Since the early 2000s, over half the world's human population has been urban which triggers cultural severance in remaining rural areas. There are issues for ecology and ecosystems as they respond to changes. Associated with global transport and communications there is ecological '*Disneyfication*' with species transported across and around the planet. Nevertheless, cities and towns and associated hinterlands are often the core zones where introduction, mixing and subsequent invasion take place. This ecological mixing is '*eco-fusion*' and forges new 'hybrid ecologies'. Yet it should not be assumed that such processes are either new, or essentially urban. Ecological recombination has been an on-going phenomenon ever since people began to colonise and manipulate the landscape. Now, with the scale of human domination over nature in the age of the Anthropocene widely recognised (e.g. Steffen *et al.*, 2007), and increasingly global, urban society, these processes are increasingly significant. This chapter provides a brief overview of the models and processes which gain importance in urban zones and in restoration ecology. Recombinance is thus an emerging paradigm in urban and future ecology.

Introduction: Hybridisation of nature is driven by long-term human-nature interactions which occur in agriculture and forestry, and increasingly by urbanisation and associated environmental change (Freedman, 2005). Changing ecology and ecosystems result from urbanisation, globalisation, climate change, and human cultural influences. The ecological consequences and the core processes are subject to ongoing research and debate (e.g. Johnson, 2010; Hobbs *et al.*, 2013; Prins & Gordon, 2014, Rotherham, 2017a, 2021). Accelerating globalisation, and both human-induced and natural climate change, speed eco-fusion hybridisation processes. Human impacts include disturbance, nutrient enrichment, habitat displacement and replacement (formation and destruction), and global species dispersal (Rotherham, 2014a; Douglas *et al.*, 2011). Nevertheless, as demonstrated by Grime and colleagues (Davis *et al.*, 2001), the ecological processes driving the changes are '*natural*' mechanisms of ecological succession and change. Within the mix there are then hybridisation and adaptation of both species and ecosystems. There is even the emergence of 'new' hybrid species.

Photograph 1: Himalayan balsam (*Impatiens glandulifera*) by Ian Rotherham

I argue elsewhere that these processes have being going on for centuries, but the key challenge today is that species mixing is at rates unprecedented in the history of biodiversity evolution. This mixing and the changed environmental drivers generate clearly novel ecologies (Hobbs *et al.*, 2013; Jørgensen *et al.*, 2013; Rotherham, 2017a). Recognised by some but not all ecologists as the '*Anthropocene*' (Steffen *et al.*, 2007), it is argued that in a new evolutionary epoch, nature is adapting to a new canvas, an altered template for future ecologies. Ecological fusion (or '*eco-fusion*') is then a dynamic, on-going process of interactions between species both '*native*' and '*alien*' to particular locations or regions. Though these interactions are formed newly combined ecological communities; some parochial in nature but others increasingly recognizable across wide areas.

Some species enter such novel communities and others are displaced (Jørgensen *et al.*, 2013; Hobbs *et al.*, 2013; Rotherham, 2017a). The wider context is the so-called '*Anthropocene*', which is typified by human-driven influences to which nature responds (Steffen *et al.*, 2007; Rotherham, 2014a). With this fluxing scenario it becomes increasingly important to understand environmental history as a context for mainstream ecology. Such knowledge then aids understanding of key drivers of change and improves predictability of future ecological consequences (Hall, 2009; Jørgensen *et al.*, 2013; Rotherham, 2014, 2017a). The need to understand better, the evolving ecologies and thereby inform planning processes has been growing over recent decades (e.g. Douglas *et al.*, 2011; Forman, 2014; Hough, 1995; Sukopp, *et al.*, 1995). The general process of invasion, establishment and recombination is illustrated in Figure 1.

The context of such change is that ecology and ecosystems are under stress at every level from local and parochial, to global and planetary (Adams, 2003; Barker *et al.*, 1994; Gaston, 2010; Rotherham, 2014a). These stresses relate to globalisation, climate change, urbanisation, intensive farming and forestry, and other human cultural influences (Sukopp & Hejny, 1990; Agnoletti, 2006; Agnoletti *et al.*, 2007). However, it is important to note that many such changes are predictable through the application of standard and accepted knowledge of ecosystems and of species strategies (e.g. Grime *et al.*, 2007; Hodgson, 1986; Rotherham, 2014; 2017a).

Understanding biodiversity is an important consideration in such processes. Ecological diversity reflects underlying biological and ecological processes around the world. For a particular locale, for example Britain, diversity results from matrices of geographical spaces (habitats with parochial environmental conditions with diverse stages and states of flux and stability), and total '*biodiversity*' is a summation of this. With innumerable sites, both species-rich, species-poor, this forms the national ecology. Importantly though, it is not fixed, but a shifting, drifting, fluxing, human-influenced, nature-influenced, climate-influenced, resource. In a context of time and space, this resource is not a fixed or finite entity.

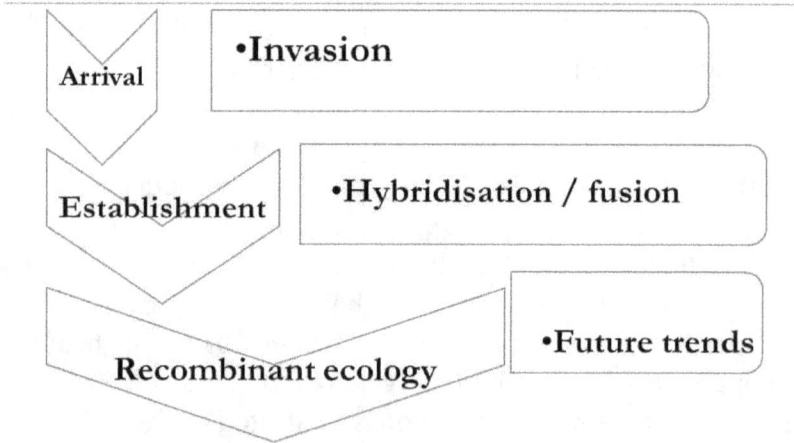

Figure 1. The general process of eco-fusion [Adapted from Rotherham, 2016a]

Over immensely long timescales, evolutionary processes generate new species and drive others to extinction. Geological forces cause massive movements of continents with extinctions and associated phases of rapid evolution. In lesser timescales, periods of glaciations, inter-glacial periods, and ice ages, stress and test ecological systems. All the other changes happen against this planetary backdrop, a *'broader canvas'* of dynamic, shifting ecologies (Rotherham, 2014b).

A cultural facilitation of invasion: Throughout history, people have interacted with nature as they exploit, modify, and sometimes destroy environmental resources (Rackham, 1986; Rotherham, 2013; Rotherham, 2014a). Human management has generated identifiable and distinctive *'cultural'* landscapes; fusions of natural and anthropogenic elements. Many of these lands have been managed with customary and traditional mechanisms to produce what we now recognise in rural areas as 'countryside'. In pre-petrochemical times such management created traditional landscapes often composed of diverse, species-rich habitats and maintained by long-established land-use applied continually over the years.
The human influences in these ecosystems include the hybridisation of species and ecology i.e. *'eco-fusion'*.

This emergence of hybrid ecology is most obvious in the world's increasingly urbanized zones, but also occurs more widely too. Although the process of recombination has only been recognised in recent decades it clearly took place at varying scales ever since people began to impact on landscape and ecology. In the modern era, vast tracts of land are dominated by forestry and agriculture. In these imposed environments, plants, animals, fungi, bacteria, and viruses move and mix beyond their natural occurrences, their core distributions and limits. The result is that old, new, native, and exotic increasingly intertwine in novel, recombinant communities within hybrid ecosystems.

Especially now, in rapidly expanding urban heartlands, this new ecology of native and alien is locked in perpetual dynamic competition for dominance. This creates novel dependencies, interactions, and communities (Rotherham, 2014a, 2016, 2017a; Gilbert, 1989, 1992a). However, although these processes are increasingly recognised, they and their consequences challenge many current ideas and debates in conservation ecology. This is particularly the case in relation to alien species and approaches to control measures. New paradigms relating to issues of perceptions, judgements, and actions are needed. Ideas of novel, recombinant, hybrid ecologies, and eco-fusion processes are rather new, and moreover, have significant implications for future ecologies. However, the processes and fact of recombination has occurred historically over centuries but this has been largely overlooked in contemporary ecological thinking (Figure 2).

Photograph 2: Grey squirrel (*Sciurus carolinensis*) by Ian Rotherham

But the processes are not new – we can see them in landscape-scale changes over centuries

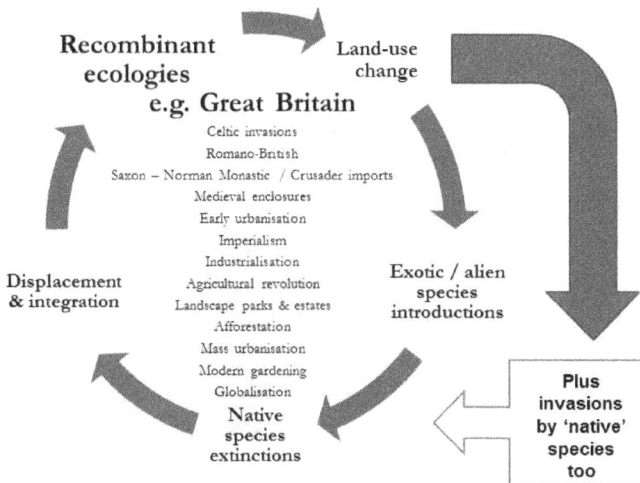

Figure 2. The flow of recombinant ecology [Adapted from Rotherham, 2017b]

Hybrid ecologies: Over centuries, non-native, introduced species have affected landscapes and altered indigenous ecologies (Gilbert, 1989; Rackham, 1986; Rotherham & Lambert, 2011; Rotherham, 2014a, 2014b, 2017a). Changes like the introduction to Britain of the rabbit (by the Normans) may have developed into fundamental ecosystem determinants and keystone species of modern-day ecology. There are many other similar examples. Nevertheless, these trends and changes must be assessed in their wider context of fluxing climate, land-use, and other human-nature interactions.

Furthermore, a brief review of British countryside shows little that is genuinely pure *'natural'* or *'native'*; indeed, even defining what these concepts are proves troublesome. The bulk of our modern environment is dominated by strongly *'cultural'* or *'eco-cultural'* landscapes (Rotherham, 2007a, 2008a, 2011, 2009b, 2014a, 2017a). This ecology is the product of many centuries of people-nature interactions to produce some *'semi-natural'* components and some traditionally-managed landscapes.

However, large areas (perhaps most) of British farmland for instance, are modern with highly exotic ecologies.

Natural changes are a part of the fluxing system but people are at the core either directly or indirectly, of most biological invasions (Johnson, 2010; Rotherham & Lambert, 2011; Rotherham, 2017a). I have written elsewhere (Rotherham, 2005, 2014a, 2017a, 2017b; Rotherham & Lambert, 2011) about two particular examples of invasion and eco-fusion that occurred historically in Great Britain and which exemplify a human component of the human-nature interaction. These two examples illustrate the wider process and its consequences.

The first example is the deliberate policy of introduction of plants and animals around the recently discovered world, by the 'Victorian Acclimatisation Societies'; both from Britain to the then colonies, and from around the globe back to Britain. The second example is the often-overlooked, case of the 'Victorian Wild Garden Movement' as promoted by leading garden writer of the time, William Robinson. In considering these two nineteenth-century phenomena there is a starting point for many contemporary issues and challenges facing contemporary nature conservation and land management. Furthermore, there is an issue of changing perceptions, attitudes, fashions, and politics in relation to nature, native and exotic. This attitudinal angle is frequently overlooked yet, from the early nineteenth century to the early twenty-first century, is very influential in shaping attitudes and responses today. Davis *et al.* (2001) wrote of changing British responses to exotic species as brought about by the seminal writings and broadcasts of ecologist, Charles Elton. Additionally, the wider influences of fashion and taste with respect to exotic species have been generally ignored. Furthermore, these changing attitudes had a great influence on the practicalities of both accidental and deliberate introductions of many of today's invasive species (See Rotherham, 2001, 2005a, 2005b, 2011, 2017a).

Facilitation of invasions by human actions and activities is very significant and both perceptions and attitudes influence processes and responses (e.g. Rotherham & Lambert, 2011). However, research on these matters is frequently lacking because the work is inherently cross-disciplinary between ecological science and history. Cleary, many if not most of the twentieth- and twenty-first century ecological invasions of Britain were culturally facilitated (e.g. Rotherham, 2001, 2005a, 2005b, 2009a, 2011, 2017a). Furthermore, the problems associated with aggressive invasive plants and animals are not new (consider for instance impacts of both black rats as plague vectors, and brown rats on medieval people and their countryside). However, the overall scale of impact combined with rapid climate change and other environmental influences, is dramatic and sometimes catastrophic. Research suggests that 15% of Europe's 11,000 exotic species together cause environmental and economic damage running to around £2bn *per annum* to the UK economy. Yet behind the often-torrid newspaper headlines, remain key questions about what is native and where, what is alien, and when. These questions run from Spanish bluebells, to eagle owls, Canada geese, ruddy ducks, ring-necked parakeets, Japanese knotweed, Himalayan balsam, and through to feral big cats, beavers, signal crayfish, and wild boar. These questions include which ones should get a *'free pass'* to a new hybrid future or honorary 'native' status, and which do not (Rotherham, 2009a, 2014b; 2017b; Rotherham & Lambert, 2011)?

Photograph 3: Brown rat (*Rattus norvegicus*) by Ian Rotherham

Global empires, acclimatisation & wild gardening: Until the 1940s and the aftermath of the Second World War, Britons and other Europeans travelled the world seeking out and collecting new species of plants and animals to take home. They also took species from Britain and Europe to populate their colonies. In both respects they unleashed a whirlwind of species mixing which still reverberates today.

These imperialist 'improvers' even went further to implement deliberate programmes of exotic species release to '*improve it*' countryside, to beautify it, and to enhance production. These movements of species to and from Europe around the world were aimed at economic gain on the one hand and landscape beautification on the other. The ideas developed and a global movement emerged from Britain and Europe and was formalised as the European Acclimatisation Societies. These mostly aimed to introduce and test new economic crops and investigate the food potential of animal introductions too. In Britain and its colonies, Acclimatisation Societies introduced animals and birds to new territories in order to enhance economies, gastronomies, and landscapes (Lever, 1977;

Rotherham, 2011, 2017a). All in all, the Victorian Acclimatisation Societies had major impacts on ecology around the world, from New Zealand, Australia, and the West Indies for example; but also back home. In many places, introduced species transformed landscapes and eliminated natives.

In Britain, this leads to the second example also associated with imperial domination of the globe and the emerging domestic interest in gardening and landscaping. With increasing imports of exotic plants from around the world, the situation was set for a dramatic transformation of countryside and ecology. Encouraged by writers like William Robinson (Robinson, 1870), Victorian 'Wild Gardeners' spread plants like rhododendron (introduced in the previous century), Himalayan balsam, Japanese knotweed, and giant hogweed, across towns, cities and the British countryside. They were aided and abetted in their efforts by foresters and estates' managers rushing to adopt exotic species for the newly-emerging European forestry with 'high forest' plantations. It was Robinson who formalised and popularised ideas of '*naturalising*' exotic plants into landscapes instead of merely planting them for effect (Robinson, 1870). Use of exotic plants was already widespread, but in the 1800s and early 1900s, he made it mainstream and popular.

Some plants were documented as local invaders at relatively early dates; an example being Himalayan balsam in Manchester noted by Grindon (1859). However, effective recognition of the conservation problems took over a century developing in the 1970s and 1980s. The early invaders are now alongside many others like *Montbretia*, *Buddleia*, and Cherry Laurel (*Prunus laurocerasus*). In most cases, by the time they were noted it was too late to eradicate them and so an effective strategy for conservation needs to involve targeted control but with benign acceptance. It seems the role of '*Wild Gardeners*' in triggering twentieth-century plant invasions has not generally been recognised. However, with the exception of broad-scale establishment of exotic conifers for forestry, it was the cause of most terrestrial plant naturalisations in Britain. From the 1700s to the early 1900s, alien plants release was first into domestic and landscape gardens, but also across forest and woodland estates. The introduction and subsequent escape of many plants into the British countryside, including spectacular invaders like giant hogweed, and giant knotweed is a direct consequence of these Victorian gardeners and landscapers. They undertook large-scale introductions of exotic and spectacular plants able to naturalise and spread. So plants like *Rhododendron ponticum*, *Heracleum mantegazzianum* (giant hogweed), *Polygonum* sp. (Japanese and giant knotweeds), and Himalayan balsam, were excellent choices. William Robinson asserted that the principle of wild gardening was '........ *naturalizing or making wild innumerable beautiful natives of many regions of the earth in our woods, wild and semi-wild places, rougher parts of pleasure grounds,* etc.' Today, a review of naturalised British exotic plants confirms how most problematic alien '*weeds*' originated as deliberate introductions. With globalisation, urbanisation and climate change, the escape of exotic garden plants continues apace and these same wild garden favourites are now the bane of nature conservation. Modern landscape architects have often carried on the trend by introducing now invasive trees and shrubs such as Norway maple (*Acer platanoides*), various whitebeams (*Sorbus* sp), *Cotoneaster* sp, and *Pyracantha* sp, to roadside landscaping and locations such as retail parks and supermarkets *etc*. Essentially, the trend continues with deliberate introductions, escapes, and increasingly recombinant ecological systems.

A history of plant importations to Britain: *Acclimatisation Societies* and *Victorian Wild Gardeners* (Rotherham, 2005a, 2005b) were manifestations of processes evolved over centuries. Throughout history, waves of settlers or conquerors of Britain brought with them new plants and animals. The Celts, Romans, and Normans, and later the returning Crusaders for instance, brought exotic animals and plants (Figure 2). Many of these aliens have become keystone species and architects of modern ecologies. Examples include the rabbit (*Oryctolagus cuniculus*), fallow deer (*Dama dama*), and brown hare (*Lepus* *europaeus*), and which then raise issues of perception and attitude (Rackham, 1986; Rotherham 2017a). Alongside active introductions other animals and plants escaped domestication to establish independently in the newly globalised world.

These processes continued throughout later medieval times since by the 1500s, traders and seafarers, particularly British and Dutch, were charting and colonising the world. They brought back exotic plants and sometimes animals with accidental imports including black rat (and Black Death), and brown rat. Later explorers spread dogs, cats, and much more to wreak untold damage to formerly isolated island ecologies. Cultural homogenisation of ecology accelerated with the collection and dissemination of exotic species as travellers sought new plants and animals for gardens and menageries.

Landscapes transformed: The changes in *'native'* ecology were not isolated from other widespread impacts and influences. During the eighteenth and nineteenth centuries for example, Britain's countryside was traumatised by parliamentary enclosures with commonland wrested from commoners, peasants, and the poor for conversion to intensive food production units. This process continued to the twenty-first century. Natural ecologies and traditionally-managed countryside were swept away by the tide of so-called 'improvement' (Rotherham, 2014a). Traditional coppice woods were converted to high forest plantations and industrialising cities sprawled over the former countryside (Rackham, 1986; Rotherham, 2014a). Areas that remained relatively intact were increasingly populated by exotic plants and animals from around the world. Other lands morphed into leisurely landscapes to pleasure landowning industrialists (Rotherham, 2014a).

These changes caused transformation from ecology dominated by native *'stress tolerators'*, to exotic species of mostly *'ruderal'* and *'competitive'* plants. This trend was noted for the twentieth century by Davis *et al.* (2001), but in practice began much earlier as disturbance and nutrient enrichment (eutrophication) emerged as dominant influences (Rotherham, 2014a, 2017a).

Transformed ecologies: This radically transformed ecology emerges now based on ecological history, as an uncomfortable truth with compounding effects of the ending of traditional and customary countryside practices (Rotherham, 2017b). This process of *'cultural severance'* grew in significance during the 1800s and into the late 1900s (Rotherham, 2009b, 2013). It equates to the ending of traditional and customary uses, values, and management of (mostly) rural ecological resources. For many landscapes, release from subsistence exploitation of centuries meant rapid increase in biomass and nutrients, so stress tolerant species (often of high conservation value) rapidly decline (Webb, 1986, 1998). Modern-day influences tend to cause abandonment or pulses of macro-disturbance which replace micro-disturbance of traditional management (Rotherham, 2009a, 2014a).

Recombinant ecologies: These ecosystem stresses are most obvious in urbanised zones, where, combined with exotic species described earlier, new ecological associations form a *'recombinant ecology'* (Barker, 2000; Rotherham, 2014a, 2017a). These emerging communities are different and distinctive from what went before with long-term vegetation trends with declines and replacements recognised at regional scales (e.g. Hodgson, 1986; Grime *et al.*, 2007).

Elements of former landscapes may remain in *'semi-natural'* (or *eco-cultural*) habitats, but even here cultural drivers over centuries of human exploitation have changed and often ended (Rotherham, 2009b, 2014a, 2017a). In some case, there may be subtle, long-term blurring of ecology, but in others, the change is rapid and dramatic. Some elements of ancient ecosystems are surprisingly resilient unless they are totally swept aside by modern mechanisation (Rotherham *et al.*, 2013; Rotherham, 2017a). However, despite this, there are major issues for conservation. The general processes and drivers are shown in Figure 3.

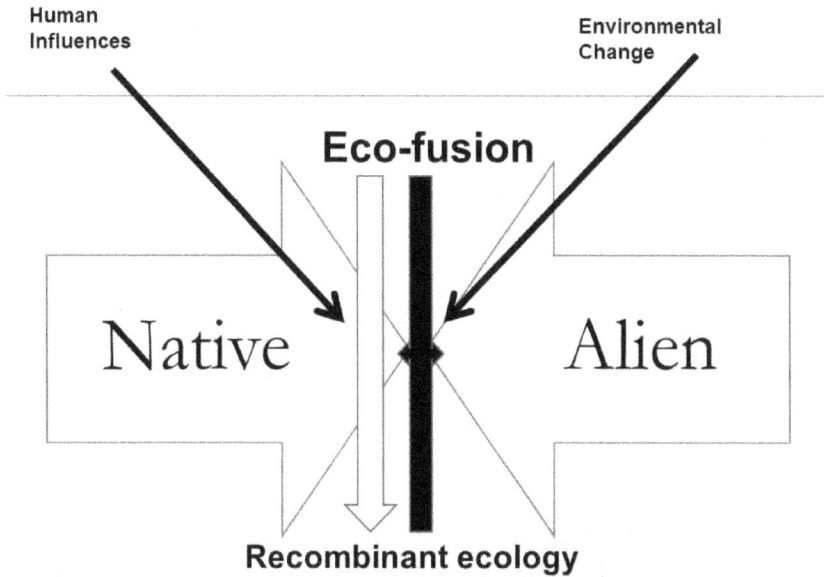

Human Influences

Environmental Change

Eco-fusion

Native

Alien

Recombinant ecology

Figure 3. Influences on eco-fusion of natives and aliens to produce recombinant ecologies [Adapted from Rotherham, 2017b]

Concepts of recombinance are very important in developing visions of future ecologies and in terms of current debates on say, wilding or so-called, rewilding, and especially advocacy for free-willed nature. Abandonment of sites to feral nature or intervention with planned release of large herbivores both present many issues and they trigger sometimes heated debates. Furthermore, in a largely urban society there is the thorny question of who gets to decide (considered further below). Whatever the model applied however, the future ecology generated will undoubtedly be recombinant; reflecting the past but different and distinctive.

The human influence is all-pervading even when we attempt to let go, the release is itself a human-determined intervention. So, to allow trees freedom to regenerate, do we fence out wild (feral) herbivores such as the Scottish Highland red deer? Ayres (2013), for example, welcomed the idea that '*When you let go of control of the land and let nature run its course it is unpredictable, often with surprising and positive outcomes.'* This is fine as an aspiration but long-term may result in dominant bracken (*Pteridium aquilinum*) stands rather than the bluebell woodland that was promised. With feral red deer (in the absence of higher-level carnivores) should we intervene or let nature run its course of animal starvation, depauperate woods, and no tree regeneration? Unpredictable outcomes may mean rich biodiversity or catastrophic loss; this is unpredictability in practice. However, the reality is that these changes are entirely predictable with current ecological science and so we do know in broad terms what the outcomes will be. In which case, do we intervene or not; and in this broader picture where do the recent (and historical) arrivals fit in?

With futurescape ecologies being strongly recombinant, will land managers, conservationists, and the wider public, accept exotic plants like rhododendron, sycamore, larch, spruce, Japanese knotweed, Himalayan balsam and giant hogweed spreading feral across the landscape. Free-willed, recombinant nature mixes these species with mink, rabbit, grey squirrel, Canada goose, ruddy duck, ring-necked parakeet, signal crayfish, and exotic or feral deer (Rotherham, 2014b) all intermingling intimately and unpredictably with the natives. From the ecological fusion processes, recombinant ecology will certainly emerge and some invasive natives (like bracken and birch (*Betula* sp)) and non-natives may be controlled. However, many conservationists remain slow to accept such inevitable changes.

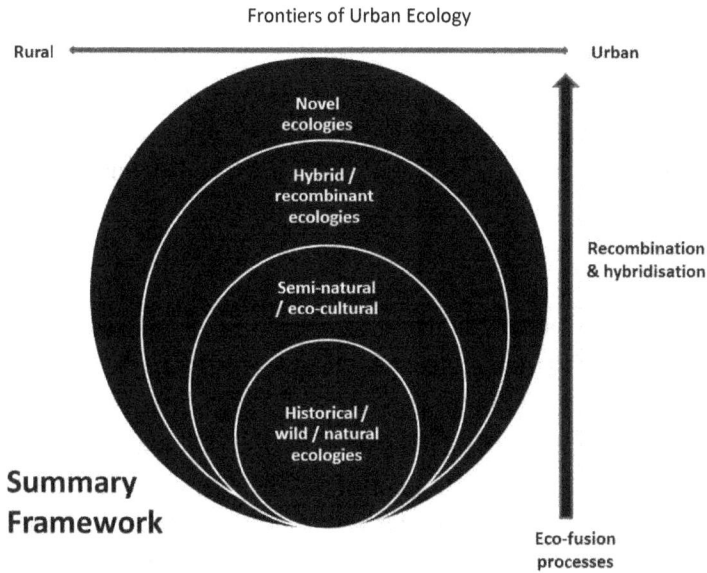

Figure 4. A summary framework of recombinant ecology [From Rotherham, 2017a]

Figure 4 illustrates the overall broad processes and context of recombinance at a landscape level. However, a key issue illustrated in Figure 2 and often overlooked in debates on aliens, is the frequently critical role of native species extinctions in facilitating invasive by non-natives and hence the generation of recombinant ecologies. Again, this is the human driver which by removing natives and introducing non-native replacements paves the way for native/exotic futurescapes.

Science, politics and environmental democracy: A point made in earlier publications (Rotherham & Lambert, 2011; Rotherham, 2017a, 2017b) is that issues of alien invasive species should be considered within the broader context of environmental change, conservation, and politics. Like it or not, we already have hybrid ecologies and the futurescapes will be more so. Bearing this in mind, then ideas of recombination and eco-fusion will grow in importance (Rotherham, 2014a, 2017a).

Conclusions: emerging paradigms & new concepts: Concepts of ecological stability depend on time-scale and spatial extent. However, presumptions of long-term environmental stasis, often assumed truths, are wrong. Even considering short periods, environmental conditions and therefore associated ecologies, fluctuate, sometimes markedly. In this context of flux, then human-led transformation of environmental conditions has radically changed past ecology. It continues to do so today but faster, deeper, and more extensively.

Along with altered and shifting environmental baselines, people move species of animals and plants in the landscape and around the world. This shifting and sifting constantly creates new possible ecological mixes as eco-fusion processes generate novel, recombinant communities. History confirms that such trends are accelerating and with globalisation and urbanisation, will have major impacts on nature conservation and land management.

Discussions of new ways to manage nature and landscape will have to engage with emerging paradigms of environmental and ecological history. Oliver Gilbert's urban studies perhaps presaged this unconformable truth for many conservationists. And whilst recombination is most obvious in urban and peri-urban landscapes, the reality is that it is all-pervading. From the urban heartlands the human influence extends more widely and recombination follows.

Long-term research into Britain's ecological history confirms the hybrid nature of our supposedly 'native' ecology. Furthermore, it suggests our future nature will be increasingly hybrid. This hybridisation or *'eco-fusion'* is at both the level of the community as aliens and natives mix and merge into recombinant ecologies, and at the species level as hybrids emerge from both deliberate and accidental fusion. Globally the competes of 'novel ecologies' have emerged (Hobbs *et al.*, 2013) but in this discussion I focus on recombinant communities because in much of Britain at least, the landscape occurs as broken habitat patches rather than fully functioning ecosystems. The degree of permanence and replication of these novel communities is yet to be confirmed.

References

Adams, W. (2003) *Future Nature: a vision for conservation*. Earthscan, London.

Agnoletti, M. (ed.) (2006) *The Conservation of Cultural Landscapes*. CAB International, Wallingford, Oxon, UK.

Agnoletti, M., Anderson, S., Johann, E., Kulvik, M., Saratsi, E., Kushlin, A., Mayer, P., Montiel, C., Parrotta, J., & Rotherham, I.D. (2007) *Guidelines for the Implementation of Social and Cultural Values in Sustainable Forest Management: A Scientific Contribution to the Implementation of MCPFE - Vienna Resolution 3*. IUFRO Occasional Paper No. 19, ISSN 1024-414X, IUFRO Headquarters, Vienna, Austria.

Ayres, S. (2013) The feral book – reintroducing rewilding. *ECOS*, **34**(2), 41-49.

Barker, G. (ed.) (2000) *Ecological recombination in urban areas: implications for nature conservation*. English Nature, Peterborough, 21-24.

Barker, G., Luniak, M., Trojan, P., & Zimny, H. (eds) (1994) Proceedings of the Second European Meeting of the International Network for Urban Ecology. *Memorabilia Zoologica*, **49**, Warsaw.

Davis, M.A., Thompson, K., & Grime, J.P. (2001) Charles S. Elton and the dissociation of invasion ecology from the rest of ecology. *Diversity and Distribution*, **7**, 97-102.

Douglas, I., Goode, D., Houck, M.C., & Wang, R. (eds) (2011) *The Routledge Handbook of Urban Ecology*. Routledge, London & New York.

Fitter, R. (1945) *London's Natural History*. Collins New Naturalist, London.

Freedman, B. (1995) *Environmental Ecology – The Effects of Pollution, Disturbance and Other Stresses*. Second Edition, Academic Press, San Diego.

Gaston, K.J. (ed.) (2011) *Urban Ecology*. Cambridge University Press, Cambridge.

Gilbert, O.L. (1989) *The Ecology of Urban Habitats*. Chapman and Hall. London.

Gilbert, O.L. (1992a) *The flowering of the cities....The natural flora of 'urban commons'*. English Nature, Peterborough.

Gilbert, O.L. (1992b) *Rooted in stone. The natural flora of urban walls*. English Nature, Peterborough.

Grime, J.P., Hodgson, J.G., & Hunt, R. (2007) *Comparative Plant Ecology. A Functional approach to common British species*. Second Edition. Castlepoint Press, Dalbeattie.

Grindon, L.H. (1859) *Manchester Flora*. [No publisher or location given].

Hobbs, R.J., Higgs, E.S., & Hall, C.M. (eds) (2013*) Novel Ecosystems. Intervening in the New Ecological World Order*. Wiley-Blackwell, Chichester.

Hodgson, J.G. (1986) Commonness and Rarity in Plants with Special Reference to the Sheffield Flora. *Biological Conservation*, **36**(3), 199-252.

Johnson, S. (ed.) (2010) *Bioinvaders*. White Horse Press, Cambridge.

Jørgensen, D., Jørgensen, F.A., & Pritchard, S.B. (eds) (2013) *New Natures. Joining Environmental History with science and technology studies*. University of Pittsburgh Press, Pittsburgh.

Lever, C. (1977) *The Naturalized Animals of Britain and Ireland*. Hutchinson & Co. (Publishers) Ltd, London.

Rackham, O. (1986) *The History of the Countryside*. Dent, London.

Robinson, W. (1870) *The Wild Garden*. The Scolar Press, London.

Rotherham, I.D. (2001) *Himalayan Balsam - the human touch*. In: Bradley, P. (Ed.) *Exotic Invasive Species -should we be concerned?* Proceedings of the 11th Conference of the Institute of Ecology and Environmental Management, Birmingham, April 2000. IEEM, Winchester, 41-50.

Rotherham, I.D. (2005a) Invasive plants – ecology, history and perception. *Journal of Practical Ecology and Conservation Special Series*, **No. 4,** 52-62.

Rotherham, I.D. (2005b) Alien Plants and the Human Touch. *Journal of Practical Ecology and Conservation Special Series*, **No. 4**, 63-76.

Rotherham, I.D. (2009a) Exotic and Alien Species in a Changing World. *ECOS*, **30** (2), 42-49.

Rotherham, I.D. (2009b) *The Importance of Cultural Severance in Landscape Ecology Research*. In: Dupont, A., & Jacobs, H. (eds) (2009) *Landscape Ecology Research Trends*. Nova Science Publishers Inc., USA.

Rotherham, I.D. (2011) *Chapter 15: History and Perception in animal and plant invasions – the case of acclimatisation and wild gardeners*. In: Rotherham, I.D. & Lambert, R. (eds.) (2011) *Invasive and Introduced Plants and Animals: Human Perceptions, Attitudes and Approaches to Management*. EARTHSCAN, London, 233-248.

Rotherham ID (2013a) The Lost Fens: England's Greatest Ecological Disaster. The History Press, Stroud.

Rotherham, I.D. (2014a) *Eco-history: An Introduction to Biodiversity and Conservation*. The White Horse Press, Cambridge.

Rotherham, I.D. (2014b) The Call of the Wild. Perceptions, history people & ecology in the emerging paradigms of wilding. *ECOS*, **35**(1), 35-43.

Rotherham, I.D. (2017a) *Recombinant Ecology – a hybrid future?*, Springer Briefs, Springer, Dordrecht, The Netherlands.

Rotherham, I.D. (2017b) *Eco-fusion of alien and native as a new conceptual framework for historical ecology*. In: Vaz, E., de Melo, C.J., & Pinto, L. (eds) *Environmental history in the making*. Volume1, Springer, Dordrecht, The Netherlands, 73 - 90.

Rotherham, I.D. (2021) *New' recombinant ecologies and their implications – with insights from Britain*. In: Francis, R., Barker, K., Fall, J., & Schlaepfer, M.A. (eds) (2021) *The Routledge Handbook of Biosecurity and Invasive Species*. Routledge, Abingdon, Oxon, 80-193.

Rotherham, I.D., & Lambert, R.A. (eds) (2011) *Invasive and Introduced Plants and Animals: Human Perceptions, Attitudes and Approaches to Management*. EARTHSCAN, London.

Salisbury, E. (1961) *Weeds and Aliens*. Collins, London.

Steffen, W., Crutzen, P.J., & McNeill, J.R. (2007) The Anthropocene: Are Humans Now Overwhelming the Great Forces of Nature. *AMBIO*, **36**(8), 614-621.

Sukopp, H., & Hejny, S. (eds) (1990) *Urban Ecology. Plants and Plant communities in urban environments*. SPB Academic Publishing. bv, The Hague, The Netherlands.

Sukopp, H., Numata, M., & Huber, A. (eds) (1995) *Urban Ecology as the basis of urban planning*. SPB Academic Publishing. bv, The Hague, The Netherlands.

Webb, N.R. (1986) *Heathlands*. Collins, London.

Webb, N.R. (1998) The traditional management of European heathlands. *Journal of Applied Ecology*, **35**, 987-990.

Chapter 8: Lead mining waste hillocks in the Peak: An archaeologist's thoughts on their character and interpretation

John Barnatt
Peak District National Park

Summary: Oliver Gilbert pioneered interest in, and awareness of the significance of former lead mining areas of contamination for ecology and especially their lichens. Lead mine hillocks are of importance for their history, archaeology, ecology, and landscape value. They have a wide range of ecological habitats of significant nature-conservation importance resulting from past mining activities, including the tipping of waste in hillocks. These can contain metallophytes (metal tolerant species) and also formerly more common species, which here have survived agricultural improvement which took place in surrounding fields and the wider landscape. In this chapter, it is argued that to understand the locally diverse communities found here there is a need to understand something of the history, development and character of these hillocks on a site by site basis, and that it is vital to recognise that hillocks are often not all the same. Some are the result of initial dumping of mine waste; others contained processed material comprising gravel, sand or clay, or are made up only of limestone. In specific places, hillocks can be made up of shale, sandstone or processed cave sediments. Each supports plant communities that are different from each other. While some hillocks are ancient, the majority have been extensively modified over the centuries when reworked to recover residual ores. Many, in their present forms, are of only nineteenth-century date, while others have been changed or largely robbed during the twentieth century.

Introduction: Today the surface remains left by lead miners in the Peak District over hundreds of years, have a range of aspects that make them important. These comprise: historical interest, including economic, technological, social and family history;

archaeological interest comprising the surviving physical remains at surface and underground; ecological interest, including metallophytes (specialist plants tolerant of heavy metals) and varied species-rich communities; and last but not least, the contribution they make to landscape character over large swathes of the region's limestone plateau and its dales.

The Carboniferous Limestone plateau at the heart of the Peak District has many ore deposits that have been worked in historic and modern times (Ford, 2004, 2005, 2008, 2010, 2012, Ford, & Jones, 2007). These commonly take the form of vertical veins running in lines across the landscape, large examples of which were known to miners as 'rakes' and smaller ones as 'scrins'. Also there is a series of deposits known to miners as 'pipes' and 'flats'. The first are irregular deposits, often either with primary deposition of mineral in palaeokarst features, or as later caves that contain transported ore-rich sediments. Flats run roughly-horizontally where mineralisation occurs that follows the bedding. Sometimes individual mines have all three types of mineralisation.

The minerals found are diverse (Ford *et al.*, 1993). The main ores of historically economic worth were those of lead, commonly galena. There were also sometimes ores of zinc, copper and iron. Most common, often comprising in excess of 95% of a deposit, were non-metallic ores, known to miners as gangue and often discarded in the mine hillocks. Most common are fluorite (fluorspar), baryte (barytes), and calcite.

Lead ores have been mined extensively from Roman times onwards (Ford, & Rieuwerts, 2000; Barnatt, & Penny, 2004; Barnatt, & Smith, 2004; Barnatt in press). Medieval mining is documented and we know output in the orefield reached a peak in the sixteenth and seventeenth centuries. From the seventeenth century onwards, mining at larger mineral deposits had extended to depth, often to in excess of 100m and in some cases, up to 300m by the end of the nineteenth century. In order to de-water deposits, drainage levels usually known as soughs, started to be driven in the seventeenth century. In places where this was unfeasible in the eighteenth- and ninenteenth-centuries, pumping was achieved using steam engines, and occasionally waterwheels. In the later nineteenth century lead mining was in decline due to rich deposits that could be feasibly reached, both in terms of depth below surface and the cost of extraction, were increasingly hard to find. A notable exception was the large Millclose Mine near Darley Bridge which was in work until 1939. In the twentieth century, some mines and many waste hillocks were reworked for gangue minerals.

Over the last few decades, much research and many conservation initiatives in the Peak have been undertaken by members of the Peak District Mines Historical Society (PDMHS). I have been actively involved with the study of Peak District Mines for three decades, as an underground explorer, a member of PDMHS, an archaeological excavator (Barnatt, 2002, 2011, 2012, 2016, in prep.) and last but not least as an officer of the Peak District National Park Authority (PDNPA). Notable works for the Authority have been 'The Lead Legacy', where a large number of mine sites in the Peak were assessed (Barnatt, & Penny, 2004; Barnatt et al., 2013), and a detailed survey of the Ecton Mines (Barnatt, 2013).

Working alongside ecologists for several decades, especially those who worked with me at the PDNPA and are well-versed in what is written here, leads me to make observations to a wider audience on the opportunities and pitfalls of studying the ecology of lead mine hillocks. Interpretation of ecological communities present, in terms of how and why they are here, cannot simplistically take mine hillocks at face value.

Figure 1: Underground in a vein working at Coalpit Rake, better known as Devonshire Cavern, above Matlock Bath

Figure 2: Sometimes vein workings are found as swarms of closely parallel scrins, as here at Slayley Corner west of Bonsal

Figure 3: Pipeworkings, where they were close to surface, sometimes have a mass of hillocks and sites of small shafts and opencast workings, as here near north of Flagg

Mine Hillocks: While some sites have important features such as engine houses, shafts leading underground and ponds for ore processing. The ubiquitous features are the waste heaps left by miners as part of the process of removing ore from the ground and concentrating this by removal of associated minerals such as fluorite, baryte and calcite. These hillocks are of great ecological interest, sometimes for their metallophyte communities and more generally for their species-richness, as havens of unimproved ground where much has been lost in surrounding pastures and meadows. The key metallophytes in the Peak District are Alpine Pennycress (*Thlaspi caerulescens*), Spring Sandwort (*Minuartia verna*) and Pyrenean Scurvygrass (*Cochlearia pyrenaica*); and there are several metallophyte lichens (e.g. *Stereocaulon nanodes*, *Sarcosagium campestre*, *Steinia geophana* and *Vezdaea* spp.). Unlike metalliferous sites in Wales and South-West England, Peak District lead mine sites appear to largely lack specialised metallophyte moss species. In addition to metallophyte communities, hillocks may support species-rich limestone grassland, and acid grassland characterised by Mountain Pansy (*Viola lutea*). The little work which has been done on invertebrates suggests mine hillocks may also support a rich fauna including scarce species. Several Peak District sites have been notified as Sites of Special Scientific Interest (SSSIs) specifically on account of their nationally

177

important metallophyte communities (Tideslow Rake, Oxlow Rake) and one site (Gang Mine) has been designated a Special Area of Conservation in recognition of its international importance. Their wonderful diversity has long been a magnet for researchers such as Oliver Gilbert.

There is a natural tendency for people who have not studied them in any detail, to regard the humble waste heaps as much of a muchness. This is far from true. Some hillocks are hundreds of years old, while others are the product of fluorspar reworking in recent decades. Their mineral content varies, as does the character of the substrate according to whether particular mounds are made after shaft sinking, initial ore sorting, or later stages of ore processing. An appreciation of the archaeological complexity is vital for understanding the ecology.

Types of Hillock: The humble mine hillocks are not all the same as each other. Understanding differences is a key factor in reaching an understanding of plant communities at mine sites, their relative rareness, and diversity within a single site. The basic types of hillock comprise:

1. Those that contain gangue minerals, mixed with some host rock (usually limestone), that was discarded after initial sorting by hand after material was brought to surface. At many mines this had been preceded by sorting underground, with obviously unproductive material left in the mine. As sorting by miners was not always fully successful, these hillocks can contain small amounts of metal ores.

2. Those that comprised 'dressed' mineral, again comprising gangue and host rock, but with this crushed to gravel and/or sand to facilitate ore refinement. Essentially, refinement depended upon using equipment that sorted material that was all of a similar size. Processing was possible because most metal ores have a higher specific gravity than gangue and host rock. Three

basic sorts of equipment were used. Firstly, a tub containing water, where the crushed material was sieved in a way similar to how gold can be recovered using a pan. Secondly, a buddle, coming in various forms but all with a sloping floor; thus, when crushed material was mixed with water, if carefully poured onto the top of the slope, heavy ore-bearing material settled out, while lighter material was washed down the buddle. The third type of equipment that was in common use, at larger mines from the nineteenth century, comprised semi-mechanised equipment (known as hotches) and mechanised equipment (usually referred to as jigs), that did the same jobs as the first two options. Using all these basic types of equipment, ore-bearing material could be separated from waste; often the resulting dumped material was similar in character irrespective of which of the equipment options had been used. Again sorting was often not fully successful and amounts of metal ores can be present.

3. Hillocks that comprise clay and/or sand which results from further processing of the fine fraction that contained some ore left after washing and buddling. This ore was initially missed as, because of its lightness, it passed through the ore refinement equipment. At some mines, particularly from the nineteenth century onwards, the fine fraction was reprocessed in settling tanks and round buddles; once the residual ore has been removed the fine waste was dumped. Metal ores in small quantities can still be present.

4. Some hillocks comprise nothing much except host rock. In the case of limestone, this often results from shaft sinking through unproductive ground. Often veins were not vertical, but 'haded' at an angle, hence to reach them at depth required sinking through host rock to one side of the vein outcrop at surface. Similarly with pipe deposits, shafts were sunk through rock to reach them.

Where cross-cuts between ore deposits were driven underground; if there was no stacking space in old workings, this material was also brought to surface. Where shafts were being sunk on narrow veins, often only a few centimetres wide, much rock was brought to surface as this needed removal in order to have a shaft wide enough for use.

5. Some hillocks, often found spaced along a line, were sunk onto drainage levels to aid ventilation and access; often they were referred to by miners as soughs. Again they were sunk through host rock and usually don't contain mineral unless this was brought out here for processing.

Figure 4: Sometimes vein workings have shafts offset because of the hade, as here at Wellfield Rake between Hartington and Pilsbury

6. Some hillocks were rich in gangue minerals such as fluorspar, in areas like Hucklow and Eyam Edges, where they have been extensively reworked, with the lead ore processing material removed, leaving a smaller hillock comprised of the shale and gritstone initially sunk through to reach the veins.

7. Some shaft hillocks are made up of clay, where pipeworkings below had ore-rich cave sediments that was brought to surface for processing. In areas of the orefield where this occurred, as around Elton and Winster, there is a specific type of hillock known as a 'buddle dam'. These have a virtually flat top where sediment mixed with water was poured carefully so that the heavy ores settled out near the point of pouring and the rest spread over the top as a whole; they grew in size and height with repeated pouring and some are particularly large. Again small amounts of metal ores can still be present.

8. There are also waste hillocks at ore smelting sites but as a general rule this was done away from the mines.

The different types of hillock are commonly found at specific locations at individual mines, for examples close to where dressing equipment was sited, or at shafts that had specific purposes.

A good example of different types of hillocks on one site is the well-known Magpie Mine. As well as the iconic engine house and other buildings, there are hillocks along veins, some partially robbed; at shaft tops including some of limestone that are the result if driving a cross-cut underground between ore deposits; and at dressing floors, including some of clay dumped after the last phase of ore processing. Not all uneven ground at Magpie is the direct result of mining underground; one area to the north comprises limestone quarries dug to provide stone and lime for building the engine houses and other buildings.

Figure 5: Some hillocks are not on veins but on drainage soughs leading to mines, as here at Old Grove Sough below Eyam Edge

Figure 6: Magpie Mine, near Sheldon, has iconic buildings, but the hillocks are interesting in their own right

A potentially important factor in understanding mine hillocks of Type 1 is a knowledge of how vein working was undertaken; while miners were working close to surface often all material removed from the vein and host rock was taken to surface for processing. However, as miners went deeper initial sorting was done underground and pieces that were unlikely to contain ore, often comprising host rock, were stacked underground. Thus, in theory later hillocks are likely to contain more discarded mineral-rich material than earlier ones. Similarly, the oldest hillocks will be those buried by later ones. However, this is unlikely to be what is found today, for hillocks were frequently turned over at a later date and this is returned to in the next section.

Other factors that influence plant communities on hillocks, which ecologists are more familiar with include edaphic factors such as the chemical and structural properties of the soil or substrate that have a fundamental influence on plant communities. The edaphic factors on lead mine hillocks can vary considerably and are dependent on the origins and subsequent history of the hillocks.

Key edaphic factors largely determined by the historical origins of the hillocks, and which in turn influence the ecology, are probably pH, levels of available toxic heavy metals, and drainage characteristics. The latter is significantly determined by particle size. All in turn influence soil nutrient levels. Aspect can be of particularly important on steep-sided hillocks. Past and present land use, in terms of grazing levels, the application of lime and modern fertilisers, and ploughing and reseeding, have significant impact. To state the obvious, the last also damages the archaeological integrity of a site.

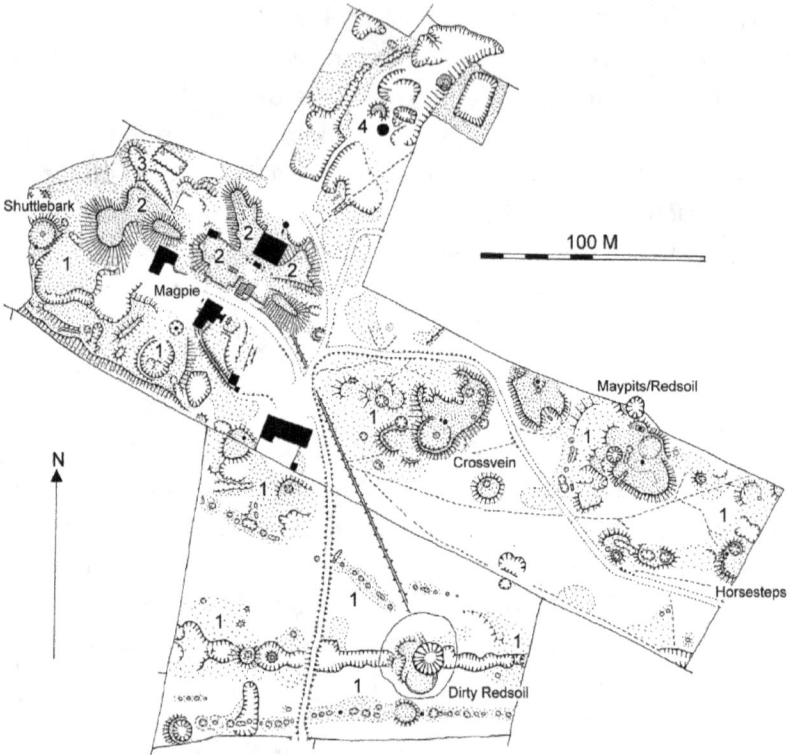

Figure 7: Magpie Mine and other mines here have (named) a diverse range of hillocks, including partially robbed mineral hillocks (1), others comprising limestone (2), and some of clay dressing waste (3). Some of the uneven ground is the result of stone quarrying and limeburning rather than mining (4)

Lead mine hillocks are potentially likely to include toxic heavy-metal material but, as we have seen, only at specific types of hillock. Where it is present, it is widely understood that metallophyte plant communities may thrive. The potential for poisoning stock is increased when there is crushed material present, since animals can use bare exposures as 'salt licks'. Keeping a good sward is important even if this is detrimental to slowing ecological succession and the potential loss of metallophyte communities. This is because it is beneficial to retaining archaeological integrity that otherwise might be lost through erosion. Another factor is whether the lead ore present is galena in its original form, or whether this has oxidised; the latter is significantly more prone to dissolution into standing water on a mine site. Again hillocks of finely crushed material are more likely to contain readily transferable toxic material, as the galena is more likely to have oxidised. Another important factor is whether particular mines were efficient at ore separation during dressing. This was sometimes the case with large mines that used multi-phased stages in the dressing process to remove even the fine fraction. Often ore recovery was only partial, as at smaller and earlier mines; this said, many hillocks were reworked at later dates to recover as much of the residual ores present as was possible.

While mine hillocks are often of great importance to ecology for their plant communities, they are also of significance to archaeologists. They have the potential for being a key resource for understanding the date of mining remains and the working methods of the miners who dumped them. This said, they often contain evidence for a multitude of different episodes and excavation needs to be carefully and systematically done to unravel sequences and changes through time. All too often, to date, the archaeological potential of hillocks has not been adequately investigated or even recognised, while more easily understood and investigated features such as engine houses and other mine structures have been targeted for study.

Hillock Age and Species Diversity: Even when a mine is many centuries old, this does not necessarily mean its extant hillocks will be. Old hillocks were periodically reworked over the centuries to recover residual amounts of ore. Particular incentives for this were provided with advances in smelting technology which allowed previously discarded material to be processed for the first time. The main advances came in the later-sixteenth century when bole smelting sites were replaced by ore hearths, and the mid-eighteenth centuries when cupolas were introduced. Old waste heaps were widely turned over as a result, with what were effectively new hillocks of waste left after the reworking was done. Similarly, in the nineteenth century, ore was becoming increasingly difficult to get from underground as veins were commonly becoming worked out; miners turned in desperation to old hillocks to see if any ore remained here. In addition, at all times, hillocks were regularly being reworked on a smaller scale by the poor and disenfranchised, independent of the main mining operations and paying a small rent, to eke out a meagre living.

All this said, the techniques used historically usually did not result in full recovery of metal ores and even when reprocessing took place they are still present in small quantities in those hillocks which contain minerals.

Figure 8: Some veins are contained within belland yards, as here at Gautries Rake and Coalpithole Rake north of Peak Forest, where they have been planted with trees

Lead mine hillocks are commonly surrounded by drystone walls, creating what known as belland yards, 'belland' being the miner's term for poisoned ground, to prevent stock from entering. These were commonly built in the eighteenth and nineteenth centuries, sometimes after mining had ceased. In these cases some landowners created plantations as a way of gaining a long-term cash-crop on ground that could not be safely grazed.

In the twentieth century, hillocks were commonly reworked for gangue minerals. At first only high-grade deposits of minerals such as fluorspar were targeted, with holes dug selectively in the old hillocks with many of the former features left intact.

However, from the later twentieth century, operators commonly fully removed hillocks to recover fluorspar and barytes that remained once the high-grade deposits had already largely gone.

Gangue recovery should not be seen as separate to the earlier lead mining, galena has often been recovered as a by-product. In the last decades of the twentieth century, Cavendish Mill above Stoney Middleton, while primarily designed to process fluorspar and barytes, produced more lead ore per year than was mined annually in previous centuries. Conversely, fluorspar has been extracted from the eighteenth century at places like Masson Hill above Matlock, with the product being used as a smelting flux at the Ecton Mine smelters. Barytes has long been used as filler in paint manufacture. Mineral extraction today is the latest phase in a 2,000-year-old tradition.

Identifying ancient hillocks which have survived post-medieval reworking is impossible from surface inspection. Similarly, map evidence can be downright misleading. Just because a wall crosses hillocks doesn't necessarily mean the hillocks are earlier than the date it was built. In some instances, temporary phases of mining have been missed by the periodic updating of Ordnance Survey maps; walls were taken down as new mining activity took place and then rebuilt afterwards. Because a map marks a mine as 'disused' doesn't necessarily mean it was not active, numerous examples can be quoted of mines that are documented as in work underground at a small scale at the dates of map editions. Such ambiguities reflect the cyclical nature of metal mining; old mines were reopened for a variety of reasons, ranging from new work because several generations down the line people had forgotten how poor the prospects at the site were, to technological advancement making new work realistic. Similarly, fluctuating lead prices affected viability, and in other instances, many specific mines were only worked in periods where there were no active rich mines in the district offering employment.

A good example that illustrates how hillocks have changed is Tideslow Rake to the west of Great Hucklow. This site has been designated as a Scheduled Monument because of the high quality of its hillocks, open cuts, etc. (and it is also a Site of Special Scientific Interest). Mining was first recorded here in the thirteenth century and there was intermittent activity, sometimes at a large scale, through into the eighteenth century. However, everything is not as it seems at superficial examination. Barmaster and other records show that the hillocks were extensively reworked in the nineteenth century after the main phases of underground mining had ceased (Barnatt, 2011). The present hillocks are largely the result of this work, as illustrated by the loss of previous mine features around the main drawing shafts such as horse engine platforms, dressing floors and small buildings known as 'coes'.

Figure 9: The Scheduled Monument at Tideslow Rake, also an SSSI, has a broad band of large hillocks which were extensively reworked in the nineteenth century

I have seen little evidence that relative species diversity is directly correlated to the age of hillocks wherever they are nineteenth-century or older in date; also, as we have seen, intact hillocks that pre-date the nineteenth century are probably going to be rare. In addition, too many other factors have significant influence on diversity, such as hillock character and modern land-use with regard to stocking levels and the use of fertilizers or manure. The often-held assumption that species diversity on mine hillocks has increased over several centuries and concomitantly that the hillocks are ancient need questioning; interpretations need to be more nuanced.

Intact Hillocks or Disturbed Vestiges: Ecologists need to be keenly aware of the history of the sites under study, understanding whether the hillocks are as left by the lead miners, or have been significantly modified in modern times.

I want to give three cautionary tales. Several years ago at Goodluck Mine in the Via Gellia, a person who was described to me as an 'ecologist' visited the site and pronounced that they had found the best display of Frog Orchids ever seen in the Peak District and that the ground upon which they were growing must have remained undisturbed for many decades and probably centuries. The people on site at the time, who had long been maintaining the mining remains, were dumbfounded for they knew they had moved this soil from elsewhere on site just a few years before. At an ecological assessment of mine hillocks on Longstone Edge, a site was initially pronounced intact on the basis of species-rich vegetation; in reality all that remained here, at a site heavily reworked for fluorspar in the twentieth century, were low mounds at the two edges of a line of large hillocks, while the bulk of material between the two had been removed. The relict vegetation was ecologically important but the site was far from intact; if this had been recognised it would have saved critical re-evaluation. At How Grove an archaeological excavation spoil heap put there only weeks before, to everyone's surprise became carpeted by the rare metallophyte Pyrenean Scurvy Grass. It was concluded that a dormant seed source had been disturbed and invigorated and for a short while the plant was locally very abundant. Initially, to the excavators' disconcertion, they were told the spoil heap could not be moved and this was problematic as restoration after the excavation could not be completed. Later, as a good example of constructive dialogue between people from different disciplines, a sensible compromise was reached and the plants together with the top layer of soil were carefully transplanted after they had seeded.

From an ecological perspective, in one sense what matters is that there are important ecological communities present on a mine hillock. However, making well-informed assessments matters if other people are to take conservation seriously; in the Goodluck Mine example an uphill battle ensued to regain peoples' trust in conservationists and conservation issues. Conversely, examples could be given where archaeologists had not recognised important plant communities before they have removed them to investigate what lay beneath. The basic lesson to be learnt, and in many quarters it already has been, is that different disciplines should talk to each other and a take a multifaceted approach whenever physical works are planned. *[This raises an important point regarding assumptions by different disciplines since many orchids, especially on post-industrial sites, thrive on disturbance and the early succession – Ed]*

Restoration of Hillocks: With transplanting of turves, or reseeding of hillocks, I do not have the expertise to say how successful such actions are. From an archaeological perspective once damage is done any reconstruction is nothing more than a poor pastiche of what went before and has no future research value in terms of heritage. Looking at the ecology, one thing is certain, given what is introduced above with regard to the subtleties and complexities at hillocks, while a new species-rich swath no doubt has great value, it will often not be the same as what was there before; nor is it likely that will it have a trajectory into the future that will bring the plant communities in-line with what was there originally, unless the detailed make up and form of individual original hillocks is carefully studied and replicated.

A Celebration of Diversity: Finally, it is worth re-iterating that metal mine hillocks are wonderful places and part of their interest is the great diversity therein. A particular mine hillock cannot simply be seen as identical to all others. It is their diversity, in terms of different origins and resulting substrate differences, and the multitude of different research and conservation interests, in terms of history, archaeology, ecology and landscape character, that should be celebrated and wherever possible retained.

Acknowledgements: Many thanks to all those over the years who have helped me reach understanding of mining remains, notable among them being Chris Heathcote, Jim Rieuwerts, Phil Shaw, Lynn Willies, and Terry Worthington. Thanks also to Ken Smith and Rhodri Thomas for commenting on a draft text. Rhodri made significant contribution to the text on edaphic factors, and on metallophyte lichens and other specialist communities.

Bibliography

Barnatt, J. (2002) Excavations and Conservation at How Grove, Dirtlow Rake, Castleton, Derbyshire. *Mining History*, **15** (2), 1-40.

Barnatt, J. (2011) High Rake Mine, Little Hucklow, Derbyshire: Excavations and Conservation at an Important Nineteenth Century Mine. *Mining History*, **18** (1/2), 1-217.

Barnatt, J. (2012) Silence Mine, Grindlow, Derbyshire: Investigating an 1870s Steam Engine House. *Mining History*, **18** (4), 1-55.

Barnatt, J. (2013) *Delving Ever Deeper: The Ecton Mines through Time.* Peak District National Park Authority, Bakewell.

Barnatt, J. (2016) The 1788 Boulton and Watt Engine House at Ecton: Archaeological Excavations 2012-14. *Mining History*, **19** (5), 38-76.

Barnatt, J. (in press) *The Peak District: A Landscape Made and Made Again.* Historic England, Swindon.

Barnatt, J. (in prep.) Watergrove Mine, Foolow, Derbyshire: Excavating a 1794-95 Newcomen engine house.

Barnatt, J., Huston, K., Mallon, D., Newman, R., Penny, R., & Shaw, R. (2013) The Lead Legacy: An Updated Inventory of Important Metal and Gangue Mining Sites in the Peak District. *Mining History*, **18** (6), 1-112.

Barnatt, J., & Penny, R. (2004) *The Lead Legacy: The Prospects for the Peak District's Lead Mining Heritage.* Peak District National Park Authority, Bakewell.

Barnatt, J., & Smith, K. (2004) *The Peak District: Landscapes Through Time*. Windgather, Bollington.

Ford, T.D. (2004) Geology of the Lead Mines around the Stanton Syncline, Derbyshire. *Mining History*, **15** (6), 1-26.

Ford, T.D. (2005) The geology of the Wirksworth mines. *Mining History*, **16** (2), 1-42.

Ford, T.D. (2008) The geological setting of the lead mines in the Lathkill Dale and Wye Valley area, Derbyshire. *Mining History*, **17** (2), 11-47.

Ford, T.D. (2010) The geological setting of the lead mines in the northern part of the White Peak, Derbyshire. *Mining History*, **17** (5), 1-49.

Ford, T.D. (2012) The geological setting of the lead mines of the Hucklow, Eyam, Stoney Middleton and Longstone Edge area, Derbyshire. *Mining History*, **18** (3), 1-22.

Ford, T.D., & Jones, J.A. (2007) The geological setting of the deposits at Brassington and Carsington, Derbyshire. *Mining History*, **16** (5), 1-23.

Ford, T.D., & Rieuwerts, J.H. (2000) *Lead Mining in the Peak District* (Fourth edition). Peak District Mines Historical Society and Landmark Publishing, Matlock Bath and Ashbourne.

Ford, T.D., Sarjeant, W.A.S., & Smith, M.E. (1993) Minerals of the Peak District of Derbyshire. *Bulletin of the Peak District Mines Historical Society*, **12** (1), 16-65.

Note

[1]John Barnatt, formerly Senior Survey Archaeologist, Peak District National Park Authority, Aldern House, Baslow Road, Bakewell, Derbyshire, DE45 1AE

Chapter 9: Restoring ecological landscapes

Penny Anderson
Penny Anderson Associates Ltd

Introduction – Habitat Creation and Repair: Although I had known Oliver Gilbert for many years as a regular associate at conferences and workshops, I had not known him socially or as a close friend as have some other contributors. Oliver contacted me in about 1996 to offer me the chance of working with him on '*Habitat creation, restoration and repair*' which he had been commissioned to write by Oxford University Press. Needless to say, I jumped at the opportunity – not only to work with Oliver closely, but also to have the chance to present my ideas on habitat creation and restoration based on my experience. I am not an academic, but had been carrying out habitat creation and restoration as part of my ecological consultancy work in various places across the country for something like fifteen years then – perhaps that was why Ollie asked me in the first place.

I have re-read what we wrote in the book for this paper, analysing the extent to which the 'ecological landscape' has changed in the intervening nearly 20 years, and identifying the major new ideas or directions that we might have applied in the book if we were writing it now.

We divided the book roughly equally between us. Ollie wrote much of the introductory chapters apart from the section on site character (soils etc), promoted natural succession as a primary method of habitat creation and presented the concluding comments. I covered wetlands (with the help of some of my colleagues), grasslands and moorlands, but Ollie wrote the rest of the habitat chapters. It is interesting to note that many of the principles, ethics and methods we set out are equally relevant and pertinent now as in 1998 and we would not have changed these significantly, although the language might be more up to date.

Promoting natural succession is still prevalent, the range of habitats that we covered are still part of the palette for practitioners, and much of the advice on how to do this still stands.

What is new in nearly 20 years? Although the book represents sound advice still, there have been changes. The emphases have altered, the challenges for nature conservation have increased, new agendas have been added, the prognostications for the future with climate change have strengthened, and the scale of and urgency for habitat creation have increased. These aspects are explored below.

The Lawton Report (Lawton *et al.*, 2010) provided change in emphasis and urgency. The 'more, bigger, joined-up, and better' headline is widely adopted and implemented throughout the country with landscape conservation the name of the game. *Habitat Creation and Repair* did promote such large-scale habitat creation and restoration through strategic schemes and reconnection of habitats as well as recommending buffering and linkages of small habitat patches. The book based this on the priorities identified in the Natural Area profiles produced at the time by the former English Nature which included recommendations for habitat creation and restoration. These principles might be written in a different language now, but we did include them in the book, but without the emphases generated by Lawton. The latter was based more on the continual erosion of habitat quality and quantity and our failure to meet biodiversity targets.

The twelve Nature Improvement Areas (NIAs) established in 2012 were as a direct recommendation by Lawton *et al.* (2010). These were partnership projects selected through competition and with some funding from Defra and Natural England which set out to establish and improve ecological networks by enlarging, enhancing, and connecting existing wildlife sites as well as creating new sites. All comprised the main components of an ecological network with core areas, habitat corridors and stepping stones to support species movement. The weakness in the vision was of course the limited political support at the time and hence only short-term funding for these initial projects.

These kinds of opportunities illustrate one major difference between habitat creation schemes now and then, which is scale. We quoted a survey showing that 75% of British wildflower seed sold was for sites less than 0.2ha in 1989. Just in the Nene Valley, Northants, (which capitalised on becoming one of the NIAs) 210ha of species-rich grassland has been created, 150ha restored and a further 60ha planned for treatment in 2014 (Field, & Johnson, 2016, pers. comm.). Flood management in the face of climate change is another means of developing large scale and interconnected habitat creation schemes. The Medmerry Flood risk management scheme in Sussex, the largest scheme of its kind so far implemented by the Environment Agency, involves 425ha of habitat creation and restoration as part of the flood control programme (Restoring Europe's Rivers website) with borrow pits for clay for the new flood bank adding to the habitat creation. An original freshwater SSSI was incorporated into the plan along with new mudflats, saltmarsh, saline lagoons, shingle islands, grassland arable, reedbeds, ponds and ditches. The scheme has won numerous awards.

Another example of large-scale imaginative and successful habitat creation is the 'Coronation and Magnificent Meadows' projects run by Plantlife. In September 2016 Coronation Meadows (a partnership with the Wildlife Trusts and the Rare Breeds Survival Trust) created their 90th New Coronation Meadow in the heart of London, bringing the area of new meadows established to over 1000acres (405ha). 'Save our Magnificent Meadows' – another partnership project- set out to transform the fortunes of vanishing wildflower grasslands through raising their profile to the public and providing support and guidance on their restoration and creation. This has resulted in 2,500ha of grassland directly restored or maintained and a wide range of other activities (Save our Magnificent Meadows, 2017).

One current conservation issue which was not specifically mentioned in the book was the plight and habitat creation needed to support bumble bee conservation. Indeed, bees were not even in the index, although there were several sections on habitat creation for invertebrates as a whole. Other animals were also covered in short sections in relation to particular habitats whilst it was mostly assumed that the animals would arrive unaided once the habitats had been created or restored. Butterflies were highlighted, along with habitat links and connectivity as important considerations. This approach to animals as a whole might be changed if the book were being written now based on more up to date information. Again the scale of current schemes is significant. The Butterfly Conservation Trust website lists many projects in all areas of the UK focusing on some of our most threatened butterflies and moths. Their work is undertaken on a landscape scale, consisting of networks of sites in a range of habitat types. Another example is the RSPB which has been instrumental in creating large reed beds and wetland habitat designed specifically for bittern and other wetland birds and their habitat requirements.

One really important addition to the list of reasons why habitat creation is so important is the health and wellbeing agenda. Although the importance of flowers, colour and habitats for people, especially in urban areas, was highlighted in our book, based on work undertaken by English Nature and organisations like Landlife in Liverpool (now the Eden Project North), the research on the value of flowers, bird song and diverse green spaces for people's health and wellbeing is new. Ollie's interest in the urban environment and his descriptions of one of the early schemes on the Lower River Don in Sheffield, which involved an 800ha scheme in the 1990s, was included, but there was no special urban chapter in the book which is perhaps surprising. There had been at that time considerable interest in the value of nature conservation habitats within the urban framework, and the positive impact this had on house prices, quality of environment and for recreation, but this lacked the current knowledge on their value for health and wellbeing which would be emphasised now.

Another advance in how nature conservation/habitats are considered is the ecosystem services or ecosystem approach, led by Defra and Natural England. Although many of the ecosystem services were recognised in *Habitat Creation and Repair,* they were not labelled as such, nor was there any comprehensive acknowledgement or consideration of their role in habitat creation and restoration. There was no specific mention, for example, of flooding, water quality, crop pollination, carbon storage and sequestration or other major benefits ecosystems provide. These would now be included as part of the arguments for habitat creation and restoration on a large scale to produce significant benefits for many. For example, there is more carbon captured in wildflower grassland than in grass monocultures (Alonso *et al.,* 2012), in heath, wetlands, newly-growing woodland and moorland than in other environments and this would have been used as another reason for extensive habitat creation. Writing the book now would rectify this.

Moorland restoration: Although there have not been major advances in creation methods or techniques for most of the habitats covered in the book, this is not the case for the moorlands, where the ecosystem services related primarily to water quality, carbon retention and sequestration in the face of climate change and downstream flood control have all increased hugely in significance. The moorland restoration outlined in the book focused on re-establishment of vegetation on bare ground, which is largely the product of wildfire and subsequent erosion. This work started after the severe and widespread fires of 1976, first in the North York Moors (1986) and then in the Peak District National Parks (Phillips *et al.,* 1981).

The Peak District's Moorland Erosion Project started in 1979 with the objectives to identify causes of bare ground, measure its extent and seek measures to restore it. It found that out of a total of 522sq km of moorland in the National Park, 25% was cottongrass (*Eriophorum vaginatum*) dominated or co-dominated, 57% was dwarf shrub dominated or co-dominated, but a massive 33sq kms (6.3%) was bare or partly bare and eroding.

The restoration experiments and larger scale trials subsequently focused on re-vegetation on very fragile and unstable peat surfaces rather than on restoring any of the damaged hydrology, as shown by the sequence of photographs in Figure 1 taken on Holme Moss of plots set up in 1988. The absence of any vegetation on the bare peat outside the plot demonstrates the need to exclude stock and rabbit grazing to establish vegetation. The plot (one of a number of different approaches) trialled the use of a Geojute mesh at 100% and 50% cover, plus the addition of phosphate-rich and slow release fertilisers, finding that the 50% cover on flattish slopes and higher phosphate fertilisers were key to maintaining vegetation. The full results are provided in Anderson *et al*. 1998. All this was covered in the book.

The photographs also show the gradual establishment of blanket bog species like cottongrasses, but not *Sphagnum*, the driver of active blanket bog. It was not until the late 1990s, but mostly into this century that re-wetting to restore active peat that can not only protect historic carbon in the peat, but capture new carbon and actively grow again was recognised as important. This was linked also to the need to reduce the colour in water coming off the peatlands for the Water Companies. Research had found that the drying of peat, through lowering of water tables in warm weather, results in the breakdown of peat in the aerobic environment into dissolved organic carbon, which then swamps the water leaving the site when water tables rise after rainfall, often exceeding colour thresholds in water treatment works. Early projects that recognised the drying of peat and designed measures to combat this were the Border Mires and the United Utilities' SCaMP[1] Projects. The former, in Kielder Forest, ran from 1998 to 2003, using an EU LIFE-fund to start the restoration of around 500ha of mires (IUCN Peatland Programme website). SCaMP, which began in 2005, was originally driven by SSSI condition targets but reducing dissolved organic carbon and maintaining carbon stores related to climate change quickly became additional objectives.

Figure 1. Holme Moss plots 1989 top left, 1991 top right, 1995 bottom left, 1999 bottom right. © Penny Anderson Associates

The SCaMP project used the measures developed in the earlier Peak District research to re-vegetate bare peat on the Dovestones/Arnfield Estate north of Longdendale, plus extensive management of water through gully and rill blocking and holding water in small depressions where possible. Grazing livestock have been excluded. In the Goyt Valley, grip blocking has been undertaken, livestock have been reduced, and cutting has replaced burning. In The Forest of Bowland, the grips on the Brennand Estate blanket bog have been blocked. The effects of these restoration measures have been monitored by Penny Anderson Associates (vegetation, water quality and hydrology)

---

[1] SCaMP = Sustainable Catchment Management Programme

and RSPB (birds). The results have so far been very encouraging, with raised water tables showing much lower perturbation from the grip blocking, elevated water tables even by just re-vegetating bare peat – although these are not yet close enough to the surface; reduced dissolved organic carbon in outflows or only low rates of increase from the more severely degraded catchments, reduced sediment loads after revegetation of bare peat associated with significant reductions in bare peat cover. After grip blocking and stock reduction on blanket bog, more key species like *Sphagnum* mosses have increased from a low 10% to up to 50% cover over 10 years on some sites along with a steady but slow expansion of other typical bog species like bog rosemary (*Andromeda polifolia*) and cranberry (*Vaccinium oxycoccus*), at least on Brennand, (Ross, & Hammond, 2018).

The key drivers for this large scale moorland restoration are now improved habitat condition, carbon and climate change, linked to water quality and downstream flooding. These are all interconnected, as shown by Defra's 'Slowing the Flow Projects', one of which was on Kinder Scout. Here, the Moors for the Future team, supported by Manchester University (Pilkington *et al.*, 2015) showed that re-vegetating bare peat and damming the associated gullies together reduced sediment runoff, slowed water runoff, thus delaying and reducing peaks in the hydrograph, increased water retention due to increased surface roughness, and resulted in identifiable reductions in flooding downstream in the River Derwent. (Derby is affected when this river floods). These kinds of results together add a much greater impetus to the reasons for habitat restoration than were expressed in our book.

The causes of the degradation of peatland, particularly blanket mire, can be blamed firmly on several factors, often interlinked. Sulphur dioxide pollution was a key factor in causing the loss of most *Sphagnum* within the blanket mire vegetation, particularly in the areas close to urban centres such as the Peak District, South Pennines and South Wales. *Sphagnum* can be regarded as the engineer of the hydrology of blanket mires, its leaves and dead leaves holding significant amounts of water and maintaining a wet bog surface. Without Sphagnum in the blanket bogs of the Peak District at least, the drier surfaces are more vulnerable to damage. Wildfire or fires during dry periods all have the potential to destroy vegetation and bare the peat surface. Once stripped of vegetation, heavy rain can result in increasingly dense and deep gully systems; and the more gullies there are, then the lower the water table (Allott *et al.*, 2009). Many moorland areas in wetter parts of the country have also been drained with herringbone or other patterns of narrow, straight grips (drains) dug out, many using government grants, in the 1950s to 1970s. These have contributed to drying of these moors, with lowered water tables close to them and diversion of overland flows as the grips intercept water across the contours. Overgrazing, reducing the biomass and litter layers, sometimes contributing to development of bare ground, also contribute to increased overland flow and reduced absorption of water, and has been an issue, although more in the past, on many sites. Managed burning when burns are too hot can also damage the surface, and there is some evidence that burning results in warmer, drier surfaces that contribute to peat decay and release of DOC (Brown *et al.*, 2014).

There are many other features of the peat mass that show degradation, including peat pipes – varying from slits and cracks to large round passageways passing through the peat, not necessarily flowing with the slopes, but which provide routes for water to erode underground and lower the water table. Most occur at the bottom of the peat layer, but on less damaged sites, many can be associated with the boundary between the peat layers (the catotelm and acrotelm). Holden (2005) has shown that peat pipes are more common on sites which have been heavily gripped, but they are also a feature of sites where multiple wildfires have occurred. Severe managed burning has also been found to result in mini pipes – like gutters, criss-crossing the peat providing new routes for overland flow to gouge out more peat (pers. obs.), Figure. 3.

Figure 2. Collapsed peat into a peat pipe marked by a depression 'upstream of the collapse, South Pennines. © Penny Anderson Associates

Figure 3. Small gutters and mini-peat pipe developing after managed burning that was too hot, Peak District © Penny Anderson Associates

With associated drainage, peat extraction on a wide scale, although not necessarily extant in most of England and Wales, also reduces water tables, leaves formerly intact bog marooned above the extracted areas, and contributes to drying out of sites.

The last 15 years has seen an increasing recognition of the importance of peat and its carbon in the country as a whole, highlighted by the Peat Inquiry instigated by IUCN in the UK (Bain *et al.,* 2011). Key facts are set out in Table 1.

Table 1: Some facts and figures on peat in the UK

1.	UK is in the top 10 nations of the world for total area of peat
2.	UK has 9-15% of Europe's peatland area
3.	It has *c.*13% of the world's blanket bog
4.	UK blanket and raised bogs store *c.*3.2million tonnes of carbon
5.	The loss of 5% of C from UK peat is equivalent to the total amount of UK man-made GHG emissions
6.	80% of carbon losses in the UK are from upland soils
7.	In the Peak District, up to 100 tonnes of C is lost/yr/km^2
8.	If all blanket bog in the Peak District was active, it could sequester 18.9tonnesC/km^2/yr
9.	Restoration of UK's peat bogs could save 400,000 tonnes C/yr =1.1billion car miles/yr

In response to the increasing awareness of the importance of peat in good condition, a large number of peatland based projects have been established across the UK and in Ireland, far exceeding the limited range known when *Habitat Creation and Repair* was written. Within the Pennines there are the Moors for the Future, Yorkshire Peat Partnership, and North Pennines AONB projects. Yorkshire Water and United Utilities are major players, along with Natural England and the National Trust. Other projects are in place on Exmoor, Dartmoor, in Scotland, Wales, Northern Ireland and Ireland. The forestry authorities are removing conifer plantations from the best areas of peatland, drains and gullies are being blocked, and management becoming more sustainable.

[Although of course, the Forestry Commission still uses peat-grown saplings. Ed]

New methods not considered in the book *Habitat Creation and Repair* are now being used on a wide scale. Re-wetting involves damming water using a variety of techniques, each suited to different conditions. Peat dams are the cheapest, plastic, wood, heather bales and coir rolls are used depending on water flows and depth of peat to imbed them.

Figure 4. Plastic dams blocking gully and raising water table on Keighley Moor, Yorkshire © Penny Anderson Associates

Stone is being used to make dams more widely where drains and gullies have extended into mineral ground. Re-profiling is being applied to overhanging and very steep gully or drain sides to increase efficacy of restoration techniques (Yorkshire Peat Partnership website). Plants like *Sphagnum* and other bog species are being added in different ways (Crouch, 2018). All this is new since Ollie and I wrote our book and would furnish a much enlarged peatland restoration section if we were writing it now.

Final thoughts: This brief look at developments in blanket bog restoration highlights some of the advances and changes in approach since *Habitat Creation and Repair* was written. It illustrates the considerable scaling up of projects throughout the country, although much more is still needed. It also demonstrates the importance of ecosystem services which has given a new perspective and new arguments for habitat creation. Furthermore, it shows the extent of resources that are being invested in peatland restoration. This is not necessarily matched in other habitat creation projects, and there is a desperate need for more, larger scale, joined up projects of all types of habitat throughout the country. Climate change is a major driver for this, both to enable species to move as their climate envelope moves, but also to sequester more carbon and reduce damaging flooding.

It is good to think that the book which Ollie and I wrote has contributed to the successful establishment of different habitats and I am sure he would be interested to see how the field has developed, gratified to see the extent of habitat creation schemes now, but equally keen to see even more.

References

Allott, T.E.H., Evans, M.G., Lindsay, J.B., Agnew, C.T., Freer, J.E., Jones, A., & Parnell, M. (2009) *Water Tables in the Peak District Blanket Peatlands.* Moors for the Future Report No. 17. Moors for the Future Partnership, Bakewell.

Alonso, I., Weston, K., Gregg, R., & Moorcroft, M. (2012) *Carbon storage by habitat: Review of the evidence of the impacts of management decisions and condition of carbon stores and sources.* Natural England Research Reports, Number NERR043NERR043, Peterborough.

Anderson, P.A., Tallis, J.H., & Yalden, D.W. (1998) *Restoring Moorlands: the Moorland Management Project Phase 3 report.* Peak Park Joint Planning Board, Bakewell.

Bain, C.G., Bonn, A., Stoneham, R., Chapman, S., Coupar, A., Evans, M., Gearey, B., ... & Worrall, F. (2011) *IUCN UK Commission of Inquiry on Peatlands.* IUCN UK Peatland Programme, Edinburgh.

Border Mires Project: http://www.iucn-uk-peatlandprogramme.org/projects/border-mires-active-blanket-bog-rehabilitation IUCN Peatland Programme. Accessed 19.04.2019

Brown, L.E., Holden, J., & Palmer, S.M. (2014) *Effects of Moorland Burning on the Ecohydrology of River Basins. Key findings from the EMBER project.* University of Leeds, Leeds.

Crouch, T. (2018) *Kinder Scout Sphagnum trials: 2018 Update Report*. Moors for the Future, Bakewell.

Holden, J. (2005) Controls of soil pipe frequency in upland blanket peat. *Journal of Geophysical Research*, **110**, F01002, doi: 10.1029/2004JF000143

Lawton, J.H., Brotherton, P.N.M., Brown, V.K., Elphick, C., Fitter, A.H., Forshaw, J., Haddow, R.W., Hilborne, S., ... & Wynne, G.R. (2010) *Making Space for Nature: a review of England's wildlife sites and ecological network.* Report to Defra, London.

Magnificent Meadows conference (2017): http://www.magnificentmeadows.org.uk/assets/uploads/1_Save_Our_Magnificent_Meadows_Introduction.pdf

North York Moors National Park (1986) *Moorland Management. Second Report*. National Park Office, Helmsley.

Phillips, J., Yalden, D., & Tallis, J. (1981) *Peak District Moorland Erosion Study Phase 1 report*. Peak Park Joint Planning Board, Bakewell.

Pilkington, M., Walker, J., Maskill, R., Allot, T., & Evans, M. (2015) *Restoration of Blanket bogs; flood risk reduction and other ecosystem benefits.* Final report of the Making space for water project, Moors for the Future Partnership, Edale.

Restoring Europe's Rivers, accessed 19.04.2019 https://restorerivers.eu/wiki/index.php?title=Case_study%3AMedmerry_Managed_Realignment_Scheme

Ross, S., & Hammond, G. (2018) *Sustainable Catchment Management Programme, Annual Report*. Penny Anderson Associates, Buxton.

Yorkshire Peat Partnership restoration techniques: https://www.yppartnership.org.uk/our-work/restoration-techniques, accessed April 2019

Chaper 10: Urban ecology: a continental European context of Oliver Gilbert's work

Jan Woudstra
The University of Sheffield

Summary: Oliver Gilbert (1936-2005) was one of the pioneers in urban ecology, who, looking at the post-industrial environment of the 1960s explored the specific ecologies of former industrial sites. These were referred to by contemporary politics as brownfield land, waste land or derelict land, but Gilbert saw them as 'urban commons'- for everyone and everything, and he celebrated them for their ecological richness. He was able to distinguish the trading histories of cities from the naturalised exotics there, and enjoyed the way they occupied a certain niche within the urban ecosystem, in contrast to more purist ecologists who aimed to eliminate exotics. The debate in Great Britain was shaped by its industrial past, but this paper highlights how this differed from the situation in three other countries, Germany, Sweden and The Netherlands. Here debates were shaped consecutively by the war, the general clearance of woodland for development, and the lack of nature and the discovery that natural processes could be restarted. These different contexts have shaped the contents and appearance of urban nature within cities on the European continent.

Keywords: urban ecology, urban nature, urban commons, new nature, urban fallow land, nature-like open spaces

When Oliver Gilbert (1936-2005) published the first of his two books on urban ecology, *The Ecology of Urban Habitats* (1989), it was not the first such text either internationally or nationally. In fact, from World War II there had been something of a natural history tradition to study the development of plants and wildlife in cities. Gilbert had not initially been part of this movement and instead studied ecological communities in the Pennines. As he was given his first academic position in Newcastle he was confronted with the effects of air pollution on Tyneside, making this a valid research topic. Later, as a landscape ecologist for the Department of Landscape Architecture of the University of Sheffield he became aware of a lack of knowledge about the ecology of urban areas, diverging here to understand the ecological capital of the city. Over a period of some ten years or so, after having been given impetus by the Nature in Cities conference held in Manchester and its publication in book form in 1979, he expanded his knowledge for the first textbook in the field, later also contributing to the burgeoning field of habitat creation.

There had been other such books, and notably Malcolm Emery's *Promoting Nature in Cities and Towns: A practical guide* (1986) but the emphasis here was primarily on creating new greenspaces in the city, while Gilbert first concentrated on what was already there. The main innovation however, and the one that has gained him enduring legacy, was that he celebrated what was generally seen as a blight, namely former industrial land. He recognised this as 'urban commons' - for everyone and everything, in contravention with contemporary politics that spoke despairingly of brownfield land, waste land, and derelict land. By applying ecological knowledge to these sites it was possible to provide detailed account of most plant and animal groups by exploring variety and dynamics, successional relationships, regional variation, and edaphic influences. A third innovation central to that of the understanding of the urban common was that they also included non-native species, which he celebrated and saw as integral to urban ecosystems.

In fact, he claimed that he was able to recognize the industrial and trading histories of cities from the naturalised non-natives occurring there. While other ecologists saw a need to eliminate exotic plants he considered this a losing battle, and instead demonstrated that even defiled plants, such as Japanese knotweed *(Fallopia japonica)* have ecological value, acting as a surrogate woodland canopy that encourages establishment of common woodland plants beneath it, and also harbouring rare insects. He was a vigorous proponent of buddleia *(Buddleia davidii).* This liberal stance provided a textbook that was readable, spiked with interesting anecdotes, and full of information.

In his analysis of landscape types in cities he took an ecological perspective, recognizing three different types that he considered complementary to each other and also far richer in variety than if only two of these three were present. He recognised 'gardenesque' landscapes, in which he misappropriated J.C. Loudon's definition for this, now meaning garden-like places 'where biological elements can function only under continuous management'. Noting how these were subject to fashion he also associated this with picturesque, and that people in Britain like to live 'in a setting not dissimilar to eighteenth-century parkland' a landscape contrived for aesthetic reasons, rather than active use. The 'technological landscape style' where artificial substitutes, unnatural landform, and alien artificial materials (concrete, tarmac, fibre glass) that lack local character and are uniform, replace the biological landscape. These are resource intensive concrete jungles, highly designed for functional purposes with a narrow range of plant material. Finally 'ecological landscapes' which are places 'where natural elements are allowed to function in a natural manner' (Gilbert, 1989; Gilbert, & Anderson, 1998). While this black and white approach may not have created an elegant set of definitions, it was helpful in caricaturing diverse urban environments and determining the types of ecological habitats. This way it enabled fulfilling the purpose of the book in providing practical advice.

This chapter sets out to put Gilbert's work on urban ecology in a continental context, concentrating on three different countries that particularly helped to shape developments in Great Britain, namely The Netherlands, Germany and Sweden. A number of different schools and traditions can be seen to be evolving that sometimes emphasise independent thought, or otherwise a continuation of tradition. Much of this, of course, is for socio-political reasons, and also the fact that in order to continue existing trends there is need to adopt new narratives and adapt them. Thus we can see this from the perspective of educational objectives through to that as a grounding for the sustainable or eco-city. Theories have been presented in the context of case studies, and through these we are able to achieve a better understanding of the development of a new profession and its field of work. As this emerges largely as a bottom-up process it also provides an alternative reading of sustainability of urban environments, which is proving to pre-date the notion of the concept itself. It is important to review this so that we can better understand these modern notions of urban ecologies, urban nature, and urban wilderness. There are currently no papers that provide a wider perspective of the various developments or trends in a socio-political context, with each fraction writing its own histories. By assembling these trends in one chapter it is possible to review urban ecology more holistically, as well as setting Gilbert's contribution within that wider context.

Ecology and the city: While natural processes within the urban environment had been a notion since the biologist and townplanner Patrick Geddes proposed this in the early twentieth century, little was done to respond to this in a creative manner, and though landscape architects were involved, city development was seen as an engineering process rather than one which had to address ecological principles also (Woudstra, 2018). This led the landscape architect Ian Laurie, on a years' sabbatical in the USA, to take a special interest in this, and on seeing the papers produced for the 'Man and Nature in the City' conference organised in Washington DC in 1968, decided to organise a symposium on the same theme back at the University of Manchester in 1974. This set out to find 'new solutions based on concepts which went beyond those of the conventional forms of landscape improvement'. The 'new design principles' that emerged 'reflected an underlying philosophy of man and nature' that was promoted in a book based on the conference published in 1979 (Laurie, 1979).

As Laurie was visiting the USA, his young colleague Allan Ruff, on finishing an MA thesis based on a series of visits to The

Netherlands between 1973 and 1978, enabled him to explore a 'social landscape, observing ecological principles' that was seen to 'compensate for an environment that displays abundant evidence of destruction, decay and material values of our society'. His notion was one that post-war urban landscapes failed to bring 'pleasure and happiness', and therefore little relevance to daily lives. New open spaces were considered to be 'without function and frequently bleak, barren, and litter strewn- yet another aspect of our modern technological society'. New urban landscapes in The Netherlands reaffirmed that they were more than just a visual amenity and restored 'a meaningful contact with the natural world, in which it is possible for children to feel earth, to touch wild flowers, to hear birds sing and to observe the passing of the seasons'. Additionally, they were 'an opportunity for children and adults to participate in the making of their external environment.' Ruff's findings, also published in 1979, were entitled *Holland and the Ecological Landscapes* (Ruff, 1979).

These publications represent an increasing environmental awareness, first dramatically addressed by Rachel Carson in *Silent Spring* (1962), later in the report of the Club of Rome, *The Limits of Growth* (1972) and translated within a broader context and for professionals, including landscape architects by Max Nicholson who viewed the development during the late 1960s as an environmental revolution (Nicholson, 1970). They would have inspired Gilbert the ecologist who had studied botany and carried on with PhD research on 'Biological Indicators of Air Pollution' (1968) that investigated different pollution levels of sulphur and fluoride on lichens and bryophytes. This pioneering work was adapted by him for teaching in schools, while it was used to develop the Hawksworth and Rose scale, a qualitative scale for measuring sulphur dioxide air pollution (Hawksworth, & Rose, 1970). Joining the newly founded Department of Landscape Architecture at the University of Sheffield in January 1970, Gilbert was the first ecologist to be appointed in a lecturer's position within a landscape architecture course. This Department had been initiated by Granada Television in order to improve the image of the north of England, which had suffered due to opencast coal mining and dereliction of old industries. As a result, Arnold Weddle, a landscape architect with experience in large scale land reclamation, was appointed professor; and Susan Cornwell, a horticulturalist and landscape designer with a PhD on 'Anthracite mining spoils as media for plant growth' (1966), was appointed lecturer (Woudstra, 2010).

The urban common: Arriving in Sheffield on 1st January 1970, with his field skills Gilbert was a notable addition to the team, able to convey his ideas and observations in succinct papers, and while he continued his interests in natural history, particularly lichens, he soon made landscape architecture his own, particularly since he noted the general lack of research in the profession. There was for example little knowledge about ecological engineering and the re-creation of plant communities, and he emphasised the need for observation and record keeping. He redefined the role of the landscape architect 'as an applied ecologist who must design changes in landscape to create complexity and integrate other forms of life with human activity.' He also saw it as a role for the profession to prevent 'fragmentation of the natural scene' and emphasised the need of large areas linked together 'for the survival and movement of many forms of life' (Gilbert, & Moggridge, 1979).

While his first job had been as a deputy warden at Malham Tarn in the Yorkshire Dales National Park, he had changed this in 1963 for the polluted environment of Newcastle, where he became a demonstrator at the university, enabling him to observe the degrees of pollution stress on lichens. The other experience gained here and when he moved to Sheffield in 1970, was the decline of the industries and increasing dereliction, which to most people was interpreted as negative, as waste land, or later brownfield land. Yet Gilbert recognized that the successional relationship, regional variation and edaphic influences in these areas and the ecological richness far exceeded those of the surrounding countryside. So instead of seeing this as a negative, he celebrated and described these urban wastelands as exciting areas in the urban jungle of the city, naming them urban commons. His concept of the urban common included officially designated commons, such as Town Moor, Newcastle, and Ilkley Moor. But moreover the extensive network of waste ground, demolition sites and vacant plots in industrial cities that had been spontaneously colonised by vegetation, constituted the unofficial urban commons. They were a major feature in former industrial cities and he defined them as places where the public have access; they were generally owned by local authorities but saw a range of flexible and informal land uses that were actively discouraged in traditional parks and open spaces.

The Ecology of Urban Habitats (1989) Gilbert's first book on the topic concentrated 'on what is already there', the various habitats of the city. From his ecological stance he envisioned three urban landscape types that were complementary to each other and provided far richer variety than if only two were present. Like in his re-use of the term 'urban common', he once again adapted the meaning of existing words to provide new meaning. The gardenesque (an early nineteenth century term that defined an emphasis on display of horticultural rarities) was given a broader meaning: 'where biological elements can function only under continuous management'. The technological 'where the biological landscape has been substantially replaced by artificial substitutes' and the ecological 'where natural elements are allowed to function in a natural manner'. Thus discussion followed not only urban commons, but also industrial areas, railways, roads, city centres, city parks, allotments, cemeteries, rivers etc., and woodland. While this book was intended for the British market its wide well-informed scope also struck a note in Germany as it addressed issues more coherently than Herbert Sukopp's first book, *Städtische Ökologie* (1980), which was more or less a series of lecture notes, not too well produced and intended primarily to his students and Berliners more generally. This appears to be the reason why it was translated (Starfinger, 2019). Gilbert's second book *Habitat Creation and Repair* (1998) not only provided a practical guide but also discussed ethics and principles. These books show that he had a good understanding of international trends, with lessons also drawn from European examples.

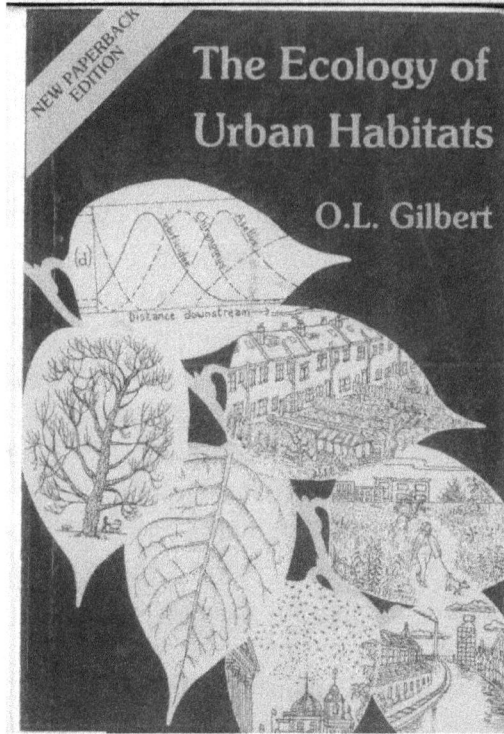

Figure 1: Oliver Gilbert's first book on urban ecology, *The Ecology of Urban Habitats* (1989) introduced the concept of the 'urban common' -for everyone and everything, in contravention with contemporary politics that spoke despairingly of brownfield land, waste land and derelict land

Continental European influences

Dutch 'new nature': The Netherlands has long been admired for its ecological approaches, as initiated first by Jacobus P. Thijsse (1865-1945) and Eli Heimans (1861-1914), both teachers, concerned with the degradation of the natural environment. In educating their pupils they selected local habitats to enable them to explain ecological principles, rather than doing this from exotic textbook examples. This could be seen to have been encouraged through the work of Frederik W. van Eeden (1829-1901), who had provided popular scientific accounts of the flora of different habitats in the region, in a series of botanical walks (Van Eeden, 1886). Heimans and Thijsse later produced individual textbooks on various habitats, having first used an urban park, Sarphatipark in Amsterdam, as an example of how an annual teaching programme might be devised using life material from there. Their concept was later extended to so-named 'instructive gardens' or 'heemparks' as they later became known (Woudstra, 1997).

The first instructive garden was Thijsse's Hof, Bloemendaal (1925) that was transformed from a potato field into a garden that displayed the vegetation of the inner dune area of North Holland, and was used for educational purposes. So, this promoted native flora for educational purposes. Within the context of the Dutch city -they were densely built up, and having been neutral during the First War, there were no derelict sites, so no ruderal plants. Nor would there – at a time when horses were still a regular feature – have been opportunity for natural regeneration elsewhere, i.e. outside parks and gardens (Woudstra, 2004).

Figure 2: In 1925 Thijsse's Hof, Bloemendaal was the first instructive garden, later referred to as 'heem'park, created from a former potato field intended to display the vegetation of the inner dune area of the province of North Holland (photograph: Jan Woudstra, 1993)

Thijsse's approach sparked a significant following and various such instructive gardens followed; e.g. the Scientific Garden, Zuiderpark, The Hague (1935); De Heimanshof, Vierhouten (1935); De Braak (1939) and Jac.P. Thijssepark (1940), both in Amstelveen and which gained international renown. Key figures of the early days of this new type of gardens were Cees Sipkes (1895-1989), the owner of a native plant nursery who laid out Thijsse's Hof; and Chris P. Broerse (1902-1995) and Jacobus [Koos] Landwehr (1911-1996), successive heads of parks of Amstelveen. Their aim was to create an attractive living environment inspired by local landscapes, while promoting natural history as a popular science. It was particularly Landwehr who developed and refined different maintenance techniques, and strongly argued for the need for such parks and park-like landscapes as an antidote to urbanisation, for the happiness and well-being of mankind (Galjaard, & Koningen, 2002; Landwehr, & Sipkes, 1974).

The main concern within these new parks was that they linked traditional landscapes with phytogeographical districts identified with these becoming the models for urban areas. Phytogeography became a scientific preoccupation with Victor Westhoff in 1942 classifying the vegetation of the Netherlands in plant communities (Westhoff *et al.*, 1942), with this being used in 1959 by Chris van Leeuwen and Henk Doing Kraft into guidelines for planting based on ecological principles, concerned mainly with woodland and countryside planting (Van Leeuwen, Doing Kraft, 1959). Ger Londo translated this to the smaller scale to 'nature gardens and parks' in 1977, in a format that encouraged extensive use by individuals for private, and groups for community gardens (Londo, 1979).

By this stage the ethical basis of these principles had been questioned by the artist and teacher Louis le Roy (1924-2012). He questioned contemporary attitudes towards the environment; inconsiderate interventions in ecological systems, through development, rationalisation, use of chemicals and fertilisers, which together destroyed the balance. Considering man as a product of nature and culture he also questioned whether conventional parks provided basic human needs, and argued that they should involve participation as a possibility for expression of creativity. He thus also rejected conventional heemparks. So, man in his eyes was a facilitator for the natural processes within the city, which he saw as an oasis, in contrast to surrounding monocultures of large-scale agriculture (Le Roy, 1973)

He considered that these two, the oasis of the city and large scale monoculture, should be separated from each other by a buffer area consisting of four elements: diverse artificial mounds that completely surrounded monocultures; small-scale agricultural areas; allotment areas and small scale buildings. This then was seen to create interconnected natural systems between cities that also enveloped nature reserves. The buffer zones were planted with a variety of vegetation, not just natives, but also exotics and cultivars as an expression of human endeavour. There would be no need to do any weeding because 'nature' orders itself, and the only maintenance required was the occasional removal of trees when the vegetation gets too dense (Le Roy, 1973, pp.135-7). Thus in Le Roy's vision the urban ecosystem of which the citizens were a part, was enriched by exotics with everything dependent on the laws of nature.

Le Roy's ideas heralded a particular resonance in the libertarian years of the late 1960s, but they also helped to popularize the debate and encouraged out of the box responses. Le Roy's project at the Kennedylaan, Heerenveen, that transformed a strip of grass and trees into a varied mound-system, was influential in rethinking landscapes for housing. Thijsse disciples Henk J. Bos (1921-2009) (head of parks Den Haag 1974-84) and J.L. Mol reported on some of the developments during the 1970s, where one housing area in Delft provided a hybrid method between methods used in traditional heemparks, versus the residential participation encouraged by Le Roy (Bos, & Mol, 1979). Thus, The Netherlands provided a rich set of methodologies which were also explored by the Englishman

Allan Ruff who provided case studies in urban ecology (Ruff, 1979), while Michael Hough has continued to explore the development of the Gillis development in Delft, noting the ups and downs of ecological processes and resident participation (Hough, 2004).

Figure 3: Louis le Roy envisaged buffer areas between large scale agriculture and the city to create havens for biodiversity and creativity. Eco-cathedral, Mildam (photograph: Jan Woudstra, 2014)

Another strong influence was the horticultural scientist Piet Zonderwijk (1924-2006), who concerned about the indiscriminate use of chemicals, concentrated his studies on the vegetation in road verges and along railway lines. He explored their significance and saw them as flowery ribbons through the landscape, developing methodologies to enrich them for flora and fauna by reducing soil fertility. It was through his student Arie Koster (1945 -) that these methods were translated to greenspace management within cities providing both theoretical and practical directions on more natural approaches intended for local authorities (Koster, & Claringbould, 1991). He emphasized that these were on an ecological basis and contributed to a healthy society by providing direct contact with nature.

A loss of nature and biodiversity had been the main concern for the Dutch government, which in 1990 established an Ecological Framework for the whole country, nowadays also referred to as Nature Network Netherlands. This recognized so-called character areas, nature development areas, and connecting zones, and it was the intention to link various areas in order to provide suitable habitats for species. The linking creates larger regions where environmental conditions and water levels can be specially adapted to particular conditions, and where it is possible to rely on natural processes to create dynamism and variety (https://www.groeneruimte.nl/dossiers/ehs/home.html).

This government-sponsored project dealt with the countryside only, leaving it to local authorities to develop their own ecological framework for urban areas.

The development of the concept of the ecological city was greatly stimulated by the urban planner Sybrand Tjallingii (1941-) who developed the ecopolis model for the sustainable city. This approach proposed strategies for ecologically sound urban development with respect to social, spatial, and ecological criteria, with policies from local to international levels. The proposed framework was captured in three key themes: the responsible use of resources and raw materials; the urban ecosystem as a living system that contributes a healthy environment; and a city for the people, belonging to the people, therefore with participation of citizens and residents (Tjallingii, 1995).

The emerging idea of an 'ecology of cities', conceptualised in the ecopolis, encouraged the foundation of the Dutch Platform of Urban Ecology in 1989. Over time this broadened to the concept of urban ecology from nature in the city of the 1970s to that being concerned with natural capital and the provision of ecosystem services in order to facilitate sustainability, with an emerging profession of urban ecologists that provides an intermediary between the various disciplines operating in the city and its residents *(Groen,* 2016). The widening of remit is also visible in the parks and gardens and the way they were presented; whereas in 1992 in providing a guide to various projects, these were still narrowly defined as *'heemtuinen'*, the term used by Heimans and Thijsse; in 2003 the guide was retitled 'nature-rich' parks and gardens. It included a wider remit, including the gardens following the Le Roy model. The cultural philosopher Rob Leopold explained that in contrast to post-modern critics of the 'nature movement' the Dutch heempark tradition has an open, dynamic and cosmopolitan character. This meant a freedom of development, for plant, animal and man, which automatically created large differentiations, and spontaneous, free interconnections. He saw this as representing Thijsse's dictum 'unconcerned' as continuing to retain currency today (Leopold, 2003).

These developments took place in the context of changing perceptions of nature generally; during the 1970s the Oostvaarderplassen had emerged as a low lying area within one of the large newly created polders, which without interference quickly developed into one of the richest nature reserves within Europe. In the highly urbanized and densely developed context of The Netherlands it showed the regenerative power of nature, and the potential for other areas to be enriched by similar processes. While the Oostvaardersplassen became an experiment in ecological management, lessons and inspiration gained here served as the basis for a prizewinning competition entry for the future of the area of the main rivers. Instead of protecting the area with ever higher dikes, the proposal was to remove more recent defence works and enable natural processes to be restored. The low lying areas here had been used by agriculture and for brick factories (as well as sand and gravel quarries), with the competition entry suggesting that while the latter might be continued the former ought to be curtailed so new materials might be deposited during high tides (De Bruin *et al.*, 1987). Frans Vera, one of the authors of the winning entry later expanded his ideas by exploring 'nature development' in the context of grazing ecology, in a book that challenged older conceptions of the history and making of the European landscape. The lessons learned here were also absorbed within urban ecology, with cattle and sheep used to create dynamic vegetation patterns (Vera, 2000).

Urban fallow land in Germany: When Herbert Sukopp (1930-), the 'father of urban ecology' in Germany, wrote his early history of urban ecology in 2002 he commenced this with an explanation of the ruderal flora found on castles and ruins, recorded since the seventeenth century (Sukopp, 2002). This was a reference to the vegetation of the rubble heaps of Berlin, which he had studied after World War II. By doing this he provided a neutral basis and convenient starting date and focus of urban ecology. But like in The Netherlands there had been an ecological tradition since the nineteenth century, culminating in a small people's park in Berlin Charlottenburg, named Sachsenplatz (later Brixplatz) that was planted according to ecological principles and contained the various vegetation types of the Brandenburg area. It was planted in 1913 by the newly appointed director of parks, Erwin Barth (1880-1933), who envisaged this as a school garden and also contained a biological garden with familiar plants and economic crops.

While Barth committed suicide at the rise of National Socialism, naturalistic landscape design was brought to the forefront of the political agenda as the Blood and Soil ideology assumed a close relationship between the Nordic race and the land. This mainly manifested itself in the new German territories -the countryside in Poland and Russia- by the landscape architect Heinrich Wiepking-Jürgensmann, and in the design of the new motorways by the landscape architect Alwin Seifert and the ecologist Reinhold Tüxen (1899-1980). The latter was also involved in the creation of a new public park, Annateich in Hanover (1936), later named Hermann Löns Park after the folkish author who popularised the north German heath. This park reproduced the plant associations of the region, something that was absorbed by the Nazi philosophy more generally in order to retain racial purity, translated in planting terms by promoting native plants in regional associations, and the avoidance of exotics (Barth, 1980).

Figure 4: In 1913 Erwin Barth laid out Sachsenplatz (later Brixplatz), planted according to ecological principles containing the various vegetation types of the Brandenburg area (photograph: Jan Woudstra, 2016)

It is clear that it would be better for a budding ecologist, such as Sukopp, to avoid such connotations and forge a new direction which emerged on his doorstep on the rubble of war struck Berlin. As in other German cities, large areas had been bombed with the rubble creating a new type of habitat that offered warmer and drier conditions for both flora and fauna. As it was colonized by vegetation it became the object of study, as it had done in Britain where E.J. Salisbury published on the flora of bombed sites in 1943, and R.S.R. Fitter included a section in *London's Natural History* (1945) (Woudstra, 2004). While this was also of interest to botanists in Germany, it was not seriously studied until travel restrictions were imposed on citizens in West Berlin in 1952, and particularly after the erection of the Berlin Wall in 1961. It was Sukopp who emerged as a leading figure of these studies and revealed the rich communities, applying Tüxen-type methodologies of plant sociology in order to characterize them. Using the term 'urban vegetation' to describe the various 'types of spontaneously occurring and cultivated vegetation in cities', the pioneering study in 1956 by H. Scholz on the ruderal vegetation in Berlin (Sukopp, 2002, p.380) was followed in 1957 with an inventory of new plants found in the region by Sukopp (Lachmund, 2012, p.53).

Over time as rubble was removed to more permanent locations it continued to provide a resource for new studies, and until the mid 1980s when redevelopment became gradually more prolific, greatly hastened after the fall of the Wall in 1989, they were increasingly valued by ecologists, who saw these areas as a prototype of an urban ecosystem. Here nature was largely determined by man-made conditions. Rather than the English word 'wasteland' to determine them they were referred to as *Brachen* or *Brachland*, 'fallow land', as in agriculture, a much more positive term. These fallow areas were of a similar character to the urban commons described by Gilbert. A remaining such area, the Dörnbergdreieck was threatened with redevelopment in the mid 1980s and vehemently defended by ecologists for the rich biotope it provided, even though being described as follows:

> *'Quite typically for such sites, it provided a space for residents to walk dogs and for neighborhood children to play and, from time to time, a space for circus owners to graze their animals. For some years, a snack bar was located at the edge of the area. During the night, it turned into a place for homeless people to sleep as well as a gathering ground for prostitutes and their clients. Trash, which could be found frequently under the trees and bushes, created a weird image of urban decay.'*
> (Lachmund, 2003)

By this time Sukopp's ecological interests had developed into a mission; he had defined urban ecology as being synonymous with sustainable cities, and saw ecology as a way 'to monitor and control the effects of human land use on urban nature and thereby create a basis for more rational planning of future cities' (Lachmund, 2012). Or in his own words, he saw ecology at the centre of environmental discussion because of the 'obviously inadequate adaptation of *human* societies to their surroundings'. As a result there was a greater urgency for 'ecological statements about the relationship between our society and its environment, based on the knowledge of the natural living conditions' (Sukopp, Hejny, & Kowarik, 1990). This was also the basis for his suggested ten principles for the protection of ecotopes and species in city development policies, which included: the need for ecological zoning in urban areas; preventing all avoidable intervention; conservation and care of all natural areas in cities; maintaining historical continuity of management; maintaining local distinctiveness; maintaining different land use intensity; maintaining larger open spaces; linking open spaces into a network; maintaining diversity; and incorporating buildings as part of ecosystems (Sukopp, & Werner, 1982).

Figure 5: The urban vegetation of the *Brachen, Brachland* or 'fallow land' in Berlin includes a wide range of exotics, including tree of heaven *(Ailanthus altissima)* here seen at a site that celebrates the ruderal aesthetic next to the Philharmonie (photograph: Jan Woudstra, 2017)

Natur-Park Südgelände: These were all principles that could be followed in the unique circumstances in West Berlin, which till reunification had only seen limited development, with abandoned sites contributing to social functions and ecosystem services, providing the city with its unique character. Yet after 1989 many of these sites were built over. However one site that was preserved was the Schöneberger Südgelände, an area of some 18 hectares of a former railyard, which had been abandoned after the war and had gradually become overgrown with woodland consisting largely of birch *(Betula pendula)* and false acacia *(Robinia pseudoacacia).* This wilderness had a rich herbaceous flora with various rare species, particularly in more open areas which were covered by dry grassland. It was also rich in wildlife. When in the early 1980s this area had been proposed for a new railway station, there had been strong local protests and the founding of an organisation that ultimately managed to achieve legal protection for the area. The area was to become a nature park that balanced conservation requirements with the need to provide access, with proposals being developed by ÖkoCan & Planland, led by Ingo Kowarik (1955-), a former student and successor of Sukopp. This foresaw continued natural growth in some areas, while in others openness was retained through maintenance, which also exposed the evidence of the former railways. A new path network provided access for those who otherwise would never had access to this type of site and thus enable them to experience the clearings, groves and 'wild woods' here (Kowarik, & Langer, 2005).

Landschaftspark Duisburg-Nord: What is perhaps most remarkable about the Südgelände project, opened in 2000 - besides the fact that it had a nature conservation designation- is that it celebrates ruderal vegetation and succession. This is also explored in another key project, Landschaftspark Duisburg-Nord, on the site of the large Thyssen ironworks, made redundant in 1985. With the regional authority revisioning the area as a modern metropolitan area the 1988 international building exhibition IBA Emscher Park was organized there in order to facilitate a conceptual restructuring of some 800 square kilometres in view of a more general industrial decline (https://www.open-iba.de/en/geschichte/1989-1999-iba-emscher-park/). The 200 hectares of the redundant ironworks was subject to a design competition won in 1991 by Peter Latz and Partners. The original landscape had been completely transformed by industrial processes and was no longer discernible and cut up by roads, railways and fences. Rather than clearing the area of waste and pollution, the status quo was accepted as a basis for regeneration; the more interesting structures and infrastructure were retained and given new purposes. The concept of the landscape park was introduced to emphasise the importance to provide new links.

Figure 6: Natur-Park Südgelände doubles as a public park and nature reserve: it is a former railyard, abandoned after the war which had gradually become overgrown with woodland consisting largely of birch (*Betula pendula*) and false acacia (*Robinia pseudoacacia*) (photograph: Laurence Pattacini, 2016).

Within this concept vegetation established by natural regeneration in various stages was seen as 'characteristic for the abandoned industrial areas' there, as a 'symbol of the post-industrial landscape' and was considered the structural element 'signalling the free and open use of areas'. Stands of birch trees on the former coke plant were a particular feature of the old slag heaps. The project foresaw retention of 'all stages of colonisation' through extensive management techniques, while creating small gardens as 'the first signs of the revival of the terrain, the taking possession of the area by human action.' In addition to other look-out gardens that provided wide views over the works and the surrounding area, they were intended as 'symbols' for smaller areas 'to awaken memories, to provoke comparisons and to make the vegetation comprehensible'. Latz saw this landscape as a basis for re-education of local people and the gardens as a basis for healing of the community through active cooperation in construction and maintenance. He envisioned special educational programmes imparting 'knowledge and skills for dealing with the vegetation typical for industrial fallow land' (Latz, 1992). It is clear that Latz thought it necessary to introduce these gardens to evoke a more general appreciation for the surrounding vegetation and create a greater understanding of the natural processes of succession, since it commonly continues to be associated with dereliction.

Preserving natural vegetation in urban areas in Sweden: Since there was no derelict land in Scandinavia, urban ecology was taken in a slightly different direction. The landscape architect Per Friberg (1920-2014), who contributed a chapter to Laurie's *Nature in Cities,* noted that the Scandinavian capitals, each in their own way, were examples of 'relationships of nature in cities'. He summed this up by quoting verbatim Geoffrey and Susan Jellicoe's description of Stockholm, who noted 'the city as a total landscape', which had benefitted from the fact that the country had not had an industrial revolution 'to blight planning and depress public standards'. The 'formidable natural landscape... was such as to enforce its character upon the urban form' of Stockholm. Green fingers 'aided by natural topography' penetrated into the city; high-rise flats had been accepted here; and 'green landscape' was 'introduced into the streets themselves' (Jellicoe, 1975; Laurie, 1979).

In Stockholm, as in other Scandinavian countries, there had been concerns about how to integrate 'ecology in planning in general and about how it can be realized in practice in the different steps of the urbanization process.' Rather than applying themselves to horticulture the new objective for parks departments was to preserve 'natural resources and to use these resources on an ecological basis in the physical planning of the total landscape'. Thus they had also responsibility for nature conservation, recreation, etc. and there was a need to align the physical planning process so as to be able to fully recognize the benefits to physical and psychological health of citizens. In order to fully understand the range of needs there were various studies of urban open spaces that investigated 'vegetation in residential areas, its appearance and use, how it satisfies the requirements of those who live with it, how it provides shelter from wind and sun and other important dimensions to the outdoor environment.'

With increasing environmental and economic concerns, one research project investigated the use of 'natural existing vegetation' during development. Intended to run over a fifteen-year period it attempted to 'elucidate the relationships between the original vegetation, the site factors, development density, the wear caused by inhabitants and the residual vegetation.' There were no instances in Scandinavia where 'the extent to which different types of vegetation and soil adapt to changed conditions in development areas, and also the features of the sites which are changed and the way these changes affect vegetation.' Järvafältet, an area proposed for development northwest of Stockholm was selected as an initial case study area, with the vegetation being surveyed prior to the project and monitored annually subsequently. The aim was to develop an understanding of how plant communities evolve and be able to provide specifications for the conservation of the natural vegetation. This was seen as a collaborative process with the residential community (Friberg, 1979, pp 334-7).

IBM Swedish Headquarters, Kista, Uppland: While initial studies established that comparisons between various sites were difficult requiring a series of further studies, one of the projects that took the concern of the existing vegetation as a starting point was the design for the IBM Headquarters in Kista, north of Stockholm (1972-6) (Andersson, 2006). The site was an area of existing pine forest with patches of heather on the thinner soils. The initial design for the area by architects Carl Nyren and Bengt Lindroos envisioned an extensive two-storey building as well as a parking garage, requiring felling of most of the trees. However, having established the qualities of the site, landscape architects Söderblom and Palm suggested an approach that would preserve the existing vegetation for the benefit of the employees and provide a unique image for the site (Florgård, 2010). This convinced the client to ask for the building to be redesigned to a narrow six-storey building that followed the contours and was integrated with the woodland. Construction of the building was confined through narrow tracks located mostly on those of proposed as permanent ways, and other areas where vegetation was temporarily removed -literally rolled up- to be replaced there after completion of the works. The approach meant that all employees would have the experience of 'untouched nature' from their office windows (Nilsson, 1996).

Figure 7: The IBM Swedish Headquarters, Kista, Uppland, were redesigned in order to preserve the existing forest in such a way that all employees would have the experience of 'untouched nature' from their office windows (photograph: Jan Woudstra, 1997).

'Nature-like open spaces' in Sweden: In 1979, Friberg still quotes G.E. Kidder Smith's 1961 description of the Swedish approach through that of the Stockholm parks as 'not merely a collection of extraordinary green fingers tying the outlying countryside to the very centre of town; they are part of the Swedish concept of life- a concept that demands contact with the freedom of nature in order to offset the indoor restrictions of man.' By that stage, however, things had changed in many parts of Sweden as observed by the younger generation of landscape architects, such as Roland Gustavsson, employed at the Agricultural University in Alnarp. He noted how from the mid-1950s and particularly in the 1960s and 1970s Swedish landscape design had entered a 'dark period' where landscape in new housing developments had become increasingly 'simple', a formulaic grass and trees with no amenities included, nor interest for wildlife. Additionally, these spaces had been designed for sunny days only, with no consideration for providing shelter from wind or rain. Any ornamental plantings were considered unsuitable for play 'if their essential qualities are to be preserved' and they were expensive to maintain. In the light of increasing environmental interest in the early 1980s, where a national newspaper spoke of a 'Green Revolution', a new approach was required. In this the rationale for change was aided by the fact that some 75% of open spaces in urban areas had been created within the past 25 to 30 years, providing wonderful opportunities for the next generation to provide a richer content and articulation of spaces.

Much of the research however concentrated on the content, not the form; there were demands that vegetation should have both closed and open rooms and that it should be 'free-growing' and increase environmental interest. Nature had traditionally been a model for Swedish garden design, which had dealt with issues at a smaller scale, for example concentrating on the 'field layer', i.e. flowering meadows, while the nature of new development required a change of scale. Earlier housing developments which had taken "nature as an approach" were located in forested regions, whereas most of the new ones were on agricultural land. These required frameworks of 'nature-like plantations' in order to create 'nature-like spaces', with a mixture of trees and shrubs rather than uniform planting blocks, or ornamental plantings of the previous generation.

'Nature-like plantations' had been the subject of a 1977 conference, which started off a process that continued into a research project administered by Gustavsson starting in 1980 that aimed to establish 'the main structures of more free-growing biotopes', their development, how they were managed and maintained, and also how plantings of the 1960s and '70s might be transformed. This gave rise to different experiments that looked at establishment of new planting, mainly at technical aspects, and involved Helsingborg parks department, contractors and landscape architects, as well as experiments at the University of Agricultural Sciences (Gustavvson, 1982). Rather than nature-like plantations this has later evolved into the notion of urban forestry and has been taken quite seriously in the Nordic countries generally (Konijnendijk, 2007).

Conclusions: This paper highlights Gilbert's position as an urban ecologist, as someone who responded to contemporary environmental issues with independent and academically argued views. He worked within the best British naturalist tradition, assimilating the latest scientific information providing easily digestible narratives that were succinct and practical. In exploring the post-industrial landscapes of northern England, he brought attention to the distinct wildlife and plants by valuing what was there and by considering habitat management or creation. The resulting textbooks included the first one in Britain in a field that is now generally known as urban ecology. Gilbert's concepts were developed in parallel with those emerging elsewhere and this chapter reviews developments in a number of west European countries to provide an idea of these various approaches.

Urban ecology is interpreted differently in different countries; in Britain and Germany being concerned with sites left derelict after industries declined. In Sweden it is concerned with retention of existing vegetation, while in The Netherlands it is about creating new environments using natural processes, new nature. In all countries urban ecology nowadays incorporates examples of these various types, inspired by each other. Moreover, it is equated with sustainability, with sustainable cities, and it is by articulating the theory and practice of those that Gilbert's legacy is to be found. There is now a much better acceptance of non-native species and the urban ruderal communities they help to compose. This has assisted, over the past decade or so, to open up and legitimise whole new fields of study into 'novel ecosystems' and 'recombinant plant communities'.

Acknowledgments: Nigel Dunnett was helpful in initial conversations and making additional suggestions. Ross Cameron furnished further comments.

References:

Andersson, T. (2006) *IBM Headquarters*. In: Taylor, P. (ed.) *The Oxford Companion to the Garden*. Oxford University Press Oxford.

Barth, J. (1980) Erwin Barth's Sachsenplatz in Berlin. *Garten und Landschaft*, **11**, 931-6.

Bos, H.J., & Mol, J.L. (1979) The Dutch example: native planting in Holland', In Laurie, I.C. (ed.), *Nature in Cities: The natural environment in the design and development of urban green space*. John Wiley, Chichester, 393-416

de Bruin, D., Hamhuis, D., van Nieuwenhuijze, L., Overmars, W., Sijmonds, D., & Vera, F. (1978) *Ooievaar: De toekomst van het rivierengebied*. Stichting Gelderse Milieufederatie, Arnhem.

Carson, R. (1963) *Silent Spring*. Hamish Hamilton, London.

Eeden, F.W. van (1886) *Onkruid: Botanische wandelingen* (1886; new edition), Schuyt, Haarlem.

Fitter, R.S.R. (1945) *London's Natural History*. Collins, London.

Florgård, C. (2010) *Integration of natural vegetation in urban design information, personal determination and commitment.*

In: Müller, N., Werner, P., & Kelcey, J.G. (eds) *Urban biodiversity and Design*. Blackwell, London, 479-496 (489).

Friberg, P. (1979) *The parklands of Scandinavian cities*. In: Laurie I.C. (ed.), *Nature in Cities: The natural environment in the design and development of urban green space*. John Wiley, Chichester, 327-349 (334-7).

Galjaard, B., & Koningen, H. (2002) *Amstelveen in het Groen: 75 jaar Amstelveense parken en plantsoenen*. Schuyt, Haarlem.

Gilbert, O.L. (1989) *The Ecology of Urban Habitats*. Chapman and Hall, London.

Gilbert, O.L., & Moggridge, H. (1974) An ecologist's view of landscape architecture. *Landscape Design,* **No.106**, 13.

Gilbert, O.L., & Anderson, P. (1998) *Habitat Creation and Repair*. Oxford University Press, Oxford.

Groen, V. (2016), special issue *'25 jaar stadsecologie'*, WUR, **72** (6)

Gustavsson, R. (1982) Nature-like parks and open spaces in housing areas in Sweden - from the view of an applied research project. In: Ruff, A.R., & Tregay, R. (eds) (1982) *An Ecological Approach to Urban Landscape Design*. (Occasional Paper No.8), University of Manchester, Manchester, 119-134.

Hawksworth, D.L., & Rose, F. (1970) Qualitative scale for estimating sulphur dioxide air pollution in England and Wales using epiphytic lichens. *Nature,* **227/5254**, 145-9.

Hough, M. (1995, 2004) *Cities and Natural Process: A basis for sustainability*. Routledge, London, 103-7.

https://www.groeneruimte.nl/dossiers/ehs/home.html   , accessed June 2019

https://www.open-iba.de/en/geschichte/1989-1999-iba-emscher-park/, accessed 8 June 2019

Jellicoe, G., & Jellicoe, S. (1975) *The Landscape of Man: Shaping the environment from prehistory to the present* day. Thames and Hudson, London, 301; see Laurie, 348-9

Konijnendijk, C.C. *et al.* (2007) Assessment of urban forestry research and research needs in Nordic and Baltic countries. *Urban Forestry and Urban Greening*, **6**, 297-309.

Koster, A., & Claringbould, M. (1991) *Natuurlijker Groenbeheer in Nederlandse Gemeenten*. Vereniging Nederlandse Gemeenten, The Hague.

Kowarik, I., & Langer, A. (2005) Natur-Park Südgelände: linking conservation and recreation in an abandoned railyard in Berlin. In: Kowarik, I., & Körner, S. (eds), *Wild Urban Woodland: New perspectives for urban forestry*. Springer, Berlin, 287-299.

Lachmund, J. (2003) Exploring the City of Rubble: Botanical fieldwork in bombed cities in Germany after World War II. *OSIRIS,* 2nd Ser., **Vol. 18**, 234-254 (235).

Lachmund, J. (2012) *Greening Berlin: The co-production of science, politics and urban nature*. MIT, Cambridge, **53**, 48

Landwehr, J., & Sipkes, C. (1974) *Wildeplantentuinen*. IVN, Amsterdam, 68-70.

Latz, P. (1992) Landschaftspark Duisburg-Nord..., *Anthos*, **31**, 27-33. (English translation corrected in places).

Laurie, I.C. (1979) *Nature in Cities: The natural environment in the design and development of urban green space*. John Wiley, Chichester, xiii-xiv.

Leeuwen, C. van, & Kraft, H.D. (1959) *Landschap en Beplanting in Nederland: Richtlijnen voor de soortenkeuze bij beplantingen op vegetatiekundige grondslag*. Veenman, Wageningen.

Leopold, R. (2003) Oase: destillaat, proefplot en toekomstvisie. In: van Lier, M., & Leufgen, W. (eds) *Oasegids: Natuurrijke parken en tuinen in Nederland en Vlaanderen*. Beuningen, Oase, 216-8.

Londo, G. (1977) *Natuurtuinen en – parken: Aanleg en onderhoud*. Thieme, Zutphen.

Nicholson, M. (1970) *The Environmental Revolution: A guide for the new masters of the world*. Hodder and Stoughton, London, 275.

Nilsson, K. (1979) Industry vs. landscape: landscape planning and the design of industrial facilities. *Nordisk Arkitekturforskning*, **4**, 37-50.

Roy, L.G. le (1973) *Natuur uitschakelen: Natuur inschakelen*. Amkh- Hermes, Deventer, 135-7.

Ruff, A.R. (1979) *Holland and the Ecological Landscapes: A study of recent developments in the approach to urban landscape*. Deanwater, Stockport.

Starfinger, U. (2019) translator of *Städtische Ökosysteme* (1994, Ulmer, Stuttgart), pers. comm., 7th June 2019.

Sukopp, H., & Werner, P. (1982) *Nature in Cities: A report and review of studies and experiments concerning ecology, wildlife and nature conservation in urban and suburban areas*. Council of Europe, Strasbourg, 42-3 (principles transliterated).

Sukopp, H., Hejny, S., & Kowarik I. (1990) *Urban Ecology: Plants and plant communities in urban environments*. SPB Academic Publishing, The Hague, 1.

Sukopp, H. (2002) On the early history of urban ecology in Europe. *Preslia, Praha,* **74**, 373-393 (380).

Tjallingii, S.P. (1995) *Ecopolis: Strategies for ecologically sound urban development*. Backhuys, Leiden, 9-10.

Vera, F.W.M. (2000) *Grazing Ecology and Forest History*. CABI Wallingford, Oxon.

Westhoff, V., Dijk, J.W., & Passchier, H. (1942) *Overzicht der Plantengemeenschappen in Nederland*. Breughel, Amsterdam.

Woudstra, J. (1997) *Jacobus P. Thijsse's influence on Dutch landscape architecture*. In: Wolschke-Bulmann, J. (ed.) (1997) *Nature and Ideology: Natural garden design in the twentieth century*. Dumbarton Oaks Colloquium on the History of Landscape Architecture, XVIII, Dumbarton Oaks, Washington D.C., 155- 185.

Woudstra, J. (2010) The "Sheffield Method" and the first Department of Landscape Architecture in Great Britain. *Garden History,* **38** (2), 242-266.

Woudstra, J. (2018) Designing the garden of Geddes: The master gardener and the profession of landscape architecture. *Landscape and Urban Planning,* **178** (2018), 198-207.

Woudstra, J. (2004) *The changing nature of ecology: a history of ecological planting (1800-1980)*. In: Dunnett, N. & Hitchmough, J. (eds) *The Dynamic Landscape: Design, Ecology and Management of Naturalistic Urban Planting*. Spon, London and New York, 23-57.

Zonderwijk, P. (1979) *De Bonte Berm: De rijke flora en fauna langs onze wegen*. Zomer en Keuning, Ede.

Chapter 11 Summary and Conclusions

Ian D. Rotherham

Introduction: In an obituary in *The Independent*, Peter Marren described how:

'Oliver Gilbert was, in his own words, a lichen hunter. His pioneering work on these humble plants as indicators of air pollution and on the lichen flora of remote and unexpected places helped create a healthy climate of field study and exploration for a whole generation of apprentice lichenologists. He was also one of the leading urban ecologists who studied and promoted the hidden wildlife jungle in and around towns and cities.'

One characteristic of Oliver's enthusiasms was an almost unrivalled focus on the task in hand. In pursuit of rare terrestrial lichens in Cornwall for example, he described how crawling on hands and knees with hand-lens at the ready around the naval airbase on the Lizard he made his way through a small gap in the perimeter fencing. This was quickly followed by his arrest by the security staff on high alert for terrorist activists. He was held for several hours until he managed to get a message from someone quite senior to vouch for him and confirm that it was 'only Oliver and he is a lichen enthusiast – not a threat to national security'! A similar incident was again a hands-and-knees episode as he made his way through dense woodland and failed to spot a tree wasp nest hanging low from a branch. With his focus on the ground he managed to head-butt a now irate nest of wasps and his error became obvious even to Oliver.

One of Oliver's former students described to me how on an urban fieldtrip in search of lichens he discovered a particularly rich community on an asbestos garage roof in someone's garden in Nether Edge, Sheffield. A keen and very nimble climber, Oliver was soon on top of the garage and extolling the virtues of this rich urban lichen site. He was blissfully unaware of the rather bemused owner of the said garage who was at the time in his back garden and looking on.

Oliver had many interests and made contributions to those fields including urban ecology, lichenology, montane juniper, exotic plants, urban and post-industrial landscapes, and even peat-bogs. Over around fifty years of active research and observation his work spanned these wide interests and he generally had some original and astute observations to make. He was for example, one of the first academic ecologists to study urban environments, establishing terms like 'the urban commons', and his book *The Ecology of Urban Habitats* (1989) is still the primary text in this field. This chapter considers Oliver's urban ecological work and activities but leaves the specific issues of lichens and related taxa to those better placed to comment.

Setting the scene: Often controversial and outspoken, Oliver challenged conventional thinking on invasive aliens like sycamore and Japanese knotweed. He effectively pioneered academic interest in urban habitats and urban ecology. I recall after an urban ecology meeting of the British Ecological Society at Leicester, Oliver made the front pages of national newspapers for his assertion that Japanese knotweed was perfectly appropriate to have growing along an urban watercourse. This came together in a paper for *British Wildlife* (Gilbert, 1992a) in which he argued for the value and novelty of distinctive 'urban' plant communities in British towns and cities and particularly along urban waterways such as Sheffield's River Don. He further noted the pseudo-woodland canopy effect of aliens such as knotweed which facilitated the growth of typical ancient woodland flowers beneath them. Oliver was not always consistent in his (often strongly-held) views so whilst advocating awareness and appreciation of exotic flora naturalising in towns and cities, he dismissed Sheffield's (nationally significant) black redstart population (McCarthy *et al.*, 1995) which developed largely in the Lower Don Valley during the post-industrial dereliction of the 1970s. This, he felt, was a Mediterranean bird somehow out of context and not appropriate for any conservation action or intervention (Gilbert pers. comm.). The species subsequently became the iconic bird of the London docklands rather than of Sheffield's Lower Don Valley.

Figure 1. The urban fig-trees as markers of the Industrial Revolution specially protected in Sheffield

Appointed as a lecturer, senior lecturer and then reader in the Department of Landscape Architecture at Sheffield University, Oliver was expected to expand his ecology into landscape design and this was a further catalyst for his urban work. In this context he became an advocate and pioneer of distinctive urban meadows and spontaneous wildflower communities in urban landscapes. It was during the studies of spontaneous urban vegetation that he coined the term 'the urban commons' and undertook studies in towns and cities across Britain (Gilbert, 1992b).

Towards the end of these researches he claimed that if parachuted blind-fold into any urban centre in the country then given five minutes to examine the flora he could tell you where he was. *Buddleia davidii* was the marker for Bath and Bristol for example, whilst common goat's-rue (*Galega officinalis*) was Sheffield. He observed how locally cultivated species and varieties of plants might escape and establish alongside natives in new communities distinctive to particular locales. Longer-term observations suggest that these communities over time coalesce into clearly replicated types but reflecting local conditions and factors such as climatic gradients.

Figure 2. Goat's-rue – Sheffield's characteristic flower of the urban commons

In his urban research Oliver also pioneered interest in urbanised 'ancient woods', something hitherto neglected. From studying the woods and their ecology Oliver became interested in the communities and their attitudes to these urban woods as the unofficial countryside, but also in the possibilities of new management interventions. Many of the eighty or so ancient woods in Sheffield had been virtually abandoned for nearly a century and Oliver in partnership with Sheffield City Council and the recently established 'Amenity Woodlands Advisory Group' undertook the first management interventions. The work was relatively small-scale but included experimental glade creation, thinning of woodland stands, and ultimately large-scale opening up and renewal through natural regeneration. None of these projects required any re-planting and indeed, the value of the spontaneous woodland regeneration would have been compromised by such an intervention. These tentative explorations into urban woodland management led the way for the later regional projects with Sheffield City Council and South Yorkshire Forest Partnership – 'Fuelling the Revolution' (South Yorkshire Forest , 1997). His main projects included Ecclesall Woods, Bowden Housteads Wood, and woods in Sheffield's Gleadless Valley. In the latter, Oliver was fascinated by the impacts and usage of the urban woods by local communities including the large-scale felling of big trees for Bonfire Night every November 5th. In his main case-study site, Buck Wood, in Gleadless, the repeated extraction of big trees was effectively removing the woodland from the landscape. Oliver's interest and activities meshed with emerging accounts of woodland history in the area by Melvyn Jones (e.g. Jones, 2009). At the time, in the early 1980s, the concept of 'ancient woodland' was only just emerging.

The Sheffield context: in the city Oliver was involved in pioneering aspects of his research which gained national and international recognition:

- Oliver was an early supporter of Heeley City Farm and the city farm movement;

- Combining his expertise in lichenology with his interest in urban environments it was Oliver who discovered the remarkable phenomenon by which once polluted urban areas like Sheffield were being re-colonised by rare lichens from as far away as Snowdonia;

- **The urban River Don** – he was the ecologist behind the greening of the River Don and the first person to understand and celebrate the famous forest of urban fig trees – the only wild exotic plant to be formally protected in Britain;

- He *'discovered'* **ancient wildflower meadows and heaths**, relict in parks and other urban open spaces, and then helped gain their recognition and conservation. Oliver pioneered new approaches to the conservation of urban parks and helped to discover relict habitats in Crookes Valley and with myself, in Graves Park. When I showed him sites in Gleadless Valley, relict hay-meadows now managed by the Gleadless Valley Wildlife Group, he declared excitedly that these were the finest he had ever seen in any city in Europe;

- A founder of the **Sheffield City Wildlife Group**, he was also a leading light in establishing what became hugely successful as the **Sheffield Wildlife Trust**, and was heavily involved in the first **Sheffield Inner City Habitat Survey**;

- **Urban ancient woodlands** – Oliver was the first ecological researcher to champion urban ancient woodlands in Britain – in Bowden Housteads, in Ecclesall woods, and in the Gleadless Valley;

- In retirement Oliver was a passionate founding member of the **Friends of the Porter Valley** – a group I was involved in kick-starting with funding from compensation and mitigation work associated with re-sewerage operation by Yorkshire Water in the Valley's ancient woodlands;

- He was one of the driving forces behind the greening of the **Lower Don Valley** in the 1980s and 1990s. We collaborated on ecological surveys along the Sheffield Canal and the River Don and in habitat creation at Tinsley Park opencast site;

- There was so much more, and this local work helped establish his wider ecological reputation.

Urban woodland ecology: Sheffield City Councils' first major foray into large-scale woodland management, at Little Matlock Wood in the Loxley Valley (early 1980s) had ended in unmitigated public disaster with an adverse reaction to the scale of disruption which left a lasting impression on council officers and elected members (see Rotherham, 2015). However, Oliver's smaller-scale pioneering research in Sheffield's ancient woodlands combined with studies by local historian Melvyn Jones (e.g. Jones, 2009) revolutionised awareness of ancient woods, especially in an urban setting. In 1979, a few experimental glades were created for Oliver Gilbert and the University of Sheffield (Gilbert, 1982) to demonstrate the speed and variety of regeneration by trees, shrubs and ground flora when group felling took place. Glades were created in Bowden Housteads Wood (see Jones, & Rotherham, 2011; Rotherham, & Jones, 2012), Gleadless Valley Woodlands, and in Ecclesall Woods; all in Sheffield. Excellent public consultation and information followed by the rapidity of re-growth assured those members of the council staff and local councillors who were sceptical about such management and fearful of the critical reaction of local residents. The outcomes of the initial works led to major schemes to rejuvenate a number of key ancient woods across the city and were also used for national training schemes for woodland managers where Melvyn Jones and I guided foresters and woodland managers around the sites. The results of management interventions in woodlands left unmanaged for many decades were dramatic in terms of bluebells and other old woodland flowers, but also for regeneration of a variety of tree species. Ultimately management plans were generated for major ancient woods, often via support from the South Yorkshire Forest Partnership, and subsequently as part of the 'Fuelling a Revolution' Lottery-funded project. Sadly little of the original or later management work was effectively monitored; a failing of much contemporary ecological activity.

Oliver produced a number of key papers in widely-read journals such as *ECOS* (Gilbert, 1982) and *British Wildlife* (Gilbert, & Bevan, 1997), and again these proved influential and especially so at a time when urban wildlife conservation was an emerging force. A typical Oliver Gilbert approach mixed his interest in urbanised woods and the phenomenon of invasive non-native species. As discussed later, the paper with Bevan (1997) presented a distribution map of Highclere Holly in one of the three main compartments of Ecclesall Woods.

Studies of an urban river: In the 1970s, the industry lining the banks of Sheffield's main arterial rivers, the Don, Sheaf, and Rother, poured uncontrolled and unregulated effluent into the watercourses. Furthermore, they used the river-water as coolant for the industrial processes. One consequence was that the urban River Don ran at a constant temperature of around twenty-one to twenty-three degrees Celsius winter and summer (Gilbert, 1989, 1992a). The overall changes in river ecology and the associated urban landscape were described in a series of key publications (Gilbert, 1989, 1992a, b). At long last by the 1980s, the environmental decline slowed, halted, and was then in part reversed. Rivers across the region were increasingly recognised for planning purposes as important 'green corridors' for people and for nature (Bownes *et al.*, 1991; Gilbert, 1992a). Additionally, some green spaces close to these rivers were acquired as nature reserves and others were protected as potential floodwater control sites. Public walkways such as the 'Five Weirs Walk' along the rivers also added impetus to improve environmental quality as did conversion of sites from former heavy industrial use to retail, leisure, sports, and entertainment. Associated with these changes there was major re-shaping of both infrastructure and landscape in Sheffield's industrial Don Valley to create a green backdrop to the post-industrial renaissance and Oliver was influential in terms of the ecological and landscape aspects of this change.

Figure 3. Shefield's River Don in the late 1800s

Nature's recolonisation of these urban riverscapes began during the 1970s and was documented in part by the local natural history society (Shaw, 1972, 1974, 1976, 1978, 1978, 1981, and 1988). However, this work was subsequently followed up by a series of surveys during the 1980s and 1990s, by pioneering urban ecologist Oliver Gilbert (1989, 1992a) and for the Sheffield City Ecology Unit (Rotherham, 1986, 1987; Bownes *et al.*, 1991; Rotherham, & Cartwright, 2000, 2006; Wild and Gilbert, 1988; Watts *et al.*, 1987). These works combined to provide a remarkable insight into urban ecological processes most recently documented by Rotherham (2020). This research provides case-study basis for ideas of recombinant urban ecological systems (see for example, Rotherham, 2017).

The long-term studies on the River Don are described and reviewed in Rotherham (2021). This ecological recovery did not represent a return to the former state of the river's natural condition but the development of a new 'hybrid' or 'recombinant' ecology. Both native and non-native species (many garden escapees) have colonised into the vacant niche now represented by the recovering river systems. As observed by Gilbert (1992a) surveying the River Don in the 1980s, this was not a case of invasive non-native species displacing the natives, but both native and non-native fauna and flora recolonizing a vacant space. Within twenty to thirty years, extensive tracts of riverbank, of riverside built structures such as walls, and in-stream shingle-banks and islands, had colonised with native trees such as alder (*Alnus glutinosa*), willow sp. (*Salix* spp), birch (*Betula* spp), ash (*Fraxinus excelsior*), and non-native trees like sycamore and shrubs particularly buddleia. The riverbank walls also have exotic cultivars of ivy (*Hedera* spp), Russian vine (*Fallopia baldschuanica*), great bindweed (*Calystegia silvatica*), and in recent years wild clematis (*Clematis vitalba*). There are also quite extensive areas of Mediterranean fig (*Ficus carica*) (Bownes *et al.*, 1991; Gilbert, 1989, 1992a; Rotherham, 2018).

Native woodland flora in a recombinant community: One of the remarkable discoveries or observations made by Gilbert and myself in the 1980s and 1990s was the recolonisation of the now improved urban rivers by indicator plants of ancient woodlands. For the first time since initial surveys of plants along the riverbanks by the Sorby Natural History Society in the 1970s (Shaw, 1972, 1974, 1976, 1978, 1978, 1981, and 1988), there were detailed vegetation assessments along the River Don. Supported by myself, Gilbert mapped the dominant stands of vegetation along both the urban River Don and the Sheffield and Tinsley Canal (Gilbert, 1989, 1992a; Wild, & Gilbert, 1988). In the pre-digital age, this exercise involved mapping the exact locations of dominant plants onto large-scale maps by hand. In part this was an exercise to map the invasive non-native plants particularly Himalayan balsam and Japanese knotweed. He and the survey team also recorded the wild figs as previously observed by Margaret Shaw and colleagues (e.g. 1988), and then followed-up along all the urban rivers by my own survey team at the Sheffield City Ecology Unit (Bownes *et al.*, 1991).

Gilbert (1989, 1992a) observed some of these changes with colonisation of the urban River Don by non-native sycamore, Himalayan balsam and Japanese knotweed into a vacant niche created by gross pollution and disruption. The new communities he suggested, were 'appropriate and distinctive' for an urban area. In the course of these vegetation surveys it was noticed that underneath the dense stands of balsam and knotweed there was a 'woodland' flora of native flowers typical of 'ancient woods'. These dense riverside canopies of invasive, non-native plants were acquiring woodland ground-floor species by dispersal and colonisation downstream with evidence of diversification under a pseudo-woodland canopy. It seemed that species such as bluebell (*Hyacinthoides non-scripta*), wood anemone (*Anemone nemorosa*), greater woodrush (*Luzula sylvatica*), greater stitchwort (*Stellaria holostea*), dog's mercury (*Mercurialis perennis*), pendulous sedge (*Carex pendula*), yellow archangel (*Lamiastrum galeobdolon*) and more, are washed down as seed or plant fragments from riverine woodlands upstream. Some of this was published by Gilbert (1989, 1992a). Today, alongside these natives there are non-native species such as hybrid bluebell (*Hyacinthoides non-scripta* x *hispanica* = *Hyacinthoides* x *massartiana*), variegated yellow archangel (*Lamiastrum galeobdolon* subsp. *argentatum*), monkey flower (*Mimulus guttatus*), and montbretia (*Crocosmia* × *crocosmiiflora*) (Rotherham, 2021). The dense stands of monoculture knotweed cast a dense shade from midsummer onwards, but as in ancient woodland, the vernal or spring flowers thrive before the canopy closes. Summer shade then eliminates from the sward potential competitors which would otherwise out-compete the woodland flowers. The result is pseudo-woodland ground flora under exotic canopies. Recent observations indicate that this process continues as flood-waters disperse ancient woodland flora and non-native invaders alike.

Mediterranean figs as markers of Sheffield's Industrial Revolution: For many local people it still comes as a great surprise that we have wild Mediterranean fig-trees along the urban rivers (Figure 1). These long-lived shrubs originated mostly from the time of heavy industry in Sheffield when river-water was used to cool the works causing streams to run at 20°C to 23°C summer and winter. This increase in the prevailing temperature throughout the riverine 'heat island' allowed exotic plants to thrive along the still heavily-polluted watercourses. Mediterranean fig (*Ficus carica*) was perhaps the most dramatic coloniser which arrived in local food products such as the ubiquitous 'fig biscuits'. Essentially the seeds pass though the human gut undamaged and end-up in the sewage system. At that time the sewage often discharged directly into local rivers and streams; sometimes under ordinary operating conditions but more often during 'storm events' from old-fashioned combined sewers. Even today some rivers have 'storm-water overflows' where raw sewage passes into the stream with flooding after heavy rainfall. With the warm micro-climate, fig-seeds deposited in river-bed silts or in crevices in the walls of canalised streams germinated to grow wild figs. Mostly originating from the mid-1800s to the mid-1900s, associated with gross industrial pollution, the plants potentially grow into quite large, multi-suckered figs. Younger plants still arise along all the urban rivers and more widely figs are now available from garden centres and popular to grow as garden plants. Some of these or their progeny escape into the 'wild', and seeds from discarded food products, aided by warmer climate, also colonise.

The Sheffield fig-trees were noted by local industrialist and amateur naturalist Richard Doncaster when he found them on the River Don near his steelworks at Owlerton. He alerted his friend, local botanist Margaret Shaw and she confirmed the identification. Richard and Margaret then led the Sorby Natural History Society's botanists on a series of surveys of the urban River Don and a good number of trees were located (Shaw, 1972, 1974, 1976, 1978, 1978, 1981, and 1988; Gilbert, 1989, 1992a). Oliver, then Sheffield University's pioneering urban ecologist, undertook detailed surveys and carried out experimental work. His studies showed that seedlings were still being produced from the sewage-contaminated river-silts as long as they were grown and germinated at high temperatures. It was his insight which then highlighted the role of pollution and temperature in the emergence of Sheffield's riverine fig forest. Following these surveys, the 'Sheffield Nature Conservation Strategy' (Bownes *et al.*, 1991) included the wild fig as a protected species in Sheffield. This eco-cultural marker of the Industrial Revolution was we felt, as significant as the ancient built archaeology of weirs, water-wheels, and mills. Indeed, as far as I know, this is the only specially-protected 'alien' plant species in Britain; and they do produce fruit. There are large established plants in the Lower Don Valley with a now-famous 'fig forest' near the Meadowhall Shopping Centre. Visitors still come from as far away as the USA to see this. Whilst the main wild sites for figs are along the River Don, it does occur elsewhere, with established plants on the Sheffield and Tinsley Canal, along the Porter Brook, and on the River Sheaf at Heeley. Young plants still establish and with climate change this is likely to continue. The River Don fig forests provide a living memorial to Oliver's riverine work in Sheffield.

Some concluding thoughts: A first thought about Oliver is that he was not always right! In challenging convention and looking at old problems perhaps through new windows, ideas can be exciting but sometimes still wrong. So for example, when looking at the spread of Himalayan balsam in Sheffield's Ecclesall Woods, he was convinced that it arrived around the 1960s because that was the first recording by the Sorby Natural History Society. However, having grown up in Sheffield I had seen balsam on the nearby River Sheaf in the 1960s, and simply didn't believe this. I ultimately traced its regional introduction to the late 1800s in north Sheffield around Walkley, and to Ecclesall Woods probably in the 1940s. The would-be Nobel Prize winner Sir Hans Krebs worked at Sheffield University where he discovered the 'Krebs Cycle'. He also took his therapeutic walks from Nether Edge and down through Millhouses bearing pocketsful of balsam seeds from a friend's garden and which he spread liberally along the way.

Also in Ecclesall Woods, a site which we both studied in some detail, a project student from Sheffield University was working with me at the Sheffield City Ecology Unit. Undertaking surveys throughout the Woods she found Norway maple (*Acer platanoides*) colonising the site from nearby roadside plantings. Until shown the specimens on site, Oliver refused to believe this because in his opinion Norway maple was not invasive. This was a case of rapid change over time and which we also found with *Buddleia* in Sheffield. When, in the 1980s, he and I began researching *Buddleia* in the city it didn't spread naturally but within twenty years it was a widespread coloniser of waste ground and on built structures. With climate change and other environmental fluxes these observation become very pertinent and informative.

Variegated yellow archangel (*Lamiastrum galeobdolon* subsp. *argentatum*) is an invasive, non-native plant, probably a Victorian variegated cultivar, and another species of interest to us both. We first studied this supercharged cousin of the native yellow archangel (*Lamiastrum galeobdolon*) (an 'ancient woodland indicator') once again in Ecclesall Woods. Thinking laterally as always, Oliver came up with the idea that this variegated species was doing so well because its leaves were camouflaged and hence overlooked on the light-dappled woodland floor, by grazing mammals. This was good until I pointed out that we didn't have any suitable grazing mammals in sufficient numbers in any of the woods. Today, both native and alien deer species have colonised but at that time they were absent, and both rabbit and brown hare were also much reduced. However, at the time, as Oliver observed, 'It was a nice idea'.

Figure 4. Variegated yellow archangel by Ian Rotherham

Controversial as always, I recall Oliver expounding to me how ancient oak-bluebell woods like Ecclesall Woods would soon become sycamore-balsam woods with variegated archangel. Essentially, in his view, we should not only accept this as inevitable but embrace it. Probably this is rather like the 'curate's egg' – good in parts! The woods have been affected by long-term acid rain from domestic and industrial air pollution in Sheffield over many decades, but today are influenced by large-scale nitrogen fallout from car exhaust fumes and power-stations. The latter may ultimately provide advantage to the sycamore (*Acer pseudoplatanus*) and Norway maple but the acidification probably favours oak (*Quercus* sp, birch (*Betula* sp), and especially beech (*Fagus sylvatica*). Indeed, in many local woods it is not sycamore which out-competes oak and establishing seedlings everywhere, but the Victorian introductions to these sites, beech and sweet chestnut (*Castanea sativa*). Furthermore, it is likely that balsam is quite effectively controlled now by the Friends of Ecclesall Woods, and bluebell will prevail. However, recent observations suggest that this may ultimately be not the native (*Hyacinthoides non-scripta*) but the hybrid (*Hyacinthoides* x *massartiana*) which is manifesting itself in hybrid swarms across the region. Oliver predicted change and indeed would have accepted or even welcomed much of it; but nature does have a way of finding its own path rather than the one we expect or predict.

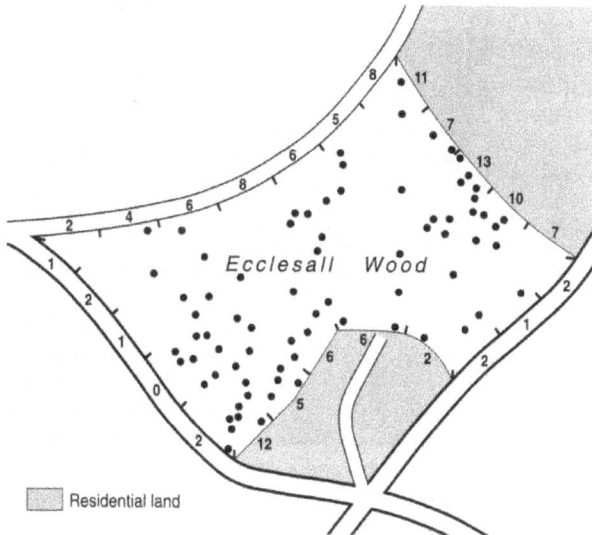

Figure 5. Distribution map of Highclere Holly in Ecclesall Woods middle section

Oliver's combination of skills, knowledge, passion, and inquiry produced remarkable insights into ecology and ecological processes. In woodlands such as Ecclesall Woods for example, he saw the split between native holly (*Ilex aquifolium*) and the garden cultivar the Highclere holly (Gilbert, & Bevan, 1997), an exotic spread by seeds from berries ingested by thrushes. He proceeded to map the occurrence of the cultivar throughout the Woods and it shows an almost universal and random distribution associated with bird defaecation! He made similar observations on exotic ivies and in both these cases this was probably a benefit from his own hybrid discipline as an ecologist and a landscape design specialist. Oliver also committed what for Mel Jones and myself was the cardinal sin for 'Ecclesall Woods' (which, as a number of named medieval woods, is plural) when in his 1997 paper he called it 'Ecclesall Wood'. However, Oliver was in good company since the Ordnance Survey also misnames the site. I have since observed the invasive non-native in woods throughout the region and liberally mixed with native holly clones which in some cases are many centuries old and forming a newly recombinant ecological community.

In nature recovery and in restoration (see Rotherham, 2017a, b, 2021), the ecological processes at work are natural but here are acting on species palettes mixing natives and non-natives without discrimination. However, for restoration ecology and conservation ecologists troubled by non-native species (see Rotherham, 2011 for example), the implications of these processes and their outcomes trigger a significant degree of angst. Yet the visionary writing of Oliver Gilbert (1989, 1992a, 1992b) predicted exactly this scenario of a 'new nature'. In his seminal 1992a paper on the urban River Don, Gilbert noted the 'natural' recolonisation by 'native' plants of the now partly self-cleansed river system. His key observation perhaps, was the appearance of typical ancient woodland flowers under the pseudo-woodland canopy provided by garden-escapee, Japanese knotweed. In the early 2000s, we were able to add the observation of native otters also back on the urban river and under the shelter of the dense knotweed canopy. Both observations are the unexpected and unintended outcomes of human-nature paradigms. At the time, Gilbert described Japanese knotweed as a distinctive and perfectly appropriate urban plant; almost as a body, the established conservation world was rocked.

Knowing Oliver as a researcher for around thirty years I was always impressed by his sharp intellect and rigorous academic discipline. He was able to identify a key ecological issue or question which he would then address, discuss, write up, and where appropriate move on. He was also able to stand back and take stock dispassionately as an academic observer of change and likely trends and this is often difficult for those involved directly in the conservation movement. However, at a time when much conservation science is less than objective, this ability often seemed to help sharpen Oliver's observational skills and acuity. Oliver observed and saw ecological patterns from which he drew objective conclusions about for example, invasive, non-native species. His ideas which emerged were not based on what he wished to see but on what he saw. This made his work such a valuable contribution to a developing science and an emerging conservation movement.

Recombinant futures: One of the on-going and still hugely controversial issues which Oliver helped bring to the fore was the matter of recombinant or 'hybrid' ecological systems (e.g. Barker, 2000) emerging through human-nature interactions (see Rotherham, 2017a for example). Throughout much of practitioner nature conservation and associated academic ecology, the issues of non-native and especially invasive species have become a cause for concern but where attitudes are often subjectively based rather than objectively established. Through his unique 'lens', Oliver's take was rather different and probably in the long-term more pragmatic. Environmental history demonstrates that in many countries and in the UK in particular, our ecological systems are hybrids and have been so for thousands of years. Furthermore, the human disruption of ecological systems means that they are altered away from any purist concept of 'native' or 'natural'. Key species believed to be native turn out not to be so and many supposed aliens may actually be native; much depends on where and when and how they are defined. Other basic considerations are that long-term non-natives such as European rabbit are now keystone species in the 'natural' landscape to the point that when they were depleted by the introduced, alien disease myxomatosis, priority habitats such as heaths, and chalk or limestone grasslands were threatened. Birds of prey such as common buzzard and red kite also suffered. Furthermore, we celebrate the European brown hare as a Red Data Book Species and worthy of special conservation measures, but it is of course non-native. Working with Oliver led to papers on Himalayan balsam and other non-natives (e.g. Rotherham, 2001, 2005a, 2005b), and the 2005 conference *Loving the Aliens?* held in Sheffield after Oliver's decline and death. The proceedings (Rotherham, 2005c) were dedicated in his honour. I am sure that Oliver's influence was looming large in the volume I edited with Rob Lambert in 2011 (Rotherham, & Lambert, 2011); and furthermore, if he had still been living his would have been a very telling contribution to the book.

Figure 6. Oliver Gilbert celebrated as an urban ecology pioneer in *Urbio* 2006

Oliver recognised these issues and conundrums for conservation but also observed that many changes were inevitable and many conservation aspirations were inherently subjective anyway. I didn't always agree with his conclusions but I valued the stimulating conversations and left-field observations.

References

Barker, G. (ed.) (2000) *Ecological recombination in urban areas: implications for nature conservation*. Proceedings of a Workshop Held at the Centre for Ecology and Hydrology (Monks Wood), 13th July 2000. UK Man and Biosphere Committee Urban Forum, English Nature, Centre for Ecology and Hydrology. English Nature, Peterborough.

Bownes, J.S., Riley, T.H., Rotherham, I.D., & Vincent, S.M. (1991) *Sheffield Nature Conservation Strategy*. Sheffield City Council, Sheffield.

Gilbert, O.L. (1982) The management of urban woodland in Sheffield. *ECOS*, **3**(2), 31-34.

Gilbert, O.L. (1989) *The Ecology of Urban Habitats*. Chapman and Hall, London.

Gilbert, O.L. (1992a) The ecology of an urban river. *British Wildlife*, **3**, 129-136.

Gilbert, O.L. (1992b) *The flowering of the cities ....The natural flora of 'urban commons'*. English Nature, Peterborough.

Gilbert, O., & Bevan, D. (1997) The effect of urbanisation on ancient woodlands the effect of urbanisation on ancient woodlands. *British Wildlife*, **8** (4), 213 – 218.

Jones, M. (2009) *Sheffield's Woodland Heritage*. Wildtrack Publishing, Sheffield.

Jones, M., & Rotherham, I.D. (2011) Management issues in urban ancient woodlands: a case study of Bowden Housteads Wood, Sheffield. *Aspects of Applied Biology*, **108**, 213 – 121.

Marren, P. (2005) Oliver Gilbert. Lichen hunter and urban ecologist in the wildlife jungle of Sheffield. *The Independent*, Wednesday 18th May 2005.

McCarthy, A.J., Rotherham, I.D., & Mawson, G.P. (1995) The black redstart (*Phoenicurus ochruros*) its current status and distribution in Sheffield. *Sorby Record*, **31**, 32-40.

Rotherham, I.D. (1987) Wildlife & Leisure in the Lower Don Valley. Natural Sciences Section, Museums Department, Sheffield City Council, Sheffield, unpaged.

Rotherham, I.D. (2001) *Himalayan Balsam - the human touch*. In: Bradley, P. (ed.) *Exotic Invasive Species - should we be concerned?* Proceedings of the 11th Conference of the Institute of Ecology and Environmental Management, Birmingham, April 2000. IEEM, Winchester, 41-50.

Rotherham, I.D. (2005a) Invasive plants – ecology, history and perception. *Journal of Practical Ecology and Conservation Special Series*, **No. 4**, 52-62.

Rotherham, I.D. (2005b) Alien Plants and the Human Touch. *Journal of Practical Ecology and Conservation Special Series*, **No. 4**, 63-76.

Rotherham, I.D. (2005c) Loving the Aliens? *Journal of Practical Ecology and Conservation Special Series*, **No. 4.**

Rotherham, I.D. (2011) *Chapter 15: History and Perception in animal and plant invasions – the case of acclimatisation and wild gardeners*. In: Rotherham, I.D., & Lambert, R. (eds) (2011) *Invasive and Introduced Plants and Animals: Human Perceptions, Attitudes and Approaches to Management.* EARTHSCAN, London, 233-248.

Rotherham, I.D. (2015) *The Rise and Fall of Countryside Management*. Routledge, London.

Rotherham, I.D. (2017a) *Recombinant Ecology – a hybrid future?* Dordrecht: Springer Briefs, Springer 85p.

Rotherham, I.D. (2017b) *The industrial transformation of South Yorkshire landscapes*. In: Rotherham, I.D., & Handley, C. (eds) (2017) *The Industrial Legacy & Landscapes of Sheffield and South Yorkshire*. Wildtrack Publishing, Sheffield, 3-40.

Rotherham, I.D. (2018) The implications of ecological fusion and cultural severance for re-wilding. *Aspects of Applied Ecology*, **139**, 91-101.

Rotherham, I.D. (2021) The impacts of recolonisation of an urbanised river by native and non-native species. *Frontiers in Ecology and Evolution*. 12 March 2021 | https://doi.org/10.3389/fevo.2021.618371

Rotherham, I.D., & Cartwright, G. (2000) The potential of Urban Wetland Conservation in economic and environmental renewal - a case study approach. *Practical Ecology and Conservation*, **4** (1), 47-60.

Rotherham, I.D., & Cartwright, G. (2006) *Water and wetlands: their conservation and re-creation in a social landscape – the vital role of project champions*. Proceedings of the IALE Conference: *Water and the Landscape: The Landscape Ecology of Freshwater Ecosystems*: IALE, Reading, 321-326.

Rotherham, I.D., & Jones, M. (2012) Managing urban ancient woodlands: A case study of Bowden Housteads Wood, Sheffield. *Arboricultural Journal*, **34**(3), 215-233

Rotherham, I.D. & Lambert, R. (eds.) (2011) *Invasive and Introduced Plants and Animals: Human Perceptions, Attitudes and Approaches to Management*. EARTHSCAN, London,

Shaw, M.R. (1972) Vegetation of the Industrial Don. Part 1. *Sorby Record*, **3**(2), 13-15.

Shaw, M.R. (1974) Vegetation of the Industrial Don. Part 2. *Sorby Record*, **13**, 54-56.

Shaw, M.R. (1976) Vegetation of the Industrial Don. Part 3. *Sorby Record*, **14**, 67-68.

Shaw, M.R. (1978) Vegetation of the Industrial Don. Part 4. *Sorby Record*, **16**, 29-31.

Shaw, M.R. (1979) Vegetation of the Industrial Don. Part 5. *Sorby Record*, **17**, 30-33.

Shaw, M.R. (1981) Vegetation of the Industrial Don. Part 6. *Sorby Record*, **19**, 30- 3.

Shaw, M.R. (1988) Vegetation of the Industrial Don: Reappraisal. *Sorby Record*, **25**, 58-78.

South Yorkshire Forest (1997) Fuelling a Revolution – the Woods that Founded the Steel Country, application to the Heritage Lottery Fund (No 96-00700). South Yorkshire Forest Partnership, Chapeltown, Sheffield.

Watts, R., Pearson, R., & Rotherham, I.D. (1987) New Life for the Lower Don Valley. *Landscape Design*, **165** (February), 16 - 19.

Wild, M., & Gilbert, O. (1988) Sheffield Inner City Habitat Survey. Sheffield City Wildlife Group, Sheffield.

South Yorkshire Biodiversity Research Group (S. Yorks Econet)
www.ukeconet.org

South Yorkshire Biodiversity Research Group is a fully constituted, non-for-profit, voluntary organisation established in the 1990's. The Group organise, run, and deliver community-based, citizen science training throughout South Yorkshire and, also nationally, in partnership with major universities and other key stakeholders. Our work involves: a) Connecting people with nature; b) work with lesser known plants, animals and organisms; and also, c) raising awareness of large-scale conservation of natural environments on land to help counter the effects of damaging human activities. (The latter are achieved in partnership with major projects on re-wetting the Humberhead Levels, on restoring the Pennine peat bogs and moors, and through our research work on 're-constructing nature', and on 'wilding' the landscape).

South Yorkshire Biodiversity Research Group provides a forum for the dissemination of information on biodiversity, landscape and environmental conservation issues. We work with a broad range of stakeholder groups, individuals, schools and colleges, including hard-to-reach groups within the community.

www.ingramcontent.com/pod-product-compliance
Lightning Source LLC
Chambersburg PA
CBHW050646270326
41927CB00012B/2901